DEVELOPMENT DERAILED

129+72

P.S.
P.S.

DEVELOPMENT
DERAILED

CALGARY AND THE CPR 1962–64

MAX FORAN

Copyright © 2013 Max Foran
Published by AU Press, Athabasca University
1200, 10011 – 109 Street, Edmonton, AB T5J 3S8

ISBN 978-1-927536-08-1 (print) 978-1-927536-09-8 (PDF) 978-1-927536-10-4 (epub)

Cover and interior design by Natalie Olsen, Kisscut Design.
Printed and bound in Canada by Marquis Book Printers.

Library and Archives Canada Cataloguing in Publication

Foran, Max
Development derailed : Calgary and the CPR, 1962–64 / Max Foran.

Includes bibliographical references and index.
Issued also in electronic formats.
ISBN 978-1-927536-08-1

1. Economic development — Political aspects — Alberta — Calgary — History —
20th century. 2. City planning — Alberta — Calgary — History — 20th century.
3. Urban renewal — Alberta — Calgary — History — 20th century. 4. Public-
private sector cooperation — Alberta — Calgary — History — 20th century.
5. Canadian Pacific Railway Company — Planning — History — 20th century.
6. Railroads — Political aspects — Alberta — Calgary — History — 20th century.
7. Calgary (Alta.) — Economic conditions — 20th century. I. Title.

FC3697.4.F676 2013   971.23'3803   C2012-906353-3

We acknowledge the financial support of the Government of Canada through the
Canada Book Fund (CBF) for our publishing activities.

 Canada Council **Conseil des Arts**
for the Arts **du Canada**

Assistance provided by the Government of Alberta, Alberta Multimedia Development Fund.

Government

To Rod Sykes, who was there

CONTENTS

TABLES, MAPS, AND FIGURES

Tables

Maps

Figures

ACKNOWLEDGEMENTS

I would like to thank the people at the City of Calgary Archives. As always, they were very accommodating in helping me locate documents and guiding me to sources I might otherwise not have consulted.

My special thanks and appreciation go to Rod Sykes. He made his private files available to me and consented to their transferral to the University of Calgary Archives following the completion of this manuscript. Blessed with an incredible memory, he was unfailingly patient and generous with his time and extremely helpful with his comments and observations. I especially appreciated his neutrality regarding my interpretation of events as they pertained to the CPR.

DEVELOPMENT DERAILED

Introduction

Life is a strange mixture of black and white, and nowhere will a person encounter more striking extremes of joy and sorrow, headaches and thrills, bouquets and brickbats than in public service at the civic level. There, close to the people, close to the wallets from which taxes are paid and close to garbage can problems, politics can be at their roughest.

Grant MacEwan, *diary entry, spring 1963*

In June 1962, the Canadian Pacific Railway Company (CPR) unveiled plans to redevelop part of its right-of-way in the heart of downtown Calgary. Covering two blocks to the east of the historic Palliser Hotel, the multi-million-dollar project envisaged retail, office, and convention facilities, as well as a major transportation centre, and it was to occupy land that was currently underused and only marginally developed. The news was received ecstatically by local political and business leaders, who foresaw increased tax revenue and a reversal of the urban blight that was depressing land values and discouraging investment. A year later, the original concept was expanded and took official form through an agreement between the City of Calgary and the railway company. The new plan would involve developing a much larger area, as well as removing all railway tracks from the central downtown area and rerouting the main line along the south bank of the Bow River. Despite the best intentions of its supporters, this grand design for the reshaping of Calgary's downtown proved too much for the unlikely partners.

Changing perceptions of the project and disagreement over details were compounded by ill-preparedness, indecision, inefficiency, poor communication, and mistrust. Calgary's most controversial and far-reaching project to date died in June 1964 amid the weariness of mutual default.

THE CONTEXT

The city's agreement with the CPR was born in optimism and rooted in the transformations that were changing Canada's urban landscapes in the post–World War II era. Two main factors were at work. Together, they combined to create an urban space much different from the industrial city, where land-use patterns were undifferentiated and concentrated around the downtown core. The first was the advent of the Central (later Canada) Mortgage and Housing Corporation (CMHC). Created in 1945 to administer federal participation in housing under the National Housing Act (1944), the CMHC implemented the affordable lending and mortgage insurance policies that helped transform the nation's spatial residential patterns.[1] The resulting suburbanization of Canada was reflected in the more than three million dwelling units constructed between 1945 and 1970. The second factor was the affordability of the car. In the period up to the 1980s, and arguably still today, planning policies and practices were built around the need to accommodate suburbanization and the automobile.[2] Every city, it seemed, had a transportation plan calling for the construction of freeways.[3] Planners Gerald Hodge and David Gordon sum up the new order of that time: "Mass automobile ownership and expressways gave Canadians a transportation alternative that was private, convenient, flexible and fast."[4] A focus on detached housing, bigger and wider freeways, the outward alignment of industrial areas, and the decentralization of retail and other services were dominant themes in the city plans that began emerging in the 1950s and 1960s.

One serious casualty in this transformation was the inner city — in particular, the downtown core. Increasingly, inner-city residents were moving out to the new suburban utopias. Shoppers were not patronizing downtown retail establishments as they once had, preferring instead to avail themselves of the newer, handier malls that included the big anchor stores and, more importantly, that offered free parking. The 43,000 suburban dwellers who worked downtown in 1963 faced traffic congestion while getting there and parking problems when they arrived.[5] In this period, the troubling question of what to with downtowns — with their limited access, their aging infrastructure, and their declining importance amid residential flight and diminishing shopper interest — was almost as important to city managers and planners as the need to accommodate outward growth.

Solutions were limited. Access to downtown could be alleviated via freeways. For example, the 1959 plan for Metropolitan Toronto provided for over a hundred miles of expressways.[6] In Ottawa, the Queensway was constructed as an east-west crosstown route in the 1960s. However, expense and rising public opposition proved to be limiting factors. Another way to bring people back to downtowns was through the enticement provided by modern new development or, to be more accurate, redevelopment. In this period, however, venture capital was scarce in downtown areas, where the attendant risks of redevelopment were high. In addition to risk, potential investors worried about higher property taxes offsetting any rental gain achieved through redevelopment.[7] In fact, many investors believed that the best economic returns could be obtained by razing older buildings and using the vacated land for parking until the development value of the site reached its maximum potential.[8]

The impetus to redevelop Canadian downtowns fell largely to the public sector. Sometimes it occurred at the local level, where civic governments promoted redevelopment on their own land and at times sold it at premium prices to encourage private redevelopment. It took the form of new civic facilities. Another intervention was through the federally sponsored urban renewal programs under the National Housing Act of 1944 and its subsequent amendments. Originally, such schemes involved the demolition of existing degraded housing in inner-city areas and replacing the demolished homes with higher-density public housing complexes. The scope of the act was later widened to include commercial redevelopment.[9]

The emphasis on redevelopment rather than on other options like rehabilitation or conservation created a mindset that saw change in terms of fresh beginnings. Regardless of its form or its impact on other variables, redevelopment was perceived as a natural good. With plenty of architects and designers willing to offer their visions for the future and many construction companies ready to enable them, any change was good change as long as it involved newness. This fixation with modernity had mixed results. Especially in terms of housing, the urban renewal movement of this period with its "bulldozer" techniques produced a "newness" that often did not stand the test of time.

Despite the later criticism of publicly supported urban renewal projects, there is little doubt about their influence as change agents in downtowns. Market Square in St. John, Scotia Centre in Halifax, Lloyd D. Jackson Square in Hamilton, Toronto's City Hall and Civic Centre, Regina Centre in Regina, and Churchill Square in Edmonton stand as testimony to public sector involvement in helping to redefine Canadian downtowns.

There was, however, at least one private enterprise with an interest in urban land, a business that had a strong physical and economic presence and was in the throes of a massive transformation. Beginning in the mid-1950s, the Canadian Pacific Railway began shaking off its "encrusted with tradition" reputation.[10] The reason was simple. Money! The company had always seen its future in terms of transportation and related enterprises, primarily the railway. However, the former mighty agent of Sir John A. Macdonald's National Policy was facing hard times. Between 1928 and 1953, thanks to a combination of locked-in freight rate agreements, competition from the Canadian National Railway (CNR), and increased use of automobiles and semi-trailers, the CPR had seen its share of the country's rail freight business decline by over 25 percent and passenger traffic by two-thirds. In 1955, when Norris Roy (Buck) Crump took over the presidency, he inherited the company's largest debt since 1941, the highest fixed charges since 1948, and the lowest return on revenue since 1922.[11] In 1960, the return on railway investment was a dismal 2.8 percent. Railway profits contributed 73 percent of the CPR's net income in 1956, but in the next four years, they plummeted from $3.76 to $1.81 per share.[12] Passenger traffic was the hardest hit. By 1962, it was contributing only eight cents for every dollar earned. The "crippled Titan" needed healing.[13]

Though he was an inveterate railway man, Crump was responsible for initiating the process that moved the CPR in a new direction. Between 1956 and 1963, he instituted a comprehensive inventory of the company's non-transportation assets, which amounted to approximately 1.4 million acres in western Canada and substantial holdings in the hearts of most of the nation's leading cities. Crump's choice for overseer of the development of these non-transportation assets was his Winnipeg-born vice-president, Ian Sinclair. It was a sound decision. With his powerful, dominant, no-nonsense personality, and without the constraints of a railway background, Sinclair was the ideal man for the job. Turning his back on the old way of doing things, in which the CPR had rented its farmlands and allowed its mineral and timber lands to be developed by third parties in return for royalties, Sinclair set the stage for the future when he declared, "We are going to start running this company ourselves."[14] This move toward diversification was helped further by the MacPherson Royal Commission, formed by the Diefenbaker government in 1959 to investigate national transportation policy and freight rates. In its report in 1961, the commission reinforced the need for further diversification by recommending a rationalized approach to uneconomic railways.[15] One immediate result was Sinclair's formation in 1962 of Canadian Pacific Investments, an umbrella company to hold all non-transportation assets. Through the late 1950s and 1960s, these included mining, smelting, other mineral holdings including potash (Cominco), oil and gas (Canadian Pacific Oil and Gas), pipelines (Bow River Pipelines), and lumber (Pacific Logging Company).

Urban land development was intended to be part of the CPR's diversification program, but it was slow to take hold. Initially, the company's interest in its substantial landholdings in cities involved sales (in Vancouver) and attempts to maintain its tax advantages (in Winnipeg).[16] Although its real estate subsidiary, Marathon Realty, was formed in 1963, the CPR was not a big player in urban land development until the late 1960s and beyond. Be that as it may, the fact remains that by 1962, the combination of the CPR's diversification program and its desire to move out of unprofitable railway enterprises had put its big right-of-way in downtown Calgary into a new perspective.

The fact that urban land development was not high on the diversification agenda had implications for the Calgary project. Its significance lay in that urban land development represented a new twist in a period of profound transformation for the CPR. Moreover, it was different from owning and operating a resource-based enterprise. It was not product oriented. It demanded judicious choices regarding how much land to own, sell, or lease; how much to develop and operate; and how to integrate significant capital investment in space and over time. In 1962, the CPR had no experience in negotiating these variables.

But that is not to say that nothing had been done in other Canadian cities where the railway tracks and facilities in downtown areas had become liabilities. The two big American precedents and models were in Pennsylvania and involved the development of the Penn Centre in Philadelphia and the Gateway Center towers in Pittsburgh.[17] In Canada, the active participant was the CNR, not the CPR, partly because the former, being a public corporation, invited closer association between levels of government. The first rail relocation project was undertaken in Ottawa in the mid-1950s when the CNR agreed to remove thirty-five miles of track and eliminate seventy-seven level crossings to enable the release of 251 acres for parks and public building sites and to provide the right-of-way for the Queensway. In 1962, the Place Ville Marie in Montréal, one of the first designs of Henry N. Cobb and I.M. Pei, grew from a railway trench dug out of Mount Royal between the southern portal of the CNR's Mount Royal Tunnel and Central Station. It was erected over a fifteen-metre-deep open cut containing the railway tracks, and, when completed, the seven-acre project combined a forty-two-storey office tower with new and existing buildings atop a public plaza. In Saskatoon, under a downtown revitalization project that began in the 1950s, the CNR yards were removed and replaced with the Midtown Plaza shopping mall and the Saskatoon Centennial Auditorium and Convention Centre.[18] Although the CPR would later be involved in similar projects, such as the Metro Toronto Convention Centre, on the city's waterfront, or False Creek, in Vancouver, the Calgary project was regarded as its guinea pig.

Calgary was a logical choice of a location in which to explore the urban land development business. The company had a significant presence in Alberta, primarily through its oil and gas interests, and its leadership believed that the province offered boundless opportunities. The vice-president of the company's Natural Resources Department, Fred Stone, a former secretary to William Aberhart, was on good terms with current premier, Ernest Manning. Furthermore, Calgary's status as the headquarters of a promising fossil fuel industry was undisputed, even if it still lacked the office towers to prove it. Of equal significance was the fact that the railway's downtown right-of-way was broad, long, and underused.

The CPR–City of Calgary redevelopment proposal was thus set against broad urban transformations that were militating against downtown economic and demographic health, and amid challenges raised by changing railway dynamics. It was also acted out in a local context where history and circumstance played important roles.

At the end of the Second World War, Calgary was a provincial city of some one hundred thousand people; its main claim to urban distinctiveness was its location within sight of the Rocky Mountains. It was thirty-three years removed from its heyday in 1912, and the value of the building permits issued in that year had yet to be surpassed by the value of those issued in any subsequent year. Its downtown was dominated by sandstone structures that, although handsome, scarcely provided the sort of skyline consistent with the truly modern city. Its urban environs stretched well beyond that demanded by population, and many of the empty land parcels and lots were owned by the city via tax default. The Turner Valley oilfield southwest of the city had brought a modicum of excitement and prosperity, but it was already a declining field and whatever interest the major oil companies had in the city was wearing thin.

Other, more promising places beckoned. There had been virtually no construction in the city since 1914, and visitors from the east alighting from the train at an unremarkable and aging station saw little to enthrall them. In all, it was a city that reflected its modest role as a distributing centre for south and south-central Alberta, an area not long removed from the ravages of a decade-long depression and whose agricultural wealth fell far short of that around Edmonton.

Local government reflected the mentality of a city that thought it was going somewhere in the years before World War I but was now stalled in a time warp. In 1914, British landscape designer Thomas Mawson had prepared a grandiose plan for the future Calgary.[19] It now lay forgotten in a file somewhere in City Hall. The only positive the city had to show for its tinkering with the idea of urban planning in the late 1920s was a zoning bylaw enacted in 1934. The senior executive consisted of a mayor who had occupied the office for fifteen years and a lone elected commissioner. Change was not in the offing. There was no civic vision in a city that fifty years earlier had seen its future as the "Chicago of Canada."

This situation was to change dramatically in 1947 with the discovery of Devonian reef oil at Leduc. The beginning of the oil boom transformed Calgary. The city entered the 1950s flexing new muscles and talking about growth. Population increased dramatically, from about 97,250 in 1944 to almost 295,000 in 1964. Construction returned. The value of building permits issued in 1944 was $7.2 million; in 1958, the figure topped $100 million. Civic revenues jumped from $5 million to $45 million between 1947 and 1963.[20] The city began expanding in all four directions, particularly to the south and northwest, where well over 60 percent of the residential dwellings were single-family, detached houses. The City Act of 1952 professionalized the civic executive by replacing elected commissioners with appointed experts. As a result, the city appointed a finance commissioner and a public works commissioner in 1953 and, in 1960, added the position of chief commissioner. A trained city planner was appointed in 1952. A mandate was received from the province to prepare a general plan. Later in the decade, a royal commission on metropolitan development gave the city the go-ahead to plan its transportation corridors to coincide with expanded city boundaries.[21] A revised zoning bylaw was in place by 1958, and the decade ended with the preparation of a new transportation plan, which included provisions for one-way couplets (that is, pairs of adjacent streets, one running in one direction and the other in the opposite direction) and inner and outer ring roads all designed to move cars around and through the city. In 1944, Calgary had 66 miles of paved roadways; in 1964, the figure stood at 559, while in the same period, the number of registered vehicles had risen from 13,035 to 124,469. Although growth had stabilized somewhat since the frenetic years of the late 1950s, in 1962 Calgary was ranked the fifth fastest-growing city with a population over one hundred thousand in North America.[22] For the first time in fifty years, the dream of greatness had returned.

Table 1 Population of Calgary, 1944–64

Year	Population
1944	97,241
1946	100,044
1948	104,718
1951	127,001
1954	156,748
1955	168,840
1956	179,711
1957	192,577
1958	206,831
1959	218,418
1960	235,428
1961	241,675
1962	269,068
1963	276,975
1964	294,924

SOURCE: City of Calgary Archives, Municipal Manuals.

Table 2 Building permits issued in Calgary, 1944–63

Year	Number	Value (in millions)
1944	2,488	$7.2
1946	3,169	$11.8
1948	2,935	$14
1949	3,710	$21.9
1953	4,972	$42.1
1954	4,042	$46.7
1955	5,515	$58.9
1956	5,425	$61.0
1957	5,389	$56.1
1958	7,278	$101.6
1959	7,521	$99.3
1960	5,846	$69.9
1961	6,491	$70.5
1962	6,421	$88.0
1963	5,659	$91.2

SOURCE: City of Calgary Archives, Municipal Manuals.

What was missing in this exciting maelstrom of change in the 1950s and early 1960s was a vision for the future. The change had come too quickly. For instance, in terms of providing housing, the city was simply playing catch-up and transferring more and more power to private developers.[23] Even an awareness of urban renewal was late in coming. A booster-type mayor with limited experience in urban issues was at the helm for most of the decade. City councils mostly comprised stolid conservative businessmen steeped in the practice of guarding the public purse.[24] Although a more dynamic executive was in place by 1960, one ready to assume leadership, its members, too, were fixated on freeways and redevelopment.

According to a contemporary planning consultant, planning in this period was all about aggregate growth and the need to accommodate and promote it.[25] The City of Calgary's planning philosophy through its first general plan clearly reflected this blinkered mentality. Released in August 1963, the plan reinforced current growth patterns by encouraging automobile use, extensive private transportation infrastructure, low-density housing, and decentralized industrial areas.[26] "No consequential changes of policy can be immediately foreseen," city planners predicted. The plan went on to indicate that future development should reflect existing trends and constraints. This endorsement of private transportation on expressways, main roads, and feeder links is best reflected in a telling statistic. In 1944, Calgary's public transit system had carried twenty-six million passengers. Twenty years later, when the population had grown threefold, the corresponding figure was twenty-four million.[27]

This lack of vision was compounded by the fact that the City of Calgary General Plan made no provision whatsoever for the downtown area. Apparently, it was to be prepared at a later date. The reason was simple: no one knew how to proceed. There was no coordinated vision of what the future downtown should look like. There was no recognition of the potential of existing natural features like the two riverbanks, no sense of the aesthetic, no thought of a new type of downtown that might cater to a different clientele. The only solution, it appeared, was simply to reverse the trend that by 1960 had given the downtown only 25 percent of retail sales and 12 percent of construction projects.[28] Not surprisingly, city officials were hoping that an outside consultant would tell them exactly how to do this.

Like many Canadian cities, Calgary operated on a commission form of government. Commissioners, the most senior executives, were appointed by City Council to head the various civic departments and to report and recommend to the council either individually or through the chief commissioner. In the power relationship between the civic executive and City Council, the former was usually dominant in prosperous times. Jack Masson, in his study of local government in Alberta, suggests that city councils in this period routinely endorsed 75 percent of the recommendations that came to them.[29] In Calgary's case, this figure was probably too low. Administrators like Mayor Harry Hays or Commissioner John Steel believed that City Council's decisions should be based solely on executive recommendations, particularly in third-party negotiations involving secrecy and confidentiality. The information gap inherent in this process was a major factor in derailing the project.

This, then, was Calgary on the eve of the big project: a city being led by its own energy toward a future where growth was the only goal. It all seemed to be about "getting there," except that no one seemed to know where "there" was. In the context of civic thought, the idea of a big agreement with the CPR was as close as it came to knowing where "there" was.

THE BACKGROUND TO THE PROPOSAL

The project was so ambitious that its scope alone was enough to make up for any lack of vision. While the long-range value of the project reached into the hundreds of millions of dollars, the CPR's willingness to invest $35 million within seven years represented a mind-boggling commitment. To put this figure into perspective, it was about three times the city's annual capital expenditures and not much less than the total civic revenues for 1962.[30] When the idea for the project was suggested in 1962, both daily newspapers could scarcely contain their joy. *The Albertan* thought it was "too good to be true" while the *Calgary Herald* labelled it as "a plan of great vision, of great imagination, of great value . . . a plan that will make history."[31] Even *The Globe and Mail* was impressed. After noting that "Calgary is a guinea pig for developments in other cities," it congratulated Calgarians for having "a straitjacket removed."[32]

Calgary and the Canadian Pacific Railway were bound together by time. The railway company had laid out the townsite in 1884 and, over the years, had continued to play a major role in the city's physical and economic development. Its transcontinental line enters the city from the southeast, crosses the Elbow River west of 8th Street East and proceeds westward through the downtown between 9th and 10th Avenues. Beyond 14th Street West, it follows the south bank of the Bow River out of the city. In the 1960s,

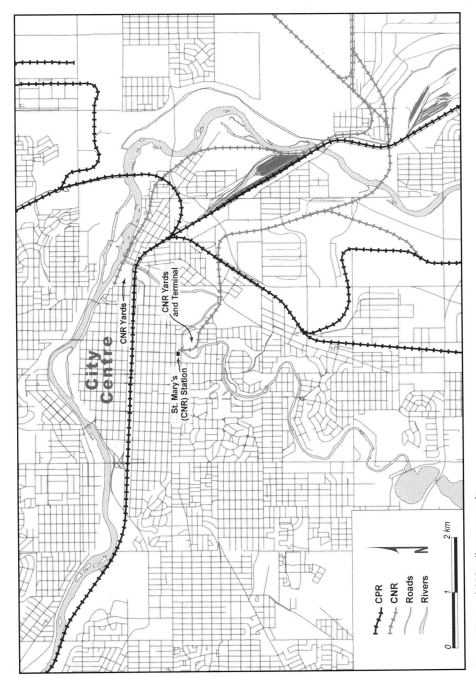

City
Centre

CNR Yards →

CNR Yards
and Terminal

St. Mary's
(CNR) Station →

CPR
CNR
Roads
Rivers

N

0   1   2 km

Map 1. CNR and CPR rail routes to city

the CPR right-of-way in the downtown area was four hundred feet wide, totalling 108 acres and encompassing twenty blocks between 6th Street East and 14th Street West. In 1960, 57 percent of this land was taken up by the main line and spurs, sidings, and yards. Another 17.6 percent was given over to railway buildings and service facilities, and 24.4 percent to one-year leases to various commercial enterprises.[33] Except for the portions under lease, this wide right-of-way, if used for railway purposes, was exempt from taxation under the 1881 contract between the federal government and the CPR.[34] It was on this right-of-way, with an emphasis on the area between 1st Street East and 4th Street West, that the CPR–City of Calgary redevelopment proposal was focused.

Figure 1. CPR right-of-way, looking east, 1962. In the foreground are the downtown station facilities; the large building in the background housed the CPR's Natural Resources Department. Under the proposed plan, this area would have been the first to undergo redevelopment. Source: Courtesy of Rod Sykes.

Calgary's 536-acre city centre was (and still is) compressed between the CPR right-of-way and the Bow River to the north. Commercial expansion had been following a westward pattern since rapid urban growth had begun after 1947. The right-of-way was a limiting factor to commercial development to the south, and it restricted traffic access to and from the fast-growing southern residential areas. On the south side of the tracks along 10th Avenue, a line of old warehouses and other structures presented a stark and ugly contrast to the city's emerging skyline north and west of the railway.

The CPR wanted to reverse its declining revenues from prime urban property in the downtown area. From 1958 to 1962, total carload traffic on its roughly 170 miles of trackage in the city had dropped from 67,214 to 59,972, with the downtown percentage falling from approximately 20 percent to 17.9 percent of the total. This trend was expected to continue. In 1962, of the carloads that originated in the downtown right-of-way, 83 percent were from three customers, with the largest, Robin Hood Mills (at 57.9 percent), destined for relocation.[35] The consolidation of the CNR's presence in Calgary via increased trackage was another worrying factor. Since opening its new industrial subdivision at Highfield in 1954, the CNR had lured forty companies, or three thousand carloads of business, from the CPR, including McCoshams and Martin Paper Products.[36] Noting that Highfield had fifty unused acres of fully serviced land, a senior official with the CPR noted, "It's just going to get worse."[37]

The City of Calgary's most degraded area was parallel to the railway right-of-way in the east end. By the mid-1950s, the area to the east of Centre Street, and particularly that adjacent to the right-of-way, was deteriorating in value and appearance. For example, between 1946 and 1963, construction on the seventy-seven acres in the two leading business districts west of Centre Street totalled $87.5 million. On Canadian Pacific property (ninety-nine acres), it was $5.9 million. By 1963, the value of construction in the two leading business districts was over $1 million per acre compared to $59,000 per acre on land adjacent to the right-of-way.[38]

Figure 2. Total downtown office construction by blocks, 1946–63. Source: Eric J. Hanson, "City of Calgary CP Railway Downtown Development Proposals," report submitted to City Council on November 7, 1963.

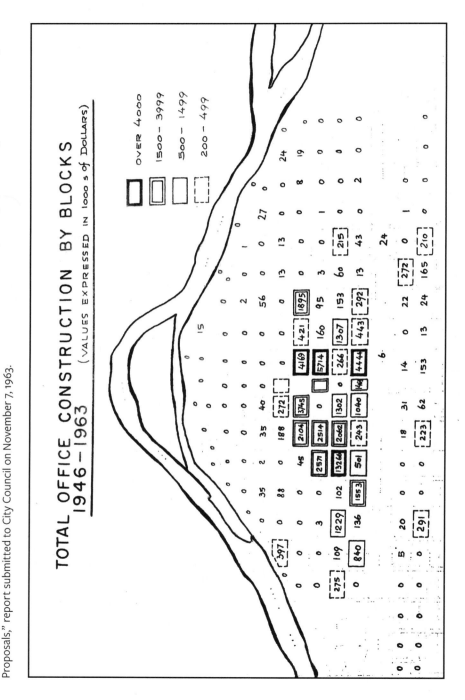

In terms of this project, it would be difficult to find a situation more beneficial for both parties. For the city, the redevelopment project promised to end blight east of Centre Street, increase revenues, remove a major physical barrier, and restructure the downtown.[39] The CPR envisaged considerable outside investment on its redeveloped right-of-way, resulting in substantial rental revenues from office towers, retail facilities, hotels, a convention centre, and transportation facilities shared with the city.

Yet despite these mutual advantages, the CPR and the city were unlikely partners. A national corporate leader, the CPR was a powerful corporation with a conservative, hierarchical structure and culture. Historical precedent had given the company a dubious reputation in the city for high-handedness. Moreover, the CPR came into the agreement with no knowledge of urban land development, uncertain long-range goals with respect to the same, and a risk-averse bargaining style. The city was equally ill-equipped to negotiate a major agreement. Civic leaders entered the agreement with an attitude toward their giant partner that may be best described as part awe, part suspicion. They were also inexperienced, lacking both preparation and an integrated vision.

As with other railway relocation projects in Canadian cities, this project has received scant academic attention. Jean Leslie devoted over fifty pages to the issue in her 2004 biography of her husband, Jack Leslie.[40] Her account provides some excellent details, while also offering some insightful first-hand observations on the local political arena and its participants. However, it is too sweeping in its conclusions, and, by beginning her discussion in 1963, Leslie fails to deal with the important background details that would contextualize the issue more fully. Similarly, historian H. V. Nelles gives a briefer encapsulation in his 2005 article, "How Did Calgary Get Its River Parks?"[41] As his title suggests, Nelles was not interested in the project itself but rather in using its failure to explain the later evolution of Calgary's river parks system. Marjorie Norris also deals with the issue in her history of the Calgary Local Council of Women (1995).[42] However, as with Nelles, her treatment, though insightful, is more a narrative than an analytical discussion. Aside from the above treatments, all enclosed within wider discussions, the story of Calgary's most ambitious downtown redevelopment project and the CPR's grand blueprint for Calgary and urban development elsewhere has not been fully told.

The following discussion deals with the proposed project from its promising inception to its quiet death. While I do try to identify pivotal points of departure between the two participants and places where both might have acted otherwise, the focus is not on who was to blame. Rather, the emphasis is on the negotiating process itself. In the final analysis, both the city and the CPR were unable to provide definitive answers to each other's questions because neither had any.

Setting the Stage

The City's Personalities and Agendas, 1953 to July 1962

As already indicated, the lack of downtown parking in Canadian cities was seen as a major deterrent to cars, people, and patronage. Calgary was no different. The need to increase the parking capacity of the downtown core focused original civic interest on the wide, underused CPR right-of-way. The parking negotiations carried out in the 1950s shed light on the attitude of the CPR and revealed the disconnect between City Council and senior administration. The failure of those negotiations also set the stage for the emergence of two vital change agents: Mayor Harry Hays and the CPR's Rod Sykes. Their combined efforts resulted in the first statement of interest in redeveloping the right-of-way.

THE CITY'S PUBLIC AGENDA: PARKING FACILITIES

The city's first interest in using the CPR right-of-way emerged in 1953, when a Planning Department report suggested building a parking structure over the right-of-way between 1st and 4th Streets West.[1] CPR officials were cool to the suggestion, believing it to be uneconomical. They also wanted assurance that rail operations would not be affected.[2] Jack Fraine, the CPR's regional vice-president, also reminded the city that a similar idea in Vancouver had been rejected as financially unsound in spite of obvious convenience factors.[3] When the idea was resurrected two years later, it was clear that while City Council and segments of the public were enthusiastic, city administrators remained as pessimistic as the CPR. The provision of public parking structures was an expensive proposition. In replying to an inquiry by Alderman Mary Dover in May 1957 on the possibility of parking over the railway tracks, the commissioners reported that the proposal would require the city to spend $10,000 to $15,000 merely on preliminary plans and consultation fees and declared that "the commissioners do not feel that such an expenditure is warranted at this time."[4] In support, they offered estimates of $423,000 for a structure with a capacity for 262 cars behind the railway station, $692,000 for a 400-car facility between 9th and 10th Avenues, and $1,091,000 for a big parkade for 783 cars between 1st and 4th Streets West. In asking Fraine for his opinion, the commissioners were openly negative, noting that "in view of the publicity this project has received we feel obliged to process it to the final stage."[5] Doubtless, the commissioners felt they had put the matter to rest by December 1957, when they reported to City Council that their meeting with the CPR had produced little co-operation. City Council was informed that if a parking structure was built to federal specifications, it would be "a very costly undertaking" involving a very large supporting structure with beams up to seventy feet in length.[6] In other words, forget it.

If the commissioners thought that the project had gone away, they were wrong. It was kept alive by interest groups like the Downtown Businessmen's Association, which began a dialogue with the CPR in 1958.[7] Then, in late 1959, the Planning Department, which had suggested the idea in the first place, came up with another proposal to build a series of six multi-storey parking buildings between 5th and 9th Streets West for six thousand cars.[8] Again, other forces within the civic administration demurred. This time it was the city's Downtown Parking Corporation, whose superintendent, Rees Taprell, believed that while the proposed facility had some merit for the future, it would not be approved by the railway company.[9] Downtown parking problems continued. The city entered the 1960s with six public parking lots, one structure, and 2,041 parking meters for a total of 2,900 spaces. In 1963–64, more than 124,000 vehicles were registered in the city.[10]

Taprell was right about CPR approval. President Crump was simply not interested. However, in rejecting the parking concept, he opened what had hitherto been a closed door: "We have no objection at all to joining with the city in a study aimed at utilizing to a greater advantage any property we may have. We will listen to anything to our mutual advantage."[11] It was an interesting comment. That Crump was prepared to wait on the city's initiative is an indication that the CPR had not yet developed any plan of its own for its right-of-way in Calgary.

THE CHANGE AGENTS: HARRY HAYS AND ROD SYKES

Buck Crump's comment was propitious, for a month earlier, in October 1959, Calgary had elected a new mayor. If one had to identify the major individual change agent behind the redevelopment scheme, it would have to be Harry Hays, the rancher, auctioneer, livestock breeder, and dairy farmer who had just unseated long-standing mayor Don Mackay in a closely fought election.[12]

Hays was an intriguing character. Self-described as "a barefoot boy from the backyard," he was born in Carstairs, Alberta, in 1909. Following the completion of a course at Garbutt's Business College in Calgary, he became a field man for the Holstein-Friesian Cattle Exporting Association. Over the years, he gained a reputation as an innovator and cattle breeder. The Hays Converter was the first breed of beef cattle recognized as a pure breed under the provisions of the Canada Livestock Pedigree Act and developed by a Canadian livestock producer. Hays was the first Canadian to ship purebred dairy cattle to Great Britain and was instrumental in introducing the modern public stock auction to Alberta. In the 1950s, he pioneered the export of cattle by plane, allowing the Canadian industry to develop new markets in Mexico and the United Kingdom. Hays was also involved with the Canadian Swine Breeders during World War II in initiating the "Bacon for Britain" campaign to increase production as part of the war effort.[13]

Homespun, down to earth, but shrewd and with a no-nonsense attitude toward business, Hays had never run for political office. It was generally believed that he finally did so at the urging of business colleagues who were concerned about the city's rising debenture debt, which reached $82 million in 1960. In 1948, it had been under $9 million.[14] Another likely motivator was the recent sale of his dairy farm (now the suburb of Haysboro) on the city's southern outskirts to a land development company for $1 million.[15] Surplus cash and a new interest in urban growth probably made running for civic office appealing to an individual accustomed to risk taking and challenge and with an established reputation for getting things done. In his campaign, Hays promised more efficiency in government, the creation of a robust business climate, and few specifics. It was enough to push him just ahead of his opponent, incumbent Don Mackay, a flamboyant character whose eight-year term had been tainted by a civic scandal involving spending improprieties and alleged kickbacks.

Hays soon gained the confidence of City Council, a luxury he was to retain for the duration of his term in office. In fact, some thought that City Council was a pawn in his hands. Nevertheless, he made good on his promise to reduce debt. Claiming that he had lowered the per capita debt by eleven dollars, he secured a landslide victory in the mayoralty election in 1961.[16] Then, at the beginning of his second term, he implemented a "hold-the-line policy" that reduced expenses further through an across-the-board wage freeze for city employees. As his mayoralty term progressed, it was obvious that City Council trusted Hays, the city commissioners trusted Hays, the press liked Hays, the public liked Hays, and, most significant for the big project that he was about to get underway, the federal Liberal government came to really like Harry Hays.

Following his second election in the fall of 1961, Hays began his campaign to do something about the CPR right-of-way. In a series of communications to Crump, he blasted the railway company for its inactivity on its wide right-of-way, arguing that CPR apathy was responsible for the urban blight that was steadily creeping westward along 9th and 8th Avenues.[17] His message was simple: something needed to be done. Although the CPR's interest in Calgary at this time mainly concerned property acquisition for outlying industrial parks, Crump was sufficiently surprised by Hays's vehemence to take action, and he turned the matter over to his right-hand man, Vice-President Ian Sinclair. Always mindful of possibilities, Sinclair directed Rod Sykes, his protégé in the CPR's Research Department, to go to Calgary and check things out.[18] Although Sykes remembers his assignment as "getting Hays off Crump's back," it is also likely that the outspoken Calgary mayor had piqued some high-level company interest.[19]

If Harry Hays was an intriguing figure, James Rodney (Rod) Winter Sykes was equally so. Born in Montréal in 1929 and educated in Victoria and at Sir George Williams University (now Concordia), Sykes began his career as an accountant in 1949, articling with Price Waterhouse before becoming a chartered accountant in 1954. He joined the CPR in 1960 under interesting circumstances. When auditing the CPR's books for Price Waterhouse, he concluded that the company's Esquimalt and Nanaimo timberlands were being grossly mismanaged. He was forthright enough to confront the formidable Sinclair with this belief. Impressed with the young man's candour and probably recognizing a kindred soul, Sinclair persuaded Sykes to leave Price Waterhouse and join the CPR's Research Department, where he was put in charge of investigating non-transportation resources. This included identification, profitability, priority assessments, and recommendations. His first assignment involved the Pacific logging industry, where he arranged the purchase of Sooke Forest Products Ltd., an investment that the CPR recovered in a year. His second was in Saskatchewan, where he worked with Stanford Research Institute to produce a detailed assessment of the company's potash holdings.[20]

Sykes brought a significant presence to his duties. Most Calgarians old enough to remember will associate Sykes with his later role as mayor of Calgary, a position he occupied from 1969 to 1977, during which time he gained a reputation for bluntness and confrontation and for being convinced of the certainty of his own opinions. One columnist described his political style as "abrasive, divisive and theatrical."[21] He was, however, highly respected and voter-friendly. In 1974, *Macleans Magazine* ran an informal survey on the popularity of Canada's mayors. Of the 359 responses, Sykes received the most endorsements. The winning entry praised "his intestinal fortitude to put the cards on the table for all to see." When he left the mayoralty in 1977, he was described by respected Calgary columnist John Hopkins as a man of sharp contrasts, a formidable adversary, and a tireless worker; Hopkins declared that "anything he did was in the best interest of the city."[22]

Sykes was to be a major figure in the CPR–City of Calgary project and his role should be put into context. With respect to land development issues, his authority in Calgary exceeded his position within the company, partly because of his bond with Sinclair, an unlikely situation given Sinclair's impersonal staff relationships.[23] Doubtless, Sykes's forthrightness earned Sinclair's respect. They also shared the same volatile temperament. Sykes's incendiary wit was once described as having the potential to "start a blaze in a fire extinguisher factory."[24] As for Sinclair, he was quoted as saying, "I don't get heart attacks, I give them."[25] While he reported to Fred Stone, who occupied the newly created position of vice-president of the Natural Resources Department, Sykes was also Sinclair's personal agent in Calgary with a mandate to push his authority as far as it would take him. As Sinclair himself once said, "If you make a decision and you're running the team, *you* make the decision."[26] The vice-president's confidence was based on more than Sykes's impressive achievements in a short time with the company. Sinclair was also aware of Sykes's proven ability as an auditor with a globally recognized accounting company, where he was accustomed to speaking his mind to senior corporate executives. In Calgary, when Sykes spoke on matters of land development, it was with the CPR's voice. The same was not as true for railway issues: the rerouting of the rails was outside his purview, and he did not lead the negotiations. He was also not given free licence to sell the project to the city.

When Sykes arrived in Calgary to deal with Harry Hays, the CPR had prepared no plans for doing anything with its right-of-way. He had no instructions beyond seeing what Hays was all about.[27] For all Sykes knew, Hays might have simply been testing the waters in a game the CPR often played with urban planners who wanted the company to spend more money in their cities. But a tour with Hays along the right-of-way convinced him otherwise. Sykes was dismayed by the sight of prime urban land languishing amid rusting spur lines and weeds. But he was equally energized by the possibilities it presented and was infused with the belief that he had a crucial role to play in a company that was moving away from railway-based enterprises. In that respect, he was one of those "clever managers" described by Robert Chodos: those who hated "to see properties lying idle and who saw the potential for Canadian Pacific to enter the glamorous and lucrative field of real estate development."[28]

Sykes recognized the potential in Calgary and told Sinclair so back in Montréal. Trusting his young protégé, who reminded him of himself, Sinclair agreed and sent him back to Calgary to research the possibilities, prepare an economic study, and make recommendations.[29] Sykes was back in Calgary in the spring of 1962 and, after taking up residence in the Palliser Hotel, began preparations for the economic study. A further priority was to reconnect with Harry Hays and to acquaint himself with key members in the city's Planning Department. He also began to get a feel for the press and the local business establishment. On April 12, Sykes met with the city's planning director, Al Martin, who, after admitting his ignorance of the talks between Hays and Crump, offered the opinion that the current right-of-way should be narrowed considerably through development. Sykes agreed but offered no details.[30] Over the ensuing weeks, Sykes worked with the Planning Department on possibilities for the right-of-way.

The city had also been reviewing the right-of-way in a different light. In October 1961, the commissioners had suggested a plan for the right-of-way involving rapid transit services and a union station for both the CPR and the CNR. They were quick to point out, however, that the scheme was "far in the future" and needed to be predicated on the railway company's co-operation.[31] But it was a start in that it marked an admission by city administrators that they were viewing the right-of-way in terms other than parking.

It was left to a rookie alderman to articulate a specific direction and to introduce the issue into political and public context. Jack Leslie's motion on March 5, 1962, was the first official statement from the city about redeveloping the right-of-way. It was prophetic. Following a preamble that referred to the right-of-way as a barrier to downtown traffic and that recognized the changing function of railways generally, Leslie moved that the city commissioners and CPR officials undertake a study to consider constructing bypass railway lines for through trains, narrowing the downtown right-of-way to a maximum of two lines, purchasing the excess right-of-way for an east-west artery through the city, and incorporating the proposals into the general plan currently under preparation.[32] It was a solid, imaginative motion, one that provided a clear direction for the city. Following a brief inconclusive discussion on March 19, City Council passed the motion on to the commissioners for report.[33]

Given his pivotal role in the negotiations to come, Jack Leslie deserves mention here. A native-born Calgarian who had served as an RCAF flight instructor during the Second World War, Leslie was well versed in the land business, having taken over his father's real estate company. He had been drawn to civic politics by his concern about inefficient land sale policies that had seen prime city properties going to private interests at undervalued prices.[34] His motion was consistent with his beliefs about the right-of-way as a constricting factor, an issue he had raised during his aldermanic campaign.[35] Although he was to be City Council's most consistent critic of the redevelopment proposal, Leslie's opposition was rooted not so much in the project itself but rather in its negotiable issues, as could be inferred from his original motion in March 1962 and his public comments in April 1963 and as late as February 1964, when debate on the proposal was polarizing.[36]

THE CITY'S HIDDEN AGENDA: AN EAST-WEST FREEWAY

As events unfolded, the proposal evolved to include both a rerouting of the rails to the south bank of the Bow River and a city parkway (freeway) running beside them. Although at the time, the parkway was touted as a way to make the best of a problematic decision by the CPR and to consolidate two types of traffic movements, the parkway concept was not new. This has implications for the blame that was levelled at the CPR for wanting to defile a riverbank. In this sense, the east-west transportation link was a hidden agenda item for the city and a possible explanation as to why city bureaucrats so readily accepted the CPR's decision in early 1963 to reroute its rails along the riverbank.

Five years earlier, in September 1957, city bureaucrats, as part of their preparation for the city's first general plan, had ordered a full-scale transportation study for the metropolitan area. The first part of this study, released on June 12, 1959, provided for an integrated freeway system that included an inner east-west ring road linking the proposed Blackfoot Trail at 34th Avenue to 6th Street East and the south bank of the Bow River.[37] Blackfoot Trail, not completed until 1962, was originally designed as an alternative truck route around the city but was consolidated into a major traffic thoroughfare pending the annexation of Forest Lawn and lands to the east. A month after City Council designated Memorial Drive, on the north bank, as the main east-west artery, Structural Engineering Services Ltd. was contracted to define the route from the Blackfoot Trail at 34th Avenue and to include a new bridge across the Bow.[38] When this route proved to be too expensive, city administrators resurrected their original south bank preference. They argued that the best and cheapest route for another east-west freeway was an alignment west from the newly completed Blackfoot Trail at 15th Street East along the south bank of the Bow River toward the proposed bridge at 22nd Street West. Although no concrete plans were considered, the suggestion was endorsed by a special City Council committee as a long-range solution to a difficult problem. At one-third the cost of the original route, it was "the most feasible and practical line to be followed."[39] It was also the exact route the later parkway was projected to take.

A road along the south bank of the Bow River jibed nicely with contemporary thought about the advantages of ring roads and more efficient traffic patterns. It also coincided with the city's plans for urban renewal. Following a CMHC symposium in Ottawa on urban renewal in February 1958, the city identified sixteen urban areas for potential attention. Area #10, the area east of Centre Street and north of the CPR main line, was described as "the most obviously blighted section of the city"; it was expected "that large-scale redevelopment will be necessary."[40] In February 1961, City Council

Map 2. Rail relocation and parkway proposal

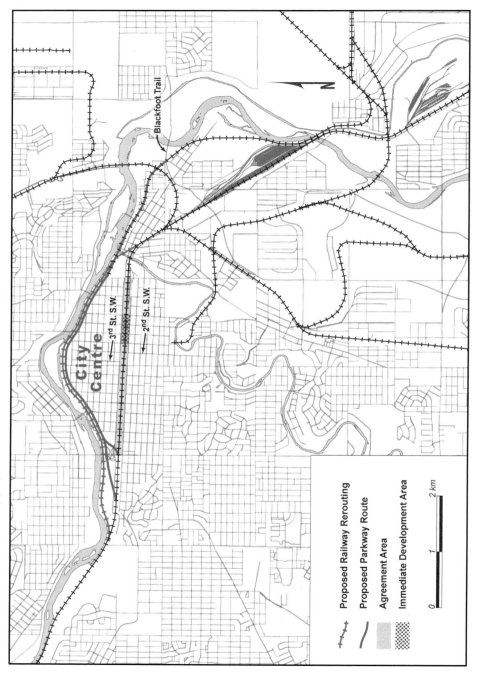

Blackfoot Trail

City Centre

3rd St. S.W.

2nd St. S.W.

N

Proposed Railway Rerouting

Proposed Parkway Route

Agreement Area

Immediate Development Area

0   1   2 km

expanded this area to include the entire area south of the Bow and north of downtown between 6th Street East and 14th Street West. In October 1961, the Planning Department announced that "a survey of the area for urban renewal purposes has been completed."[41] In March 1962, City Council approved a $22.2 million urban renewal project for Area #10.[42] Included in the breakdown of multi-use land use for the project was a road along the south bank of the Bow River. At this stage, however, the south bank east-west freeway was a concept only.

THE ANNOUNCEMENT

By June 1962, Sykes, with Sinclair's backing, was ready to announce the CPR's entrance into urban land development. Reasoning that it was best to test the waters and begin in an area where direct control and minimal risk were involved, Sykes orchestrated an announcement that focused on the existing passenger terminal and the land immediate to the east of it. The announcement date was set so as not to interfere with the federal election. Harry Hays would be there to lend his support. The press was notified and the excitement began.

On June 20, 1962, the *Herald* published its front-page story under the banner headline "CPR to Put Millions into 9th Ave. Project." The story unfolded beside a photograph of Harry Hays and Rod Sykes "confer[ring] over long-range conceptions for the development of land east of the Palliser Hotel."[43] Tentative plans for the two-block area included a transportation centre that combined the present railway terminal with airline offices and a bus depot, a high-rise office building with a helipad on the roof, banquet facilities with a serving capacity of three to five thousand, and a central transit installation for city-run services. Although nothing specific was offered in terms of start time or completion date for the two-block project, it was hinted that much more might be done along the right-of-way pending the results of the CPR's economic study and that this redevelopment project in Calgary was to be the first in an overall national development plan for CPR properties.

The June announcement marked the informal beginnings of the CPR–City of Calgary project, yet even at this initial stage, it is possible to discern some of the fundamental elements that were to plague the proposal during its more formal phases. First, despite the impressions it gave to the contrary, the CPR had given little thought to its new enterprise in Calgary.[44] The announcement was made months before Canadian Pacific Investments was set up and a year before Marathon Realty was formed — two subsidiaries of the CPR. True, the idea was probably in Sinclair's mind, since urban land development was part of his mandate to optimize non-transportation assets, but it was not a high priority. In this sense, the idea of beginning the implementation of its development plan in Calgary came out of the blue. According to Rod Sykes, the company had no specific plans whatsoever for its Calgary right-of-way when he went to see Hays in late 1961. The short time frame between Sykes's visit to Hays and the June 20 announcement seems out of character for a conservative company like the CPR. The only reasonable explanation is that Sykes (and Sinclair) and the CPR felt that attention to its existing landholdings in a growing urban centre like Calgary was a practical way to ease into an area of future interest. Be that as it may, the CPR's decision to entertain the redevelopment of its right-of-way in Calgary had virtually no planning behind it.

The second element of the proposal that would become problematic was the CPR's reluctance to be forthright, despite Sykes's enthusiasm for the project and his ability to push it forward. One sees this in the June 20 announcement, when Sykes refused to make promises regarding start times or even timelines, causing even the supportive *Herald* to note: "News of the development is most welcome. But more welcome will be the assurance that it will indeed be completed."[45] Yet Sykes was also prepared to use fulsome phrases like "we are here to stay," "we are going to change the face of the city," and "we can't be prosperous if our customers aren't."[46] These sorts of comments underlay what was to be the CPR's major problem in the negotiations to come. That the company had an interest in redeveloping its right-of-way was certain. What was far less certain was how. On the one hand, the company sought to direct and control its development as much as possible.

On the other hand, the degree to which it could do this systematic-ally and attract venture capitalists to develop on land they would not own was far more problematic. The best alternative, therefore, was to temporize.

The city's role in the lead-up to the big announcement showed executive dominance and, aside from Jack Leslie, a compliant City Council. Mayor Harry Hays was a one-man show in that he acted independently of the council. For example, aldermen were not informed of the June 20 announcement. After a gentle vote of cen-sure that barely passed and that called for administrators to pay more attention to submitting required reports before they were leaked to the press, Hays's ringing response informed the alder-men, "You will be getting these projects from me as long as I am in the chair."[47] The aldermanic reaction to this challenge was pure capitulation and demonstrated who was really in charge at City Hall: comments like "You're the best mayor Calgary has ever had," "You're doing a good job," and "We are not meaning to criticize" spoke for themselves.[48] The CPR deal was Harry Hays's baby. The possibility and implications of his ever leaving office were never considered.

Executive indifference to City Council was revealed in the way that city administrators handled Jack Leslie's motion of March 5. Although the commissioners claimed to have prepared the required report within a week, they failed to present it to City Council until after the announcement of June 20. In the report, the commission-ers admitted that informing City Council was "deemed inadvisable in the light of the current discussions the mayor was conducting at the time with the CPR."[49] The commissioners then stressed their future close liaison with the CPR. While there was nothing untoward in this latter comment, it could be argued that it implied a continuance of the status quo already established. Apparently, City Council had no problem with this, and the report was shelved. It was clear at this stage that civic administrators considered City Coun-cil marginal to the process. It was equally clear that City Council did not mind.[50] Nothing much was to change until it was too late.

As for City Council, its members simply lost interest following the June announcement. They left their mayor to his own devices and concerned themselves instead with city business that did not involve the CPR. And in the spring of 1963, when Hays announced a major change of direction in his dealings with Crump, the council was as surprised and overjoyed as the public. Its erstwhile leader had come through again. Only Jack Leslie might have been dismayed but, like his mayor, he had additional personal ambitions in that momentous spring.

Heady Days of Hope

Two Announcements,
June 1962 to April 1963

This period began and ended with an announcement. The first, on June 20, 1962, told the public about the CPR's interest in redeveloping the area around its station in downtown Calgary. The second, in April 1963, announced an agreement in principle involving a partnership with the city to develop a larger area. In the months that led up to this Heads of Arrangement, as the agreement was called, the civic executive dovetailed the city's interests with those of the CPR, despite the latter's dramatic and surprising decision in early 1963 to reroute its tracks. Although the CPR's research had endorsed the merits of redevelopment, the company did not commit to a timeline in the Heads of Arrangement. City bureaucrats maintained their enthusiasm for the project, even though there were signs that the city was emerging as the junior partner.

THE CPR'S PUBLICITY

In the summer and fall of 1962, Rod Sykes concentrated on promoting the project. Securing the right publicity was crucial to him, a priority that was reflected in his correspondence and personal jottings. No one with the company was more aware of the CPR's poor reputation in the city, and from the very beginning, he felt that the CPR was not persistent or thorough enough in convincing people of the seriousness of the company's intent.

The announcement in June 1962 provides an excellent case in point. Sykes decided that to ameliorate the CPR's reputation in the city, the announcement would be made as detailed as possible and would be accompanied by several media interviews; he noted that this approach was "a complete break with the usual channels." For certain elements within the corporation, this was going too far. After noting the success of the announcement in terms of publicity, Sykes wrote: "[The publicity] led to some unfortunate results for us since some Company officers referred to for comment on the news announcement apparently said it should not be taken seriously, and one went so far, I have been told, as to say I wouldn't be back as a result of it."[1]

Here we see the breakdown in communication that dogged the CPR throughout the negotiations. Sykes had no railway background but was a chartered accountant with a strong financial and business sense; he therefore understood the principles of effective marketing, especially in the volatile domain of land development. According to him, the CPR — Sinclair included — tended to adopt the attitude of "affronted dignity" if the company's integrity was ever questioned. Steeped in a philosophy that equated success with reliable and cost-effective service, CPR executives felt that results spoke for themselves. In the meantime, their statement of intent was sufficient. Thus, they saw no need for the president or Sinclair to support Sykes by visiting the city to glad-handle the locals and give personal assurances that their man in Calgary was speaking the truth. They saw no advantage in providing a conceptual model showing the company's vision in three-dimensional terms. And putting a shovel in the ground and making a beginning, however tentative, was simply not done. Sykes railed against this attitude, and the tenor of frustration is discernible in his correspondence.

In the summer of 1962, Sykes maintained public interest by providing as much detail as possible. While still offering no specifics about commencement, he referred to selecting a specific developer while stressing Calgary's fortunate position as the chosen city and as the guinea pig for prospective ventures in other Canadian cities.[2] Also suggested were rebuilding the Palliser Hotel and a possible location for the proposed convention centre.[3] Most significant were the hints that redevelopment, including office buildings and retail facilities, was to occur to the west of the railway station between 1st and 8th Streets West.[4] For the first time, depressing the tracks below ground level was mentioned, and details were added concerning joint use of the new transportation centre by the CNR, Greyhound Bus Lines, and city transit vehicles.[5] Expectations also included crossings over the tracks on every street from 6th Street East to 14th Street West.[6]

Favourable press comments on these announcements were the norm; the mutterings of opposition did not make the front page. The *Herald* called the proposal "a plan that will make history," and *The Albertan*, "one of the boldest and most promising projects ever to face the city."[7] A popular *Herald* columnist declared it "so startling in its concept that it is almost beyond comprehension."[8]

Sykes was delighted with the favourable coverage, noting in early September, "The CPR has received better publicity in the last eight weeks than it has over the past ten years."[9] During the fall, he consolidated his position in the city, becoming a member of the Chamber of Commerce Business Development Committee and the chair of the Calgary Master Plan Subcommittee. He was asked to address dozens of businesses and other organizations, once even filling in for Mayor Harry Hays. His format rarely varied. Following lighthearted opening remarks, he detailed the CPR's interest in Calgary in terms of its legacy in the city and then used this base to project a vision for the future. He believed that this approach allowed him "to maintain a proper balance in the picture we present to the public: the newspapers have taken care of the 'glamour' and the talks offer an ideal opportunity to control excesses of newspaper publicity without in any sense detracting from its very real and valuable positive aspects." For example, he told one organization, "This project is not a pipe dream, and, what is more it is going to be successful regardless of the comments to the contrary you have heard from some of the many sceptics with which this world abounds."[10] Sometimes he did not want reporters present. Occasionally, he was forthright. In November, he told the Downtown Businessmen's Association that, speaking as a private citizen and not as an employee of the CPR, he "had no doubt there would be development but it would be premature to hazard a guess as to what it might be and when."[11] Interestingly, while he was willing to address City Council or a meeting of aldermen, he declined to discuss the project with individual aldermen.

Privately, his concerns about necessary discretion were very clear. In his June progress report, he placed them front and centre: "Outside support and co-operation are essential. We can only obtain this co-operation if the people we talk to believe that we are serious." In the same month, he wrote: "It would be difficult even with publicity for Canadian Pacific to convince people that it meant business at last after years of inaction and opposition to outside suggestions for development of the right-of-way."[12] Clearly, Sykes held a very different view of public relations than did his superiors in Montréal. This disconnect was to continue into the formal negotiations.

One wonders how much leeway Sykes actually had despite Sinclair's mandate to push his authority and make his own decisions. For example, on at least one occasion, he had to secure prior approval before addressing a group.[13] Although he had excellent relations with his immediate superior, Fred Stone, whom he admired immensely, he also felt that Stone was somewhat nervous about what he might say that was not entirely in line with CPR gospel. In fact, when in Montréal, Stone often had to defend Sykes against critics.[14] Other comments in his progress reports indicate that he thought he was not getting his message across: "We must promote the idea that the Company is serious in its intentions and really means business. If we fail to follow through effectively in Calgary it will be doubly difficult to undertake a similar project elsewhere. We must talk the planners' language and express our problems in their terms."[15]

THE CPR LAYS THE FOUNDATIONS

Led by Sykes, the CPR's main aim in the fall of 1962 was to pave the way for long-range development along the right-of-way. In many ways, Sykes was in a catch-22 situation. On the one hand, potential investors had to be convinced that CPR-led development was going to go ahead before they committed themselves; on the other hand, the CPR needed to know that outside money would be forthcoming before beginning construction. This tentativeness on the part of a major corporation like the CPR shows just how wary and inexperienced its leaders were with respect to commercial development in an urban area. Faced with an unpalatable task, Sykes used a two-pronged strategy. First, knowing that tangible proof was some time in the future, he still needed to convince interested parties and stakeholders that the CPR was serious in its intentions. Here, his ace in the hole was city support and, better yet, involvement. Second, he needed to test the investment waters at the same time that he prepared an economic feasibility study, reasoning that he could use one to support the other.

The Calgary Land Use Study

The feasibility study, begun in June 1962 and completed in March 1963, was conducted by a team of four led by Rod Sykes. They worked first out of the Palliser Hotel and later out of the CPR's Natural Resources building. The team's objectives were to evaluate the development potential of the company's real estate in the city and to formulate a plan to promote this development potential. Specifically, the study involved a real estate inventory, an assessment of the city's economic future, the impact of financial and taxation considerations, and engineering studies.[16] The research conducted was impressive. Based on a wide array of sources, many supplied by the city, and consisting of dozens of interviews and regular progress reports, the study was an exercise in due diligence. When completed, it contained a wealth of statistical information on Alberta with respect to oil and gas development, construction, forestry, and mining. Information on Calgary included a detailed office space analysis in the downtown area, a breakdown of commercial and industrial activity and potential, a traffic study that analyzed trends in downtown freight activity, and a cost-benefit analysis (from the perspectives of both the CPR and the city) of development on the various sections of the right-of-way. The Land Use Study's conclusions were optimistic:

> Opportunities for profitable commercial development of Canadian Pacific's downtown Calgary land within a context of forecast market growth and prosperity for Calgary are such that the scale of potential benefit in value added by development can be conservatively measured *in terms of present value* at between $31 million and $39 million plus a variety of other important advantages upon which a dollar value has not been placed.[17]

The study also concluded that at full development, and assuming a conservative long-range value of $1 million per acre, net after-tax profits from rental alone could reach $4.5 million for the CPR, and the city would gain annual tax revenues of $13.5 million. It also conveyed the CPR's intention to exert control over all development and to maximize the value of its land by maintaining ownership.

Forecasting an annual 4 percent population increase over the next fifteen years and an increase in demand for office space of over two million square feet, the authors of the report reasoned that the redevelopment project would capitalize on that demand and provide the quality and prestige that was presently lacking in roughly 50 percent of commercial buildings in the downtown core. They also assumed that the modern commodious office space, which the project would provide at competitive rents of five dollars a square foot, would lure higher-profile tenants from their existing quarters.[18]

Based on conservative projections, statistical data on railway traffic, and a balanced assessment of the benefits to both parties, the Land Use Study was a solid piece of work. It was distributed to the nation's leading power brokers: the CPR board of directors and the chairs of the major banks, insurance companies, and large corporations interested in making mortgage loans and sponsoring investment in urban real estate. According to Sykes, the report represented fifteen man-years of specialized work.

From the CPR's point of view, the Land Use Study justified redevelopment of the right-of-way; its optimistic tone was an enticement to potential investors. Yet despite its statistics and rosy forecasts, it did not satisfy city officials seeking tangible assurances. First, it made no estimates as to when actual development would begin or how many years (or decades) it would take to complete.[19] According to the report, much of the right-of-way would continue with its present use for some time, and surface parking "would be preserved and considerably extended."[20] Nothing would be done at the extreme east of the development area, despite contrary wishes in City Hall: as Sykes put it, "The pious hopes in this direction have been effectively extinguished by the simple statement that 'we are in business.'"[21] Even the three blocks immediately east of the proposed redevelopment were described as being "too far east to be attractive and downright discouraging to investors." Spur lines would still be in place for downtown freight and would, according to the report, be required "for many years to come."[22] Of interest, especially in light of later skepticism over exactly where CPR was going to allocate its spending priorities, was the recommendation for an aggressive campaign to spend money developing competitive industrial areas in various parts of the city.[23] The report concluded that the city "must co-operate" and give priority to certain capital projects not presently being entertained.[24] The fact that the final draft of the study contained details of the rerouting alternatives shows that its authors were clearly anticipating the agreement to come.

Investor Interest

Sykes's philosophy of land development called for the company to act as a catalyst. He felt that the CPR should retain control of all land in the development area and must be prepared to involve itself directly by investing in construction. As he wrote on July 25, 1962, "Going it alone in real estate development on a large scale seems unnecessarily risky and unrewarding. . . . Emphasis [should] be placed on attracting outside capital to construct facilities on Canadian Pacific land, but there has to be some direct Canadian Pacific investment from time to time which should be looked upon as a catalyst designed to get development started and keep it going."[25] The CPR's reluctance to commit to this philosophy was to be one major stumbling block in Sykes's attempts to attract investors to the project.

On October 4, 1962, Sykes advised his superiors that even though economic studies were well underway, there remained a strong need

> to command the serious attention of investors upon whose intentions profitable commercial development largely depends. Without their serious interest we will be unable to evaluate the development potential — the marketability of our land. What is more, if we fail to follow through effectively in Calgary it will be doubly difficult to undertake a similar project elsewhere since this project is being closely watched by every developer in this country.[26]

That not one investor ever made a specific commitment to the project or invested a single dollar says more about the way the CPR handled the issue than about Sykes's lack of initiative or energy. Most investors took the attitude adopted by the Guinness family, who told Sykes that they would put up money "under the right conditions," conditions he was unable to assure.

In the fall of 1962, Sykes's appointment book was filled with meetings, phone calls, and correspondence with a wide variety of individuals. Not all of these individuals were solicited, but they all had one thing in common: they were potential investors. Some were renters; others were developers. Some were consultants and architects; others were speculators and fly-by-nighters. The most promising investor and the one pursued most aggressively was the Guinness family — specifically, Arthur Onslow Edward Guinness, or Viscount Elveden, who owned and operated Calgary's tallest structure, Elveden House, on 7th Avenue. Other interested investors were STW, the British-based partnership of Standard Life and Taylor Woodrow Construction; Monarch Investments; and Hartford Insurance. Also approached were Tankoos Yarmon, Webb and Knapp, Crédit Foncier Franco-Canadien, Campagnie Financière de Suez, Power Corporation, and three major Canadian banks. Construction companies like Dominion Construction, Poole Construction, and Marwell Construction also expressed interest. Like the investors, these companies predicated their participation on the outcome of the CPR studies. The same applied to Gamble-Skogmo (owners of the Winnipeg-based Macleods Hardware), General Supplies, and Beaver Lumber. Major companies already in Calgary that were interested in erecting new facilities on CPR land were Socony-Mobil Oil, California Standard Oil, and Calgary Power.[27]

Some interested parties were not received so warmly. In November, Sykes was approached by a representative of Chartered Investments, an Edmonton-based company. The proposal was to build a high-rise apartment building on CPR land on 9th Avenue west of the Post Office. Sykes gave the proposal short shrift, arguing that the site was wrong for a high-rise and that CPR land was too expensive for the sort of parking arrangements needed for the project. Apparently, the representative threatened to go over Sykes's head, claiming to have close liaisons with senior CPR management in Montréal. In an angry letter to Fred Stone, Sykes's philosophy was made clear: "This is straight bullying. Canadian Pacific has to travel first class. It can't afford not to as I see it, and these people are simply speculators. . . . We should not be stampeded into anything by a high-pressured approach."[28] Not surprisingly, this company was included in a list of six that Sykes later advised that "we should not do business with," adding a recommendation "that we should be extremely cautious in dealing with any approach they might make."[29]

Three specific negotiations managed by Sykes deserve special mention for several reasons. The first two involved efforts to relocate the site of the Calgary Inn and to secure an agreement in principle to put the city's proposed convention centre on CPR land. Both of these show a concerted intent to enhance land values in the original redevelopment area. The third was the soliciting of North America's leading consultant to guide the entire redevelopment proposal. The latter was a revealing departure by the CPR, a company that had habitually sought its own solutions.

Anchoring the redevelopment area was the historic Palliser Hotel. Adjacent to the railway station and opened in 1914 at a cost of $1.5 million, the magnificent twelve-storey (later fifteen) structure had long been recognized as Calgary's finest hotel. By the 1960s, however, its age was beginning to show, and to developers like Rod Sykes who believed that a hotel's importance was linked to its role in raising surrounding land values rather than to the amount of revenue it generated, the Palliser was simply not doing its job. In light of the grand redevelopment scheme, Sykes was in a quandary as to what to do with the Palliser. He was wary of demolition, since it would leave a void and invite competition until a replacement could be built. He saw two solutions: buy time until a final decision could be made on the Palliser by building another hotel in the vicinity or enhance the Palliser and the value of its site by extending it and linking it with a convention centre.

Mayor Harry Hays had long wanted a convention centre for the city. He also knew that the $14 million cost was a daunting sum and that it needed to be very near a major hotel that could not be

Figure 3. The Palliser Hotel, on 9th Avenue. Situated immediately adjacent to the main railway station, this impressive edifice was a landmark in Calgary for several decades after the CPR completed construction in 1914. Had the original redevelopment plan gone through, the city's first convention centre would have been built directly behind the hotel. Source: Glenbow Archives, NA 5093-238.

built with public money. His first move was to secure a site in the west end. It was not the best site, admittedly, but it was one that was likely to prove its worth in the long run, given the fact that the city was expanding west. He also hoped that Western Hotels, a management company that was seriously considering a hotel in Calgary, just might provide the answer to his problems. He was half right. The actual developers, Marwell Construction Company of Vancouver, did intend to build the Calgary Inn, a nine-storey, 260-room hotel modelled on Vancouver's Bayshore Inn, complete with swimming pool, parking for 255 cars, and convention facilities for a thousand people. Moreover, planning and design for the hotel had been completed, financing was not a problem, and the proposal was ready to go to tender. The problem for Hays was the fact that Marwell Construction had already chosen a site a few blocks north and just slightly west of the Palliser on 4th Avenue and 3rd Street West. The one-and-a-half-acre site had cost Hugh Martin, the owner of Marwell, $685,000. The projected new hotel was also a problem for Rod Sykes: with its attractive design and favourable location, it promised to be a major threat to the Palliser, a fact that Hugh Martin had made quite clear.

Sykes's twofold solution to the dilemma that both he and Hays faced was simple: persuade Hays to build the convention centre right behind the Palliser and Hugh Martin to sell his site and build the hotel in partnership with the CPR on land elsewhere in the redevelopment area. The former showed Sykes's vision; the latter revealed difficulties inherent in his middleman status.

Hays's response was favourable. He agreed with Sykes that the convention centre on railway land adjacent to the proposed new transportation centre and redesigned railway station presented an opportunity too good to turn down. In a report to his superiors, Sykes outlined the incredible benefits to the CPR, benefits that would solve the "Palliser problem" and upgrade land values:

> Let us ask the City to build the new convention centre behind the old Palliser and to build it with foundations for a major hotel, and public rooms designed to be flexible enough for eventual conversion to the public rooms and offices of a major hotel with

extensive convention accommodation; then let us pay the city for the extra foundation and design cost and take an option to purchase the convention building. When we decide to replace the old Palliser we can then exercise our option and build another eight or ten storeys of bedrooms on top of the convention building: when the new Palliser is in operation we can tear down the one in front. As to what could be done with the vacant land then in front of the new Palliser there are several possibilities — in the long run the land could serve for a third Palliser when the second is replaced some seventy years hence but in the meantime we could establish a Crystal Garden type of facility together with a circular driveway leading to an impressive hotel entrance and a beautiful garden. That would give the new Palliser prestige such as no hotel in Calgary will ever have.[30]

Sykes felt that the prospect of having the city's first convention centre on railway land and linked to the Palliser Hotel was tantamount to "a free gift."[31] Although the site was later changed before the city ultimately backed off completely in one of the few instances in which it successfully held its ground against the CPR, the Palliser–convention centre arrangement showed how persuasive Sykes could be, how the city was willing to respond to external initiatives without consultation or discussion, and how serious the CPR was about consolidating its position.

The Calgary Inn issue followed a similar route. Sykes, initially unaware of Hugh Martin's involvement in the Calgary Inn project, first approached Martin as a potential investor. An astute and highly respected businessman, Martin had promoted the Bayshore Inn in Vancouver and remained a part owner. In addition to his ownership of Marwell Construction, he wholly owned Georgian Towers and was active in pipeline construction. Another of Marwell's acquisitions was British Columbia Bridge and Dredging. Like many savvy investors, Martin was not convinced that the CPR was serious about redevelopment — hence, the location of his proposed new hotel in the city. However, in a meeting in Vancouver, Sykes convinced Martin that his choice of hotel site was unfavourable given the scope and potential of what the CPR was intending to do along the right-of-way.[32] When the meeting was over, Martin had tentatively agreed to sell his land, move to a CPR site, and build the hotel west of the Post Office in partnership with the CPR on a long-term lease arrangement that, as Sykes pointed out, offered many of the advantages of ownership. It was also agreed that a third party should be manager. For the pragmatic Sykes, this was the best he could do. He did not want another hotel on CPR land and was aware that Martin saw it as upstaging the Palliser. But at the same time he feared the competition that Martin would provide if the Calgary Inn went ahead on its original site. Even though Sykes recommended the partnership, however, CPR senior management turned it down — so hard that, in Martin's words, "[I] bounced."[33]

In January 1963, Martin came back with another proposal, this time to build and operate a smaller hotel on CPR land in the core redevelopment area, arguing that a Western Hotel was going to be built in Calgary anyway and that the CPR would derive rental revenue from an establishment that would supplement more than compete with the grand Palliser. Again, Sykes liked the idea, but he clearly did not expect Martin's offer to be approved: he admitted that any favourable recommendation "would come as rather a shock."[34] He was right. His recommendation was turned down. In the end, Martin retained his original site and built his Calgary Inn (now the Westin) there.

In his correspondence on these negotiations, Sykes presents himself as having the authority to push as far as he could. Although he knew that CPR philosophy was opposed to partnerships on CPR land, he went ahead anyway. Apparently, the head of CP Hotels was not happy with Sykes dealing in areas that were ostensibly beyond his authority. The fact that Sykes could not close a deal without authorization is a further example of how the compartmentalized nature of the CPR disadvantaged its on-site supervisor of land development.

Probably the first tangible evidence of the CPR's intention of doing something with its right-of-way came in October 1962, when Sykes and Fred Stone, CPR's vice-president of Natural Resources, visited New York for an interview with a major North American consultant and designer, Robert Dowling. They met first with several prominent individuals, including Ieoh Min Pei of I.M. Pei Architects and William Zeckendorf, president of Webb and Knapp Inc., both of whom had been involved in the Place Ville Marie project as architect and developer, respectively. Sykes and Stone also met with James Boisi, a vice-president with the New York Central Railroad, and Robert Field, a partner with Price Waterhouse. The person they had primarily come to see, however, was Robert W. Dowling, president of City Investing Company. Renowned for his energy and versatility, the sixty-seven-year-old, who swam long distance as a hobby, was an impressive figure. The recipient of more than twenty awards, from a 1948 Tony Award for his contributions to theatre to the Order of Merit of the Italian Republic, and for everything from civic public service to his role in the glass construction industry, Dowling also held directorships in more than a dozen companies, including Macy's, Waldorf Astoria Corporation, Hilton Hotels International, Knickerbocker Investing Company, and United Artists. He was also chair of the American National Theatre and Academy and a trustee of the American Heritage Foundation.[35] In fact, his involvement in organizations such as these led Sykes to comment privately, "Mr. Dowling has made a lot of money out of culture."[36]

But it was Dowling's experience as a consultant and developer and, equally important, his investment contacts that had brought Sykes and Stone to New York. Dowling had been involved in many major projects, among them New York's Stuyvesant Town and Peter Cooper Village. Although Sykes had met Dowling some years earlier and had an enormous respect for his abilities, it was Dowling's work with Pittsburgh's Gateway Center and the Penn Center in Philadelphia, the urban models that had inspired the CPR in the first place, that drew Sykes and Stone to New York. They must have had trepidation, given the mixed messages they received before their meeting with Dowling. On the one hand, they were advised by those close to him not to expect too much: the "great man" was difficult to interest and very frank. On the other hand, they were assured that if he did become interested, there was no one better.[37]

Not surprisingly, given the practice they had been getting in Calgary, Sykes and Stone were very persuasive. Dowling was clearly interested; he strongly advised that, without question, the CPR should remain landowners and retain full control of the project, sentiments that were echoed by Pei and Boisi. Dowling also expressed interest in visiting Calgary in the second week of November to see for himself.

"This is not a social occasion," Sykes wrote about Dowling's visit to Calgary on November 23–24.[38] Apart from a few CPR personnel, Dowling met only Mayor Harry Hays, the city commissioners, two Bank of Montreal officials, a Guinness family representative, and Marwell Construction's owner, Hugh Martin. Lunch at the Bank of Montreal was followed by a visit to Elveden House, where Dowling was shown "an unparalleled view of the city" from the nineteenth floor. Later, the small party visited City Hall and met Mayor Hays and Commissioners Batchelor and Steel, all of whom waxed eloquent on their support for the CPR project and how it was being carried out in an atmosphere of mutual co-operation and assistance. The three city officials, Hugh Martin, and Charles Morley, the superintendent of the Bank of Montreal (Alberta District), were the only non-CPR personnel at a dinner that evening hosted by Fred Stone in Robert Dowling's Palliser Hotel suite.

The next day, Dowling inspected the CPR's land and viewed the surrounding area from a helicopter rented at $120 an hour. Later, he walked around the downtown area. He declined to inspect Eaton's department store beyond the ground floor, describing it, in Sykes's words, as "a waste of time. Atmosphere all wrong, no merchandising know how apparent."[39] That afternoon, Dowling was on a plane back to New York after lunching at the Palliser, but not before his accompanying vice-president told Sykes that thirty hours was the longest he had ever seen Dowling spend in one place.

The visit was a success. Dowling was impressed with Calgary, describing it as "raw" but holding great potential and challenge. He left the door of communication open and offered to provide advice on land values and how to enhance them. Sykes recommended Dowling to his superiors: "We should take advantage of his offer of help; we should keep him informed. And . . . we should attempt to keep him sufficiently interested to be able to secure his services as consultant when we have made the decision to go ahead." This time, the CPR agreed. Sykes's recommendation was interesting for two reasons. First was the veiled recognition that no decision to develop had been made by the company. Second, and probably unwittingly, Sykes had handcuffed himself. For as long as Dowling was a potential consultant, Sykes was limited with respect to specific commitments from major investors who might want to erect facilities on the right-of-way. This was evidenced in January 1963, when he temporized over endorsing Hugh Martin's idea for a smaller hotel on CPR land, noting that it might not be wise since as long as there was a chance of securing Dowling's services, "we should avoid confronting him with a such a fait accompli as a commitment to accommodate a hotel."[40]

CITY-CPR RELATIONS

Sykes was well aware that the plans announced by his company to redevelop an area immediately east of the railway station did not warrant the sort of active city involvement that he envisaged. The announcement on June 20, 1962, had been nothing more than a public statement by a major corporation that it intended to develop part of its land in a prime downtown area. Mindful of its marginal reputation, the CPR had orchestrated the announcement by garnering as much business and press support as possible. Included in this orchestration was the mercurial Calgary mayor, Harry Hays, who wanted to take the credit for finally igniting a hitherto reluctant tenant into action. But in terms of city involvement, it was little different from any other major redevelopment project by private interests. Under normal circumstances, the redevelopment proposal would be subject to due process, which involved the submission of a preliminary plan that specified overall land use and zoning considerations and that included provision for utilities and recreational areas. The plan would then be circulated to relevant department heads for review and comment subject to final approval by the city's Technical Planning Board and, ultimately, by City Council.

But this project was different for several reasons. First, its potential for increased civic revenue had no precedent, and this alone was enough to induce a starry-eyed compliance on the part of the city. Second, although city planners were nearing completion of the city's first general plan, they had decided to omit the downtown area pending further study and recommendation by outside consultants. In terms of automobile traffic movement from the south, the CPR's long-range redevelopment plans regarding traffic access under or over the tracks would have a decided impact on the Downtown Master Plan. And finally, Sykes had allies who shared his vision, including Harry Hays. Equally fortuitous was the presence of Chief Commissioner Dudley Batchelor and Public Works and Utilities Commissioner John Steel, both of whom saw the long-range potential of the plan. The highly regarded Batchelor was a municipal finance expert who strongly believed in executive power. He was also close to retirement. Unfortunately, little is known about John Steel, a Scot who had come to Calgary from Regina, where he had been city commissioner and director of planning. It is difficult to get an accurate picture of him or of any private agenda he might have had. In terms of personality, he was mercurial. On the one hand, he could be abrupt and domineering. David Russell, then a rookie alderman, recalls Steel taking him aside after a City Council meeting and setting him straight classroom-style. On the other hand, he could be charming and enjoyed the respect of many aldermen. He would also succeed Batchelor as chief commissioner within a year. Two things are certain about Steel in the context of this discussion. First, he could be very, very convincing. Second, his highest priority was finding solutions to Calgary's traffic problems, and he felt that the CPR held the best solution.

Sykes carefully cultivated commonalities of interest with the city. Through public utterances and conversations, as well as telephone calls to Hays and City Hall executives, he let it be known that his company was in for the long haul, that sound planning principles necessitated close co-operation, and that the city would gain more than the CPR from redevelopment. At a luncheon meeting at the Palliser Hotel on September 14, 1962, attended by the mayor, the commissioners, several aldermen, Rod Sykes, and Fred Stone, the foundations for close co-operation were laid.[41] But by whom? It was a very interesting meeting.

After introductory remarks by Harry Hays, the meeting was opened by Fred Stone, who alluded to the CPR's greatness and its changing policies regarding urban land development. Sykes spoke next. In calling for the city to co-operate with the company for mutual gain, Sykes elaborated on the company's Land Use Study, then underway, to demonstrate the CPR's seriousness of intent. It was a low-key address clearly predicated on the assumption of city co-operation. During questioning by aldermen, however, both Sykes and Stone were vague in their responses. They did not know how long the Land Use Study was going to take; the time frame for the removal of facilities was like "opening a Pandora's Box"; details on the new station were under preparation; the timeline for retention of spur lines waited on engineering studies. And when cost-conscious alderman Grant MacEwan asked about the cost to the city and about whether there was any merit in participating at all, Hays decided enough was enough. He asked Stone and Sykes to leave the room so that the commissioners and aldermen could discuss the issue.

There was little discussion. Both Batchelor and Steel went into persuasion mode and focused almost entirely on the pending Downtown Master Plan. Batchelor explained that the city could now implement the plan itself in co-operation with the CPR rather than paying for expensive consultants. With the CPR now in the picture and involving itself so heavily in the downtown core, Batchelor stressed "the fantastic" impact that the project would have on the city and the opportunity to turn Calgary into a New York rather than a Los Angeles. Steel was no less enthusiastic. The peerless convincer agreed with Batchelor that integration of planning with the CPR was imperative, noting that the railway "can't do anything without our downtown study; we can't solve our problems without knowing what the CPR is going to do." He proposed postponing the current urban renewal study for the east end of the city and forming a team to work exclusively on the downtown plan, adding, "I would personally supervise our study and would meet weekly with Mr. Sykes to dovetail our thinking. We would depend on them [the CPR] for engineering studies and we would undertake planning studies and then dovetail them together."

It was all too much for the aldermen, who sat in stolid silence. After Steel exulted that "this is the greatest thing that has ever hit the City," Hays adjourned the meeting by saying, "If everyone here is agreed we will bring a recommendation to Council for formal approval." An interesting meeting indeed!

Steel was true to his word. If he had any doubts, a visit to Philadelphia in October to see what had been done there with the railway tracks reinforced his belief that close co-operation with the CPR was the only way to go. Under his impetus, the city did back off on its plan for urban renewal in the east end by securing approval from the Central Mortgage and Housing Corporation to postpone the requisite preliminary studies. Steel and Batchelor then set up a six-person planning team (referred to as the Downtown Study Group) led by Deputy City Planner Geoff Greenhalgh to work with the CPR and the commissioners to develop a Downtown Master Plan. The team met monthly with the mayor, the Board of Commissioners, and the planning director, and weekly with Steel. According to the terms of reference of the planning team, this level of co-operation between Steel and Sykes was expected to result in a "complete liaison between City and C.P. Staffs."[42] Thus, for all intents and purposes, planning for Calgary's downtown core was not just to provide "a workable staged plan for future growth" but also to "develop an inner core incorporating land made available by the Canadian Pacific Railway."[43]

Interestingly, the planning team prepared for its work by re-examining the Mawson Report, a grand scheme for the development of the city on the "City Beautiful" model prepared by British town planner Thomas Mawson in 1914. The team doubtless took heart at Mawson's view of the railway as a major barrier to integrated development. Yet one wonders what team members thought about his strong feelings about the aesthetic value of the riverbank with respect to restaurants, promenades, boating facilities, and park spaces.[44] For his part, Sykes was delighted with city co-operation "in a project we initiated and along lines we suggested."[45] And although he thought the planning team had a "preoccupation with aesthetics, social planning and noble-sounding academic approaches" and that the CPR needed to inject the necessary "practical, commercial and economic factors," he was under no illusion as to the proper path of action.[46] In urging his superiors to "stay in step" and work closely with the city "to achieve what we both want: prosperity and growth in the Central Business District," he warned: "It is one thing to share and have influence in the development of thinking and policies and quite another to change minds already made up — especially when the minds are committee and specialist ones."[47]

In retrospect, the brief period in the late fall of 1962 represented the apex of city-CPR co-operation. The city was preparing a Downtown Master Plan in concert with its long-time major tenant and sometime adversary, and, for its part, the CPR seemed prepared to align its major redevelopment plans for underused land on the right-of-way with city policy. Although it seemed too good to last, one cannot help wondering what might have happened if the CPR had not dropped the bombshell that changed everything.

REROUTING THE TRACKS

In addressing a local business association in October 1962, Sykes had this to say:

> Well in closing at long last I will just say that we are looking for all the help we can get. We're thick-skinned and take criticism as well as advice — we're doing our best not to tread on anyone's toes in the course of our work, but there are so many darned toes about that I'll remind you of the traditional old-time dance hall notice and ask you to apply it to us if necessary: "Don't shoot the piano player — he's doing his best."[48]

Although Sykes was not personally responsible, nothing mocked the integrity of those remarks more than the decision in early 1963 to reroute the railway tracks along the south bank of the Bow River. This decision was flawed in its conception and arrogant in its presentation. Ultimately, it was pivotal in dooming the project.

From the outset, all sides agreed that redevelopment costs and the need for more efficient traffic movement meant that the existing railway tracks could not remain at grade. The general consensus was that they would be completely or partially depressed in their present location or possibly moved a few yards to the south to enable more redevelopment on the downtown side. By August 1962, this assumption was common knowledge. And while it was true that the CPR maintained that nothing was certain until engineering studies were complete, company executives allowed this belief to stand uncontested, as evidenced by comments in the press, from the city, and from Sykes himself.

On August 14, 1962, *The Albertan* informed the public that the CPR intended to reduce its trackage "to one or two sets of tracks cutting through an open cut in place of the 400' right of way."[49] A similar statement appeared in the *Herald* on August 17.[50] The article in *The Albertan* also quoted Sykes as saying that "the Company plans to put the main line in an open ditch and use the rest of its downtown right-of-way for commercial development." In the September 14 meeting with city officials, Sykes said that "there was nothing to suggest that the rails would be removed from downtown."[51] City officials seemed equally convinced. In a progress report on the CPR Downtown Study dated November 9, Dudley Batchelor referred to the depression of the tracks as "a basic premise."[52] As late as November 30, at about the same time as the CPR engineers were wrapping up their feasibility studies, Sykes told the Downtown Study Group (the city's planning team) that its design proposals should be based on the assumption that the tracks will be depressed.[53] Nothing was further from the truth.

In November 1962, the CPR sent engineer Fred Joplin and a team of engineers under his direction to Calgary to study feasibility options concerning the tracks. An honours graduate in civil engineering from the University of British Columbia, where he had played quarterback for the UBC Thunderbirds, Joplin was a twice-decorated squadron leader in World War II. He joined the CPR in 1947 and was promoted from divisional engineer to special engineer for the Calgary project.[54] Apparently, he developed a good working relationship with Steel, a poor one with Sykes, and none at all with the city's Engineering Department.

Joplin and his team completed their study in a very short time, given the scope of the recommendations, and with no external input from any city official or department, or from the Mannix Company, a local major contractor who had offered to do a pro bono cost analysis of track depression. Sykes was left in the dark, but according to Sykes, Steel was not, although how much the latter actually knew about the study is conjectural. In December, Joplin returned to Montréal, where he presented his findings and recommendations to CPR's vice-president, Ian Sinclair.

In addition to the feasibility of the project and costs associated with the anticipated partial or full depression of the tracks in their present location, Joplin's team had studied three other alternatives. First, a complete bypass of the city was considered. Under this alternative, the main line would follow the CPR's Edmonton line and be diverted north of the city in the Beddington area. The diverted line would follow Beddington and Big Hill Creeks and rejoin the main line near Cochrane. The other two alternatives called for the main line to diverge just east of 9th Street East and follow either the north or south bank of the Bow River, rejoining the main line near 14th Street West. Of these latter two options, the one recommended was a two-mile diversion along the south bank of the Bow River. Indications are that Sinclair liked this recommendation but wanted more details before taking it to the CPR president and Board of Directors for a final decision. For all intents and purposes, however, the south bank alternative was an accepted fact by mid-January 1963.[55]

Being an engineering study, the recommendations were based on the costs associated with feasibility.[56] Although the Beddington diversion, at $7.5 million, was nowhere near the most expensive alternative, it was rejected because, in the engineers' opinion, it would cost the company more in the long run since steepness of grade in some areas was the equivalent cost of adding a few miles to the transcontinental main line. Full depression of the tracks in their present location was also dismissed on engineering grounds because of water table problems and the $13 million expenditure needed to address them. According to Joplin, four to seven feet of water would be encountered in the requisite twenty-eight-foot trench, necessitating retaining walls, waterproofing, and pumping. Even with these restraints, Joplin believed that the pressure would be too great over a long distance. Partial depression in an open cut thirteen feet deep was the cheapest option at $7 million, but it, too, would encounter water table problems, according to the engineers, while also presenting grade issues for the street crossings. Another reason for rejecting the depression options concerned the loss of revenue due to interference in rail operations during construction. The north bank of the Bow had no advantage over the south (which makes one wonder why it was considered in the first place) and would require extra bridges. This left the south bank, with its $9.5 million construction costs and the unequivocal recommendation to adopt it.

Although it is unclear exactly when they became aware of the south bank recommendation, civic officials reacted with a mixture of shock, dismay, and surprise. According to Sykes, "the planners were horrified."[57] Mayor Harry Hays made a plea for reconsideration in favour of track depression. Chief Commissioner Dudley Batchelor summed up what he probably thought was a betrayal when he wrote: "The acceptance of this proposal by the City meant, for all practical purposes, the abandonment of much planning and thinking which had been engendered."[58] It is small wonder that Sykes told Robert Dowling on January 18 that he expected "stormy weather ahead."[59]

But within ten days, all had changed. In a letter to Steel on February 1, Sykes acknowledged an official turnaround at City Hall: "I was very glad to hear from you yesterday afternoon that the proposed South Shore diversion appeared to be feasible from the Commissioners' point of view."[60] Apparently, Sykes had been trying to convince Steel of the merits of the south bank while "listening to his complaints about lack of co-operation and lack of liaison."[61] But were Sykes's formidable powers of persuasion the sole reason for commissioners buying into a deal from which they had recoiled a week earlier or for their realization that track depression was not a viable option? Possibly not. Maybe they saw how the decision could be turned to advantage or, to use a Sykes metaphor, how

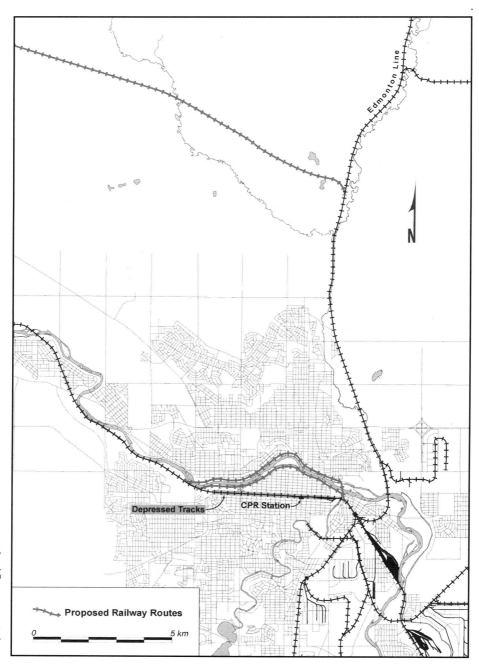

Map 3. Rerouting proposals

Proposed Railway Routes

Depressed Tracks

CPR Station

Edmonton Line

N

0   5 km

they could make lemonade out of lemons. A railway running along the banks of the Bow River could serve to justify the long-desired but seemingly forgotten east-west freeway — or parkway, as it was called — alongside the tracks. Batchelor later wrote:

> We were quite satisfied in our own minds . . . that the relocation of the *railway in itself could not be recommended*. . . . The more we examined this scheme, particularly having regard to the bene-fits of the roadway to our traffic system and the long search and study we had experienced over four years in endeavouring to get a connection from the Blackfoot Trail in the East to the down-town area, the more we were satisfied that the overall benefits of the entire conception, namely relocated railway, new parkway, vacant CPR right-of-way and potential development on such, were beginning to take shape.[62]

Such pragmatics did not apply to the Planning Department, which responded angrily to the proposed railway diversion.[63] In a strongly worded critique, it argued that the south bank route would consume far too much land in excess of right-of-way needs through ramps, junctions, and overpasses. It would also effectively wreck development planned under urban renewal since the CMHC would not grant money within two hundred feet of a railway right-of-way. Commenting that railroad functions in the downtown area were no longer of prime importance in Calgary and that "in many famous cities, a river is a valuable natural asset," and stressing the need to examine other alternatives, the Planning Department defined a philosophical position that ran directly counter to that held by the commissioners: "All objective studies dedicated to creating a better urban environment have carefully reserved the river as an integral part of the city. The possible selection of a rail route that would divide the city and the river destroys a concept that we hold valid and necessary."[64]

Given Sykes's statements many years later about his private beliefs regarding the rerouting issue, his response to the Planning Department's position appears overly acerbic.[65] He dismissed the objections "as a somewhat emotional reaction." It was, he wrote to Stone, indicative of "the kind of thinking with which we have to deal" and of "the calibre of some of the planners."[66] Not surprisingly, the city planners' concerns were given short shrift in City Hall. The Planning Department's report was filed away, not even reaching City Council for comment. The commissioners' minds were made up. All that remained was to get City Council onside.

A meeting with City Council was set up for the morning of February 19, 1963, in the penthouse of the Palliser Hotel.[67] In attendance were the city commissioners, Mayor Hays, and eleven of the twelve aldermen. The usual CPR complement was there, but with one important addition. Accompanying Stone, Sykes, and Joplin was Vice-President Ian Sinclair, the man who was to be the CPR's chief negotiator. It was Sinclair's first visit to Calgary in this capacity, and his presence at the meeting added an authoritative dimension. Described by columnist Allan Fotheringham as "a linebacker who stumbled into the chairman's office by mistake,"[68] the burly, workaholic, no-nonsense Sinclair, a.k.a. "Big Julie," had the mind to match his physique. A graduate in economics and law from the University of Manitoba, he was both articulate and incisive. A formidable and intimidating force, he guarded his company's interests zealously and held the "old school" belief that a bargain once made should not be violated by subsequent concessions. This was the larger-than-life man whom the city had to ultimately face across the bargaining table. This was the adversary. Not Stone, not Joplin, and not Sykes. From the city's point of view, this was hardly a pleasing prospect!

The purpose of the meeting was "to advise the Council members of the progress that had been made between the city and the CPR with respect to the development of the CPR right-of-way and to secure their comments thereon." Sinclair spoke first, telling the group that he hoped an agreement in principle would be in place within a month. Those aldermen wondering what agreement Sinclair was talking about were soon to get their answer, but it came not from Sinclair, Stone, or Sykes — or even Joplin, for that matter. The honey-tongued John Steel took the floor, delivering his message as a fait accompli and as the reasoned opinion of a man who had "done his homework." He went through the various alternatives that had been studied but gave the most detail to the south bank diversion, which he described as "the most feasible." He minimized any difficulties and left the aldermen with the impression that they were facing a minor disruption. No difficulty was foreseen in the complex bridge modifications necessary to accommodate the new right-of-way: as Steel succinctly stated, "The mechanics of getting to this location can be worked out and no difficulty is seen in rerouting the tracks."

Following an address by Joplin, who provided further details about water table problems in the present right-of-way, with an aside about a perfunctory consideration of a tunnel under the exclusive suburb of Mount Royal, the meeting was opened to questions from the floor. Although the answers to queries about crossings, the new station, and time of completion generally lacked details, the aldermen were left with two very important assumptions, assumptions that doubtless guided the decision they were to reach at meeting's end. First, despite being given no figures, they were told that costs to the city "would be slight." Second, they were under the impression that the old right-of-way was to be taxable once the diversion was complete. The following comment was part of a written summary of questions and answers, and was contained in an official description of the meeting signed by Hays, Batchelor, and Steel: "The CPR propose to retain ownership of the existing right-of-way, and make it available for development. Under their charter, the right-of-way and station are tax free. Their existing right-of-way would be removed from the charter and be taxable."

As he had done at a similar meeting six months earlier, Mayor Hays took over, focusing on what the meeting was all about and what needed to be done. He asked the aldermen if they would give Sinclair the go-ahead to take the new proposal to his board and if they would be prepared to endorse it if it ultimately came to City Council. And as before, he got what he wanted. Alderman P.N.R. Morrison went even further, moving an informal motion authorizing the mayor and commissioners to assist in the presentation of this scheme (ostensibly to whomever) and adding that it was so far reaching that he anticipated no opposition from the council. No one objected and Hays noted the unanimity. The meeting closed on that note. It had consumed about an hour and a quarter.

Negotiations continued when Hays, Batchelor, and Steel visited Montréal in late March and conferred with Sinclair and CPR President N.R. Crump. Although the details of the meetings are not known, we can surmise from comments made by Batchelor that they left Montréal much better informed and more convinced than ever about the merits of the project.[69] Both sides agreed to a Heads of Arrangement, an announcement of broad objectives subject to further negotiations and approval by both parties. Since the project involved expropriation and deviation from subdivision regulations, the approval of the Alberta legislature was necessary. The representatives of the city and the CPR at that Montréal meeting also agreed that the announcement of the agreed-upon Heads of Arrangement should be made in Calgary. The city officials arrived back in the city on or around April 1. Ian Sinclair was either in tow or a day or two behind them. Secret talks took place in the mayor's office on April 3 and 4. Although an announcement was expected on April 4, nothing was forthcoming, but it was apparent that the whole city was in high anticipation. On the morning of Friday, April 5, *The Albertan* referred to "the curtain of silence" that had descended on City Hall. The well-timed announcement came in late morning, in time for the *Herald* to get the scoop on its morning competitor. Just above a photograph of Sykes, Stone, Joplin, Sinclair, and Hays, all with beaming smiles, ran the headline, "$35 Million Face-Lift for Calgary Revealed."[70] The article extolled the mammoth redevelopment program being planned by the CPR, including a $3 million futuristic-looking convention centre right beside the Palliser Hotel. The $35 million was merely for the initial development and was expected "to soar higher." It would result, crowed the article, "in a rebuilt downtown within two decades." The announcement was made by a jubilant Harry Hays. It was his finest hour. It was also three days before a federal election.

Around the same time as the Palliser Hotel meeting in late February, the minority federal Liberal government fell on a non-confidence motion, and an election was called for April 8, 1963. The federal Liberal party, desperate for an attractive candidate in a city well-known for its allegiance to Tory blue, seized upon Calgary's popular mayor, Harry Hays, who, though hardly a staunch Liberal with higher political ambitions, was a Liberal nonetheless. Doubtless induced by assurances about a potential Cabinet post, Hays agreed to stand as the Liberal Party candidate in Calgary South. A Conservative Party stronghold, Calgary South represented hazardous country for even the popular Hays, especially given the fact that the Conservative Party had an attractive candidate of its own: Jack Leslie, the alderman most skeptical about what Hays and the CPR were planning, had also agreed to stand for election. Under normal circumstances, Leslie would have won easily. But these were hardly normal circumstances.

Hays, a persuasive fundraiser, was backed by substantial money, some of it put up by disaffected Conservatives.[71] The reason was clear, and it had nothing to do with a lack of faith in Leslie's abilities. Hays gave the reason in his campaign platform: "There were a number of rather persuasive men and women in Calgary South with various political beliefs who were kind enough to suggest that the principles which we had tried to follow municipally could and would be applied to government in Ottawa."[72] Hays had a powerful team behind him. His sixty-person "Citizens for Hays Committee" included almost half of his City Council, among them P.N.R. Morrison and Grant MacEwan, and leading businessmen like Carl Nickle, Harry Cohen, Jack Pierce, Peter Rule, and Jim Gray.[73] On the campaign trail, while he advocated Liberal principles such as stronger ties with the United States, as well as job creation and the social security benefits it promised, his main message, as in his civic campaigns, called for stability and efficiency in government.

Although results from advance polling stations later showed that he was actually leading Leslie by about the same majority as that of his victory, Hays did not let his work on the CPR redevelopment project stand for naught. According to Jean Leslie in her biography of her husband, Hays's carefully orchestrated announcement of April 5 was designed to ensure his victory at the polls on April 8.[74] When the results were tabulated, Calgary South voters had given Hays a 1,300-vote margin of victory over Leslie.[75] Moreover, in spite of the Liberal Party's national triumph, Hays was the only Liberal elected in Alberta. There can be no doubt that Jean Leslie is correct: the April 5 announcement was a blatant political ploy. What is not so evident is whether it made the difference she thought it did. An examination of the various polling stations shows a stronger level of working-class support for Leslie, who actually topped more polls than Hays did. The big difference came in the more affluent areas, where Hays was popular and where voter turnout was higher.[76] But be that as it may, the CPR had indirectly helped Hays get elected, and — ironically, as it turned out — his CPR-assisted election removed him from the power base that the company needed. By July, Hays had resigned as mayor and was off to Ottawa, where he assumed the position of minister of Agriculture.[77]

THE HEADS OF ARRANGEMENT

The newspaper publicity that engulfed the city during the first week in April focused primarily on the tremendous implications of the redevelopment proposal. Ian Sinclair commented that it was the "most unique" and had the most potential of any development in Canada.[78] John Steel said it would solve the city's downtown traffic problems "virtually overnight."[79] While reference was made to the removal of the tracks and some guidelines given as to when the process might begin, the implications of a major realignment of CPR trackage did not command much media attention. Nor did the way the agreement had been reached, for that matter.

Even a cursory glance at the Heads of Arrangement document should have been cause for alarm at City Hall. Yes, its brevity was to be expected given the fact that it was supposed to be an agreement in principle only. Despite this intent, however, it was ambiguous and contained far too much detail favouring the CPR to be an "only in principle" agreement, a regrettable imbalance that was exacerbated later when CPR officials began referring to it in binding terms.

The document that Hays signed was a little over four pages in length (see appendix A).[80] It opened with three main statements. The first outlined the CPR's plan to divert the rail lines to the south bank of the Bow and the company's intentions to prepare and implement a comprehensive master plan for development. There was no mention of any obligation to the city. This sentiment was not reciprocated in the second statement. The agreement was said to be in the public interest and promised city co-operation "to the fullest extent of its powers in assisting the Canadian Pacific to implement the plan." The third statement committed the city to acquiring land for the new right-of-way.

In the rest of the document, the CPR did not make a single specific commitment beyond agreeing to development and assuming the costs of new railway bridges needed for the diversion. The same could not be said of the city. Although there was some ambiguity, the city agreed to continue to exempt the present right-of-way from taxation until the CPR chose to develop it. The new right-of-way would also be exempt from taxation. The city agreed to set aside the entire redevelopment area as "an area for special development" subject to separate zoning considerations that included waiving the normal requirement that 10 percent of the redevelopment area be reserved for community purposes such as parks or recreation. To this end, the document stated, "The City will co-operate to the fullest extent in facilitating the specific development plans." The city also agreed to construct its convention centre on CPR land, to consult the railway company if land being bought on the CPR's behalf for the new right-of-way exceeded 10 percent of market value, and to assume the total costs of any bridging arrangements that affected both the rail lines and the parkway. The redevelopment area was defined as being between 6th Street East and 14th Street West, but the agreement failed to include the fact that the CPR was not planning to develop most of it for at least twenty years. One did not need to possess a legal mind to conclude that the city was not starting from a level playing field.

But in those heady days of early April, the future was roseate and the blinkers were on. The concept was simply too big, too magnificent, and too promising to induce anything but raw optimism. All that remained was to work out the details, formalize the final agreement, and get it approved by the legislature in Edmonton. In the ensuing months, though, the blinkers would come off.

IMPLICATIONS

Several points arise out of the foregoing discussion. The main ones relate to the rerouting of the tracks, but others are worth considering as well. The first and most significant matter concerns the proposal itself and the planning context in which it was placed. The CPR redevelopment plan essentially defined the long-range planning strategies adopted by the city rather than the other way around. What should have emerged as but one possible alternative for downtown development in terms of civic goals became not only the sole driving force, but also one that originated with a private corporation. Thus, the downtown plan as it was evolving in 1962 and 1963 was built around an incoherent and uncertain proposal. In terms of long-range planning vision and objectives, the city was in default mode. As stated earlier, the city's compliant attitude toward the proposal evinced the fact that city leaders had no vision whatsoever for the downtown.

The second point concerns CPR managers and the fact that they, too, had little idea of what they wanted to do. City officials and the public knew little more about what was going to occur, and when, on the right-of-way than they had a year earlier. The role of Rod Sykes is a good example. At first glance, delegating him to conduct a land-use study seemed to be good corporate strategy, but why would the company send a man to Calgary with the task of soliciting investor interest and then give him nothing with which to convince them beyond vague allusions to redevelopment? And why would a potential consulting developer be solicited, a developer with such prestige and influence that any potential investor commitment waited on his as-yet unprepared design plans? It seems that the only tangible results Sykes secured in the summer and fall of 1962 — beyond the Land Use Study, then underway — concerned lease renegotiations on the present right-of-way. Sykes thought that present rents were too low and raised them, even those of Max Bell, the owner of *The Albertan* and the soon-to-be member of the consortium that was to become the CPR's largest shareholder.[81]

The strained relations between Sykes and Fred Joplin epitomized the tensions within the company between the railway and non-transportation interests. Sykes was resentful of the elitist status of CPR engineers and felt that Joplin was uncommunicative and had private agendas of his own. According to Sykes, this resulted in mixed messages to stakeholders and the public, especially over the rerouting issue. Joplin's behaviour in not keeping Sykes informed of his engineering studies, the private negotiations with Hays of which Sykes knew nothing, and Sykes's own frustration over lack of direction all point to internecine divisions within the corporation. Furthermore, Sykes believed that the company was too hierarchical in nature and was dominated by railway interests and "riddled with the cult of cronyism." This seems to be reflected in a comment that Sykes heard about himself: "Sykes thinks he is rowing the boat when he isn't even in it."[82]

For all his geniality and good fellowship, Harry Hays remains an enigmatic figure. A man who once told the House of Commons that "statistics was for losers," he probably saw only "the big picture."[83] While his secretive negotiations with Crump, Sinclair, and other CPR executives are not part of the archival record, his hold over City Council invites speculation about what the project's outcome would have been had he remained mayor for another term. The *North Hill News* commented that his was a regime that ruled aldermen.[84] A letter from the Calgary Labour Council to City Council just after the Heads of Arrangement was announced noted, "It is high time that our aldermen stopped idolizing one man."[85] Yet Hays's staunch supporters on City Council also included strong individualists like Grant MacEwan and P. N. R. Morrison. But still, one wonders. How much was Hays an opportunist who simply brought a good idea to the table? Was he aware of how difficult the negotiations would be? Was he even planning to be around? According to his federal election campaign statement in 1963, he did not intend to seek another term as mayor in the fall of 1963 when, ostensibly, the negotiations toward the formal agreement would still be ongoing. Also, when he accepted the Liberal nomination in early 1963, he asked the aldermen to vote on whether he should resign in order to campaign. Then, after he had signed the Heads of Arrangement and won the election, several aldermen wanted him to remain as mayor to see the CPR issue through while also serving in Ottawa, an untenable situation once he became minister of Agriculture. He did not press the issue but stressed that it should be at the will of City Council. While it could be argued that he was certain of his support in the latter two instances, some conjecture remains over how much Harry Hays was prepared to stay the distance.

City Council's minimal involvement was maintained. Between its tacit approval of negotiations with the CPR and the Heads of Arrangement announcement in April 1963, the council was directly involved in only one briefing. Here, the aldermen learned little beyond grand assurances. No alderman met Robert Dowling; probably none of them was even aware of his presence in the city. Neither Sykes nor Joplin addressed City Council. Following the Heads of Arrangement announcement and the jubilation that followed it, one alderman noted that his only criticism was the fact that — as was the case in June 1962, when the CPR announced its urban development intentions — the press seemed to know about it before City Council did.[86] City Council's ignorance of the proposal would prove to be a gross disadvantage when Harry Hays left and a new mayor took over. Its solution was to trust its administration and try to play catch up. That proved to be an impossible task.

But the decision to reroute the tracks along the south bank of the Bow River is far and away the most difficult to understand and reconcile. It was a bad decision. One element of the rerouting decision that is puzzling is the CPR's insensitivity and arrogance. Here was a private company suddenly announcing without prior discussion or consultation that it intended to usurp prime city property within city limits virtually on its own terms and on the basis of its own unshared engineering studies.[87] Of course, this was not stated so unequivocally but the message was clear: give us what we want or forget the whole thing. Ian Sinclair said exactly that less than a month after the Heads of Arrangement was announced.[88] Second, on learning of this insensitive and arbitrary decision, why did city administrators yield so readily? It could be contended that the commissioners were blinded by the dazzle of potential tax dollars. They may also have realized the validity of the CPR's reasons for not depressing the tracks. But this does not explain their sudden anger followed by an equally sudden capitulation. The change of heart may simply have been due to the sudden realization that the parkway was back in play.

The question as to how early in the negotiations the CPR knew it was going to reroute the rails needs to be considered. A contemporary University of Calgary geographer thought the decision had been made before the engineering studies began in November.[89] A map inserted into a draft of the Land Use Study and dated June 1962 shows two potential routes for the railway along the Bow River, one reaching the riverbank by following 6th Street East and the other through the existing Fort Calgary site, then the property of the Canadian National Railway.[90] Arguably, this was not conclusive evidence that the CPR knew where it was going to go fully six months before the rerouting was announced. The two routes could have been two of many possibilities. However, if this is an indication of serious CPR thinking as early as June 1962, then the press, the public, and the city's downtown planning team had been misled into thinking that the tracks were going to be depressed.

Sykes was also misled. An examination of his correspondence to his superiors supports his claim that he believed that the tracks were to be depressed. A memorandum to his superiors as late as October summarizes his opinion that three engineering solutions were available: depressing the tracks, either completely or partially, or leaving them at grade.[91] He heard about the rerouting only in early January, the same time as the city learned about it. If the engineers' studies justified what the CPR intended in the first place and Sykes was not informed, this is additional evidence for the company's blurred focus.

Perhaps the most unfortunate outcome of the engineers' studies was the fact that they actually pointed the way to a solution that, if pursued, would have allowed the project to proceed to completion. The bypass route through Beddington would have freed up the existing right-of-way and preserved the riverbank. Furthermore, the Beddington plan was feasible in terms of expense and offered no construction problems. According to Sykes, the reasons for rejection were not valid and evinced the hidebound thinking typical of CPR engineers. Although he agreed with the engineers about the non-feasibility of track depression, he felt that minor alterations to grade at several places elsewhere along the main line would have negated the engineers' concerns about the extra length posed by the Beddington route.[92] The city and the CPR had enough on their plates with respect to the present right-of-way without introducing a second sensitive issue. The question as to why a viable and studied solution to a problem involving a massive project that promised all sorts of financial windfalls was dismissed so easily in favour of a controversial alternative remains at the centre of any serious debate about the CPR's grand plan for the city.

It is also possible that the CPR was very worried about another matter entirely. Its contractual tax-free concessions on its rights-of-way were becoming of concern to western Canadian premiers, who had already begun proceedings to have the offending clause removed from the 1881 contract.[93] Briefs to Ottawa were expected, and possibly a legal challenge. From the CPR's viewpoint, another tax-free right-of-way within the city under a special agreement and with no relation to the contract of 1881 was a sure way of hedging one's bets against a potentially damaging outcome.[94]

In conclusion, the Heads of Arrangement symbolized the end of rhetoric, mutual backslapping, and the luxury of basking in a sunny future. It was now time to negotiate. And when this began in the summer of 1963, it was time to see how much of the "win-win" rhetoric was true.

From Arrangement to Agreement

*Dodging the Negotiation Potholes,
April 1963 to January 1964*

April 1963 marked the beginning of the negotiations to transform the Heads of Arrangement into a formal agreement. However, instead of the evolution of a common understanding, irreconcilable divisions developed and insurmountable difficulties arose that ultimately doomed the project. Problems arose with both rights-of-way. New issues emerged. Opposition developed and battle lines were drawn. Despite these obstacles, on January 22, 1964, City Council gave its official go-ahead. The following discussion is an attempt to explain how this bizarre decision came about.

Following the Heads of Arrangement announcement in early April, it took the city another four months to begin actual negotiations. During this time, City Council appointed a new mayor to replace Harry Hays and, despite a lack of unanimity, reinforced its enthusiastic support for the project. The CPR, after waxing enthusiastic, gave hints of the entrenched position it would be adopting. Voices of concern were raised. In short, the battle lines were defined.

THE CITY COUNCILS OF 1963 AND 1964

Some mention should be made of the two city councils that were to preside over the redevelopment scheme as it unfolded. Although the most active role belonged to the 1964 council, the two councils overlapped strongly in terms of membership. Eight of the twelve aldermen served on both councils, and, of the newcomers in 1964, three had formally served as aldermen in the past. Despite the bitter criticism that both councils endured for their ineptitude, the individual aldermen (all men) brought considerable experience to the table. They were also long on both ambition and public service. Although their party affiliations varied, eleven had already sought or filled higher political office or else would run in the future. Three would occupy cabinet posts in the provincial government, another would be elected mayor in 1965, and the new acting mayor, Grant MacEwan, would go on to become one of the province's most popular lieutenant-governors. Three were lawyers. Two were decorated former soldiers — one an Order of Canada recipient and the other a British SAS commando who had been awarded the DSO, three MCs, the Croix de Guerre, and the American Legion of Merit, and whose wartime career had mirrored a Hollywood action movie. Eleven owned their own businesses, another was a household name in radio, and yet another had been a prominent member of the CCF. Most were in favour of the project, but they also had their own political and personal agendas along with their strong ties to community and business power bases. With the major project they were facing and like city councils everywhere, they needed a leader who had both enthusiasm for the project and the ego to make it a career capstone. Grant MacEwan, whom they selected from their number to replace Hays as acting mayor and who would subsequently win the fall election on his own popularity, had neither.[1]

In the above context, Grant MacEwan also deserves comment. He was a highly respected agriculturalist who had left his position as dean of the Faculty of Agriculture at the University of Manitoba to run in the federal by-election for Brandon in 1951. Like Hays, he had been assured a cabinet portfolio if successful. Unlike Hays, he lost. After serving as the editor of the *Western Producer* and as manager of the Canadian Beef Producers Association (Western Section), he came to Calgary in 1952 and entered municipal politics the following year. Over the next ten years, he served as alderman and, after securing a seat in the Alberta legislature in 1955, led the provincial Liberal Party into the elections of 1959. On City Council, he earned a solid reputation for his cost-consciousness and common sense. Initially, MacEwan liked the redevelopment plan, seeing it as a tax-dollar windfall, and he continued to support it through his aldermanic and mayoralty terms. Although known for his strong views on conservation, he went along with the riverbank route because it meant cleaning up a despoiled area where industrial waste, dilapidated housing, discarded rusted machinery, and other junk had turned the shoreline into an ugly, unsightly "dumping ground."[2] According to the *Herald*, the riverbank was "undeveloped, unimproved, a repository for junk and a haven for weeds."[3]

MacEwan, however, was never as enthusiastic as Hays about the project and did not share his faith in the CPR. Like many with rural backgrounds, he mistrusted the CPR and its self-serving policies. Thus, as negotiations bogged down and public anger mounted, his enthusiasm waned. MacEwan was also a true populist who believed that a major issue with long-range implications like the CPR plan should ultimately be decided by plebiscite rather than by the politicians whose job, he believed, was to debate, educate, and recommend. Despite being good friends, Hays and MacEwan were poles apart when it came to the CPR and to the democracy of decision making.

There is also the matter of MacEwan's propensity for leadership. He had no ego, despite his success as an author, his national reputation as an agricultural expert, and his growing number of awards and honours that ultimately included five honorary doctorates, the Order of Canada, the Premier's Award of Excellence (Alberta), the Governor General's Conservation Award, the Sir Frederick Haultain Prize, and shortlist considerations as western Canada's and Calgary's Man of the Century. He was essentially an individualist who believed in following one's conscience and was therefore no consensus builder. He also lacked the instincts for political infighting. This project demanded both. MacEwan's leadership in this issue is better assessed against the person he was rather than what his detractors wanted him to be.

In summary, the members of the two city councils that accepted the 1963 Heads of Arrangement and presided over the tumultuous events of 1964 were experienced, disparate in their backgrounds and politics, and generally in favour of the project, some more enthusiastically than others. The voices of concern were in the minority, and only one was persistent throughout. However, their collective knowledge of details respecting the CPR proposal was lacking; there seemed to be little interaction or strategizing, especially among opponents of the redevelopment plan. Finally, although Acting Mayor Grant MacEwan was a supporter, he did not share his predecessor's enthusiasm and made little attempt to influence the council either way. Thus, executive control prevailed, and only when the swell of public opinion began mounting in the late winter of 1963–64 was this dominance challenged.

RESPONSES TO THE HEADS OF ARRANGEMENT

The Heads of Arrangement (see appendix A) was a brief document. In spite of the fact that its announcement was news to them, as it was to the general public, the aldermen's response to the Heads of Arrangement was generally favourable — so much so that, in the opinion of the *Herald,* the only area of disagreement concerned who should get the credit. Inspired by Harry Hays's comment that "the benefits so outnumber the liabilities that any thinking Calgarian will go along with it," several aldermen were equally enthused. "This is the biggest and best thing that has ever happened to Calgary," said Clarence Mack. To veteran Ernie Starr, it was a "dream come true" — that one he had been anticipating since he had joined City Council in 1945. Future Member of Parliament Ray Ballard thought it was "a terrific deal" and one that he was 100 percent behind. Ted Duncan was "really excited about it," noting that "it's the obvious and only answer to remedy stagnation and blight creeping into the business district from east 8th and 9th avenues."[4] Six weeks later, City Council voted to appoint a three-man coordinating committee, all pro-redevelopment, to work with the CPR "to ensure the scheme's accomplishment."[5]

The City of Calgary

Like the original announcement a year earlier, the Heads of Arrangement carried the signature of a crusading mayor. It was different, however, in that it announced a formal agreement. The first stirrings of uncertainty appeared early on City Council, stirrings that quickly got the attention and response of senior administration. Roy

Farran told the press on April 6, "It's pretty hard to comment on something when you don't know who is footing the bill."[6] Then, on April 29, Jack Leslie introduced notice of a comprehensive motion that called for further economic and engineering studies to determine both the total cost to the taxpayer and the effects of the redevelopment project on the downtown area in terms of taxation structure, land values, and retail vitality. He wanted engineering studies to re-examine the feasibility of alternatives to the riverbank route, the implications of alterations to bridges, and the merits of an east-west freeway running along the riverbank. Leslie also wanted to know what other cities in North America were doing in similar circumstances. The motion was put on the agenda for May.[7]

Leslie's notice was enough to get his fellow aldermen thinking and raising issues of their own. Clarence Mack wanted to know details respecting taxation along the new right-of-way. Ted Duncan inquired about the possibility of provincial contributions and the effect of the scheme on the city's mill rate. Ray Ballard was concerned that all streets across the present right-of-way might not be open to automobile crossings. Roy Farran wanted a projection on how much the CPR would pay in annual taxes and details of their building commitments. He also called for an independent opinion on the reason for abandoning former long-range plans for riverbank development and urban renewal in the neighbourhood of Prince's Island.[8] Motions were also passed calling for a public hearing and asking for details on CPR contributions to bridge-work alterations to allow the new right-of-way and the company's schedule for development.[9] Other concerns were being raised by at least two planners, while the city's Parks Department was openly critical, saying that the scheme was deficient in landscaping and provided inadequate access to Prince's Island while obscuring the river from public view.[10]

While the Chamber of Commerce, the Calgary Stampede, and the Calgary Labour Council were quick to endorse the proposal, it was not long before other groups and individuals began expressing concern.[11] Letters began pouring in to City Hall protesting the redevelopment plan. The Local Council of Women was upset about the new route, arguing that it violated long-range concepts for riverbank development and asking for a strip at least a block wide between the river and the railway.[12] Labelling the provision for a convention centre adjacent to the Palliser "a gift to the CPR," a spokesman for the Hilton Hotel chain expressed concern that it would severely prejudice the hotel business elsewhere.[13] The Calgary Real Estate Board was nervous about the impact of the redevelopment on property values, a sentiment echoed by landowners on or near the new right-of-way, including the Bow Valley Ratepayers Association.[14] Others were worried about taxation, the east-west freeway, the impact of the railway line on surrounding residential and commercial areas, and the abandonment of projected urban renewal in east Calgary. These concerns continued to mount.

Figure 4. South bank of the Bow River, 1955. Described by the *Herald* as "a repository for junk and a haven for weeds," the degraded condition of the riverbank area led many to support plans to reroute the railway and build a parkway along the banks of the Bow. The Local Council of Women was the only major group to argue that a beautification plan would be the better long-range solution. Source: Glenbow Archives, NA 5093-206.

The rumblings of opposition caught the city commissioners by surprise. The last thing they needed was a full-blown public issue over the project before negotiations had even started. Their counter-strategy was twofold. First, they needed official authorization to commence negotiations as soon as possible. Second, the merits of the project required independent endorsement. It is a tribute to their seriousness of intent that they had achieved both by the end of June.

On May 20, the commissioners reversed due process by inviting City Council to a closed meeting — not at City Hall, as one might expect, but at the airport. It was an unprecedented action accompanied by a persuasive report, high-powered rhetoric and an opening act by a supportive University of Alberta economist.[15] The meeting bore fruit. In a special meeting on May 23, City Council unanimously authorized the commissioners to begin negotiations with the CPR toward a general Agreement of Intent. Jack Leslie's motion — which, if it had passed, might have redefined the entire issue — died on the table for want of a seconder.[16]

Interestingly, since City Council had not validated the Heads of Arrangement through a formal vote, its instructions to the commissioners on May 23 were on tenuous legal ground. It was not until June 27, 1963, when a motion was passed instructing the commissioners "to prepare a money bylaw to cover proposed borrowings for the CP project," that any legal improprieties were removed.[17]

Over the next month, as the commissioners attempted to defuse aldermanic concerns, they demonstrated their own vagueness, lack of knowledge, and considerable faith in the CPR. They erred in telling Ray Ballard that all crossings were to be open. They also thought that the CMHC would be providing money for the freeway, under its provisions for urban renewal, even though the prerequisite study had not been completed. Despite having little idea of the total costs to the city, they told Ted Duncan that the mill rate would not increase. As for Leslie's suggestion that reconsideration should be given to depression of the tracks, the commissioners informed Leslie that the decision was not the city's to make: "It has always been assumed that while the City would provide planning schemes relative to this project, the responsibility for cost and feasibility would be the responsibility of the CPR." Only Clarence Mack's question about current annual taxes on the new right-of-way was answered directly: $49,317.[18]

In June, three external reports were commissioned. The Stanford Research Institute, Van Ginkel Associates of Montréal, and economist Eric Hanson were asked to evaluate different aspects of the project. Their timeline was short — too short. In fact, all three reports were completed by the end of the month, although Eric Hanson's was an abbreviated version of his later and much more detailed study. All were positive. The fact that two contained qualifications did not matter to the commissioners or to those City Council members in favour of redevelopment. The reports gave them enough of what they wanted.

The Stanford Research Institute

The California-based Stanford Research Institute (SRI) was contracted to produce an economic evaluation of "the reasonableness of the proposal of the CPR to free its downtown right-of-way for development by relocating CPR trackage to the south bank of the Bow River." At the time that the report was requested, SRI was also working with the City of Calgary on a study of municipally owned industrial areas and thus had some familiarity with the city.[19] The report on the CPR proposal was commissioned on June 17 and completed by a two-man team a week later.

The six-page report concluded that "the proposal under consideration would be desirable from the City's point of view." Doubtless, this assertion by a highly reputable organization was all the commissioners needed, especially when half the report contained supportive information.[20] The chief author, economist E.C. Harvey, noted that the CPR had already accumulated "a large unit of downtown land," that "the owner (CPR) has a vested interest in the growth of Calgary and possesses considerable financial and management capabilities," and that "international publicity will be obtained from the announcement of a development as promising as this." As for benefits to the city, Harvey referred to increased tax revenues; a consolidation of the central business district (CBD) through rising land values and increased competitiveness, both internally and with other cities; improved access to the CBD via extra crossings and an east-west freeway; and the removal of manufacturing and wholesale establishments from downtown to modern industrial areas elsewhere in the city. In discussing the cost to the city, Harvey argued that heavy short-term expenses would be more than offset by long-term gains.

The report, however, was deficient in that it was prepared under severe constraints and based on assumptions that were far from assured. Harvey acknowledged in the report's preamble that in view of the short time period during which the report was prepared, the evaluation contained no new data and no engineering studies, and was based on existing material and on-the-spot surveys. In his final recommendation, he noted that the report was "subject to the assumptions listed earlier in this letter." These included acceptance that the riverbank route was the only feasible option, that the parkway faced no problems in connecting to Blackfoot Trail and would be completed as a single unit and not incrementally, and that the CPR would make available the necessary crossings across the tracks. All of these assumptions were wrong. Finally, in referring to the loss of potential recreational areas along the riverbank, the report assumed that other aesthetics would be considered in the plan for the CBD. At the time the report was presented to City Council, there were no such provisions. In short, the Stanford report was deficient in lending authority to the merits of the proposal.

Van Ginkel Associates

Like SRI, Van Ginkel Associates was commissioned in June and given a short timeline to complete its report. A husband-and-wife team with wide experience in several European countries and the United States, Van Ginkel Associates was currently involved in planning studies for the City of Montréal and for Bowring Park in St John's, Newfoundland. It was the firm's experience in planning and landscape architecture that led to a request for their services in assessing and recommending on the issues associated with the physical aspects of the plan.

The report was completed by June 24. As with SRI, the authors recognized the time restrictions placed on them and the fact that the project had a great many aspects that could not be worked out in detail.[21] Despite these limitations, the van Ginkels were positive toward the plan, describing its basic principle as "very sound indeed" and "likely unique in North America." The authors were also very impressed by the opportunity afforded by the proposal for the development of Calgary. Specifically, they declared that the plan had immense potential for developing and consolidating the downtown area and recommended immediate and imaginative implementation. As for the riverbank, the report intimated that its underuse and degraded condition justified any improvement. However, it fell short of total endorsement. After noting that "one would never project a railway along a riverbank if one had to design a new town," the authors were careful in their subsequent wording: "This may be the best solution providing that the design of the riverbank is treated very carefully." The report concluded: "We, on our part, have no reservation whatsoever in recommending that the City proceed with this scheme forthwith."[22]

This seemingly unequivocal concluding statement is misleading, since it was predicated on two alterations to the proposed plan, alterations that the authors felt were "of cardinal importance to the success of the total scheme." The first was debatable. The second showed that the van Ginkels were not convinced that the scheme gave proper integration to the downtown and the riverbank. They thought that the plan proposed too many downtown connections to the parkway and that only two were needed: at 14th Street and at the Elbow River, both for westbound and eastbound traffic. More significant was the recommendation that 4th Street West should be widened and continued north across Prince's Island (and the river) to connect with the Trans-Canada Highway at 16th Avenue North. The van Ginkels believed that this would link the downtown with the parkway and riverbank, reinforce the central area, and provide access to residential areas north and south of the river.

The van Ginkels' implicit reservations were further qualified in late August when Daniel van Ginkel informed the city commissioners that he had reconsidered the report with respect to the riverbank. In his opinion, the scheme was viable without track relocation and should be focused entirely on the present right-of-way with whatever modifications could be negotiated with the CPR. He received short shrift, being informed tersely, "We have devoted all our efforts to the river bank scheme."[23]

Eric Hanson

Since only final recommendations count and, for that matter, are often all that are read, the SRI and Van Ginkel Associates reports provided the city with ample ammunition to throw at critics of the scheme. But the commissioners had another ace in the hole. Economist Eric Hanson was already a consultant with the city. A fiscal expert with several publications to his credit, including a history of local government in Alberta, and the former head of the Department of Political Science at the University of Alberta, Hanson was a highly respected academic. Along with SRI and Van Ginkel Associates, he, too, presented a report to City Council in late June on the economic implications of the project.[24] Using words like "sound," "valid," and "reasonable" to describe the CPR's economic and land-use studies, Hanson concluded that "the net benefits of the redevelopment scheme appear to be so substantial on the basis of information available that a detailed major study is not required to prove the point."[25]

However, the city commissioners, with adverse publicity still on their minds, disagreed, arguing that "while it is difficult to assess the exact degree of reservation which may exist in the public mind, the commissioners feel that if additional economic information could offset this doubt then we should proceed with the proposed survey."[26] The $25,000 study, commissioned to Hanson and the former chair of the Board of Public Utilities, Ivan Robison, was to be ready by September 1963. Delayed for two months, the 236-page report, submitted on November 7, was replete with detail, statistics, and analysis, and mapped out a rosy future for the two partners if redevelopment occurred. Divided into four main sections — Economic Base, Physical Base, Taxation and Assessment, and Fiscal Base — the report provided the most unequivocal endorsement of the proposal:

> We have arrived at an entirely favourable view of the redevelopment project with particular reference to the people of Calgary and the Municipal Corporation of the City of Calgary. The proposal is imaginative and forward looking and it constitutes an attempt to adjust to the changing economic and social conditions in the western Canadian economy in the decades ahead.[27]

The report projected figures and statistics based on what might ensue with or without redevelopment and used population and income growth, and land availability within the CBD as variables to demonstrate a better and financially healthier city if the project went ahead. As for increased civic revenues, Hanson and Robison argued that by 1981, annual taxes would amount to $4 million if the plan was implemented and only $451,000 if it was not.[28] They cavalierly dismissed criticisms of the riverbank route with the comment: "We are aware of allegations that the new right-of-way should not run along the Bow River. We are also aware that we live in an imperfect and not an ideal world."[29]

The Hanson Report, as it came to be known, became the bible for those supporting the project. But it had its critics. A prominent geologist, J.C. Sproule, believed that Hanson's preliminary June report to City Council was the work of "a man who had already made up his mind."[30] Another critic, this one with a satirical bent, after calling Hanson "a run-of-the-mill teacher of economics," described his detailed report as "a hypothetical evaluation of taxation on a hypothetical situation; the hypothetical consequences of a hypothetical city rearrangement due to the hypothetical effects of a hypothetical agreement with the CPR."[31]

An academic rebuttal of the detailed Hanson Report came in a thirteen-page document released a month later by three University of Calgary geographers.[32] The Coulson Report, as it was popularly called, disagreed with Hanson's comparative points about future population growth and income with and without the redevelopment project. The authors' main criticism focused on Hanson's argument that the redevelopment project would alleviate the potential shortage of land in the CBD. After breaking down figures relating to available land in the present CBD and the amount of land the CPR was likely to actually develop, the Coulson Report writers presented a completely different view from that of Hanson, arguing that "during the next 10 years the need for CBD land can be easily be satisfied without the re-development of CPR land." Furthermore, they suggested that the availability of the CPR right-of-way for redevelopment could depress rather than stimulate parts of downtown Calgary.[33]

By the time negotiations began on August 6, much had changed since the Heads of Arrangement was signed. Specific questions were being asked in City Council. Voices of concern were being heard outside City Hall. External reports had been received that, on the surface at least, were pro-redevelopment. But what of the CPR? What had its executives done to bolster the cause?

The CPR

The answer to the above is not a great deal. Following the usual endorsements after the Heads of Arrangement announcement, the CPR gave the impression that it was prepared to bargain, but on specific terms. Both Sinclair and Stone were on hand to offer their praise for the proposal after the big April 5 announcement. "You've got a chance to build a city," declared Fred Stone. Ian Sinclair was more effusive, calling the proposal "the most unique and with the most potential of any development in Canada," and adding, "you won't recognize Calgary in thirty years."[34] A day later, he equated the projected convention centre with making Calgary a major international convention venue and with lifting the city's tourist revenues fivefold in five years.[35]

By the beginning of May, however, with the emergence of critical comments, the mood of the CPR began to change. Fred Stone referred to the press "getting its licks in" and to the "political dust" of disturbance.[36] Rod Sykes was equally concerned. He attributed the "dirty politics" of City Council in part to the loss of Harry Hays and the illness of Dudley Batchelor. He felt that the CPR needed to get the facts out as soon as possible to counter those who were turning the whole project into "a source of suspicion and distrust."[37] Sykes's concerns were echoed by the influential oilman and ardent supporter, Carl Nickle. In a letter to Sykes on May 29, Nickle expressed his surprise and concern over the negative press coverage; like Sykes, he believed that an information deficit was responsible. Nickle felt that the CPR response should take the form of public education through models, maps, and a "question-and-answer sheet," noting that in matters involving both private and public enterprise, it behooved the former to exercise extreme care.[38]

On June 7, three days after the city voluntarily dropped its lawsuit against the CPR over the responsibility for a washout west of 14th Street "in order not to jeopardize any other major agreement,"[39] Ian Sinclair gave a hint of how the CPR might bargain in the upcoming negotiations. He had been asked by the Board of Commissioners about the feasibility of abandoning the riverbank route in favour of track depression should the city contribute toward the extra cost.[40] His reply was terse, almost confrontational: "I think our position has been stated. In summary it is this: We would not proceed with the project if the tracks were to be depressed whether in whole or in part in their present location." He gave as reasons the dislocation of main line operations during construction and *possible* water table problems.[41]

Three days later, the CPR gave its official response to mounting criticism in a ten-page statement delivered to City Hall.[42] As was to be expected from Sinclair's tone just days earlier, it was an aggressive document. Heavily underlined and punctuated with phrases like "we make no apology," "we have done our homework," and "we know what we are talking about," it was more a bludgeon than a rapier. It focused primarily on the rerouting aspect and used misleading "facts" to argue that the decision to reroute was consultative and transparent. It was a forerunner of what was to come.

The CPR's response opened with a section titled "Studies," which led with a sentence that referred emphatically to the *"exhaustive engineering economic planning and other studies that have been carried out by Canadian Pacific and by the City of Calgary. This has been no secret."* It went on to say that *"in every question* that arose, every alternative was carefully evaluated and *the best possible solution was selected in joint consultation."* The section closed with another emphatic sentence: *"The rail location will be carried out in a manner completely acceptable to the City in all its aspects."* As it turned out, the last statement was completely wrong and the first statement misleading. True, there had been consultation between the city and the CPR with respect to planning, but as for the city being part of the engineering studies that led to the rerouting decision, this was simply not so. Steel and Hays may have had unofficial prior knowledge of their results, but no city department was part of the studies themselves.

The main portion of the next section, titled "Rail-Parkway Development," was discussed under the heading "These Are the Facts." Fifteen heavily underlined "facts" followed telling the public that the rail-parkway system would not destroy the riverbank or access to it and would be aesthetically pleasing as a result of extensive landscaping. The CPR probably made its most accurate statement about the partnership in its justification of the rail-parkway tandem:

> *The road and the parkway were combined for one simple reason:* far-sighted City officials saw a golden opportunity to solve the major downtown traffic problem at one stroke *for a far lower cost* than had ever been thought possible, because the opportunity to carry out necessary work jointly, and to share costs equitably where work is shared, permits both projects to be carried out far more cheaply than either could separately. *This is sound business. It is also common sense.*

CPR executives were probably sincere in their belief in cost-efficacy based on sound business principles. To them, the railway-parkway scheme was valid solely on economic and practical grounds and was therefore the right decision for the city. No wonder planners and critics like Michael Coulson were appalled.

The next section told the public that there never had been a plan to depress the tracks. It stressed again the joint decision-making with the city, noting that the choices were either to abandon the project or to find a suitable alternative. After listing ten obstacles to track depression, the section concluded: *"All thinking persons . . . will understand the magnitude of the problems. . . . Individually they are complex and serious. In total they are overwhelmingly adverse."* The final section touched on consultants, claiming that the best independent advice had been sought. The closing sentence acknowledged, "It is easy to ignore the facts and indulge in fanciful criticism, *but the facts won't support any such criticism.*" Two "facts" that were not mentioned were that the public had been led to believe for six months that the tracks were to be depressed and that the final decision had not been based on any independent advice.

Two weeks later, the CPR followed up this lengthy statement with a presentation to City Council by Robert Dowling and an associate.[43] In early May, the CPR and Dowling's City Investing Company had formed a company to develop the right-of-way. In addition to holding 20 percent of the shares in the new company, City Investing agreed to act in a consulting role through a specially created Board of Design.[44] Apparently, news of the CPR's publicity problem was unsettling enough for one company insider to suggest that Sykes form a group to "look after diplomatic and political work and who would also serve as an Intelligence department since it was important to know what was going on in the backrooms among the politicians."[45] Sykes, however, did not possess the authority to implement this suggestion.

If nothing else, the combination of Sinclair's letter to the commissioners and the official CPR defence of the rerouting scheme gave notice that the CPR was going to be a hard bargainer. Yet when negotiations began in early August, the city seemed optimistic.

THE NEGOTIATIONS

The first formal negotiations began on August 6 and would continue through the rest of the year and into January 1964. They were conducted primarily by the city administration and functioned on two levels. At one level were the negotiations between the mayor and city commissioners and the CPR, usually Sykes and Joplin and sometimes Stone, although Sinclair was the lead company official and was often in Calgary. At another level were the detailed legal negotiations between CPR lawyer Herb Pickard and the city's team headed by Deputy Solicitor John DeWolfe.

The negotiations were flawed from the outset. First and most significant were the differing interpretations of the Heads of Arrangement. City administrators saw the agreement as a negotiable document; they based their view on the summary statement, which specified: "These Heads of Arrangement are subject to negotiations as to detail and subject to approval by both parties of a formal agreement, which agreement will be validated by the

Alberta legislature." To the CPR, however, the document's terms were binding. A second flaw was the isolation of City Council from the negotiations. True, traditional local government process was followed in that details involving major matters were carried to completion by the administration before being presented to City Council for approval. Yet in this case, with so much at stake, one might have expected more ongoing dialogue between City Council and the administration through the former's coordinating committee — a body that seemed to have little influence and that produced no regular reports. In fact, on October 21, City Council disbanded its coordinating committee and decided that future matters concerning the negotiations should be left in the hands of the commissioners, with the city's aldermen being called on as required.[46] Thus, for all intents and purposes, City Council was allowed to retain certain misconceptions about the agreement as it unfolded during the fall of 1963. A final mistake was limiting the negotiations solely to the existing and the rerouted rights-of-way between 6th Street East and 14th Street West. Crucial components to the east and west of these boundaries were pushed to the background.

The Proposal

The proposal comprised two components: the existing right-of-way and the new riverbank route. As discussed earlier, the Heads of Arrangement provided for the present right-of-way to be cleared of the main line tracks immediately, prior to development. It was, however, silent on two major areas of contention and ambiguous on a third. First, the Heads of Arrangement did not mention road crossings over the existing right-of-way, an important point since the city had been led to believe that every street would traverse the right-of-way. In fact, on June 17, Rod Sykes informed Chief Commissioner Dudley Batchelor that the CPR would defer to the city's Downtown Master Plan with respect to north-south roads across the existing right-of-way: "I have no hesitation in saying that a road will undoubtedly go through everywhere the Master Plan calls for a road to go through."[47] Second, there were no details as to when or where the CPR would begin construction and at what speed the rest of the right-of-way was to be developed. And finally, the wording of the tax exemption provision as "retain[ing] its present tax status *as set out in agreement* or statute until any parcel therein is leased or sold for commercial development" introduced an ambiguity strong enough for the city to contest.[48] However, in accordance with the Heads of Arrangement, the city did agree both to waive the normal requirement for developers to give 10 percent of gross acreage for recreational areas and to treat the freed-up area as separate and distinct and demanding special zoning provisions.

The riverbank route fell into two areas for negotiations: the new right-of-way and the parkway. The Heads of Arrangement was silent on the details regarding both, but it had been agreed that the two would run side by side, with the railway tracks paralleling the riverbank and running north of the four-lane parkway. The city's share of the costs was estimated at $7.6 million; the CPR's at $10 million, including $2.2 million for land. The rail line was never to rise above the parkway and was originally projected to go through the area occupied by Mewata Park and to rejoin the main line in the vicinity of 14th Street West.[49] At fifty feet in width, the new right-of-way comprised only fourteen acres in total. It would also be tax free in perpetuity. Both the right-of-way and the parkway were to be landscaped, although it was still not clear how the associated costs would be divided. The railway tracks and the parkway were to pass under the existing Langevin, Centre Street, Louise, and 14th Street Bridges. The Heads of Arrangement seemed to assign the costs of modifications to these bridges to the city, although even before negotiations began, the city had indicated that this was an area open to debate. The CPR was responsible for all bridges necessary for the rail line and for the bridge over the parkway at the 6th Avenue and 14th Street interchange. East of the Elbow River, the city was responsible for the costs of the parkway passing under or over the rail line.

The negotiations focused only on the area between 6th Street East and 14th Street West. The new right-of-way would diverge from the main line east of 8th Street East, but no details had been worked out as to the route the tracks would take to get to the riverbank. To the west, the diverted line was to rejoin the main line near 14th Street, although the location later shifted farther west, after passage through Mewata Park was denied. Again, details of the exact location were not specified. References to the parkway were vaguer still. Plans for the parkway were limited to the area between 14th Street West and 6th Street East. The parkway was designed to continue west past 14th Street, but whether it would join the designated access roads to the new Crowchild Trail Bridge (11th and 12th Avenues South) or connect directly to the bridge itself was unclear.[50] It was considered likely, though, that it would fork just east of 14th Street. The north fork, which would parallel the river west of 14th Street, would handle westbound traffic, while the south fork would join 9th Avenue after diverging from the main parkway and would accommodate eastbound traffic. To the east, the situation was less certain. The parkway was to extend to Black-foot Trail, but no route had been finalized beyond 6th Street East. Nor had a time frame been set for construction. In fact, the connection to Blackfoot Trail might have to wait ten years or more.[51] Small wonder, then, that skeptics called the parkway "a road from nowhere to nowhere."

It had been decided before negotiations began that where the new right-of-way and the parkway were to be in tandem, the city would acquire the land by purchase — or expropriation, if necessary — and share the costs equitably with the CPR. This looked simple on paper but it proved to be anything but. Finally, there was the matter of the new passenger station, about which there is scant information. Its specific location changed several times. Initial projections had it somewhere east along the main line before the proposed divergence. Later, it was to be located on the new line somewhere between 4th and 6th Streets East. By the time negotiations ended, it was to be built on the present Fort Calgary site, at the time occupied by the Canadian National Railway's freight yards. Information on the station's size, type, and function is even sketchier. The only available map shows it to the south of the diverted rails and running almost the entire length of the CNR site. Ian Sinclair was vague on how the new facility was to function. He told the *Herald* that it "will not be a station in the normal sense. Passengers will report at the new transportation centre and [be] transported to the new station." He admitted that since direct access would also be available, some duplication in services could be expected. Clearly, the CPR had not given much attention to how train passengers to and from Calgary would be accommodated along the new right-of-way. Although this may have been related to the company's plans to phase out passenger service on its main line, it could also be interpreted as another example of the CPR's ill-preparedness.

Drafting the Agreement, August–December 1963

On August 6, 1963, Mayor Grant MacEwan wrote in his diary:

> We have this day started the C.P.R. redevelopment negotiations which we hope will lead to the relocation of the tracks now severing the city and rendering almost a hundred acres of land at city centre tax free for the past eighty years. They call it a $35 million undertaking. The city's undertaking in acquiring and renovating bridges and building a new parkway will cost something like eight millions. It promises to be a highly controversial issue however partly because many people do not trust the railroad company.[52]

How right he was! Protracted, bitter, inconsistent, and highly emotional, the negotiations degenerated into a morass of confusion and mistrust. Yet when one examines the evidence, the conclusion seems inescapable. It was all over and done by the end of August. In that month, the city administrators made their case and lost. From then on, they were on the defensive and, if anything, lost ground.

MacEwan was not quite correct: the negotiations actually began a day earlier, on August 5, when the CPR submitted a draft of the proposed agreement. It followed the terms of the Heads of Arrangement and, ostensibly, waited only on details and refinement. A meeting between the two parties to discuss the draft was set for the next day at 10:00 a.m. in the commissioners' board room. The city representatives present were MacEwan, Batchelor, Steel, and the other two commissioners, Ian Forbes and A. H. Nicholson. Herb Pickard, Fred Joplin, and Rod Sykes represented the CPR.[53]

Without much ado, the commissioners dropped their bomb-shell. In rejecting the CPR draft, they clearly indicated their belief that the Heads of Arrangement was a starting point only. Pointing out that relief of taxation on two rights-of-way was highly questionable, they asked for amendments allowing for the taxation of railway lands on the existing right-of-way. Using a complex formula based on the net acreage on the new right-of-way and applied to the present right-of-way, they suggested that the CPR pay annual taxes of $104,000. In addition, they proposed taxing undeveloped lands on the existing right-of-way at a release rate of three acres per year, asked the CPR to bear the entire cost of landscaping on the new right-of-way to a maximum of $500,000, and suggested that the company assume the costs for all work and land acquisition associated with the railway underpass at the 14th Street Bridge as well as for the construction necessary on the south approaches at the Louise, Centre Street, and Langevin Bridges. The city commissioners also wanted wide flexibility in selecting the locations of the north-south traffic crossings, and they stressed the need for a specific time commitment for development on the vacated right-of-way. That these requests were unexpected is an understatement. Incredulous and stunned, the CPR negotiators sought a quick adjournment while they consulted their superiors in Montréal. After agreeing to meet the following day, the meeting broke up with one side surprised and the other in utter disbelief.

The August 7 meeting was as startling as its predecessor, and its outcome even more surprising.[54] It was held in the same place with the same people and began at 1:30 p.m. This time, it was the CPR's turn to attack. Herb Pickard spoke for the group, doubtless deriving his confidence from the written statement he held in his hand. He opened his address by explaining the long hours his delegation had spent considering the city administrators' extraordinary behaviour in rejecting the terms of a signed agreement. He reminded them that his delegation had the power to negotiate only within the framework outlined by the Heads of Arrangement. In light of the city's breach of faith, he had contacted CPR management in Montréal for direction and had forthwith received a response, which he was authorized to read. Not surprisingly, it came across as an ultimatum. Under Fred Stone's name, the response described the city's proposals as representing "a broad and significant departure" from the Heads of Arrangement, one that, in effect, meant shifting "a heavy burden of costs to the C.P.R. in areas where the City had agreed to share responsibility." In stating further that its Calgary team would only negotiate within the Heads of Arrangement and that any modifications had to be submitted to CPR senior management for approval, the CPR threw down the gauntlet. For the senior city administrators, it was a moment of truth. Ostensibly, they had been prepared to bargain with Pickard, Sykes, and Joplin within a climate of flexibility. However, the tone emanating from CPR's head office held a menacing message: either back down or risk losing a golden opportunity to reshape the city. The commissioners chose the former option, hoping that all was not lost. They reassured the CPR delegation that their requests from the previous day were "considerations only." It is not too much to conclude that with that statement, it was game over.

One wonders at this sudden capitulation. The CPR's contention that the specifics of the Heads of Arrangement were ironclad was open to interpretation. The last sentence in the document, which stated that "these Heads of Arrangement are subject to negotiation as to detail," seems to indicate that the city might have had a contestable point. Clearly, the CPR interpreted the word "detail" to mean minor additions and elaborations on clauses that themselves were not contestable. Yet why city officials did not argue more strenuously for a wider interpretation is puzzling. As for the CPR, its on-site representatives had essentially been denied any future negotiating flexibility. Montréal had spoken.

The ensuing discussions thus proceeded on predictable grounds. The CPR showed little inclination to give ground on any major point of contention despite frequent and sustained discussions. By August 30, a draft "acceptable to both parties" was announced, one that mocked the city's original initiative of August 6.[55] In this draft, the CPR rejected any change to the tax exemptions. With the exception of $182,250 for the Louise Bridge, the company would not assume any of the $3.5 million costs for bridge construction and modification. It was not prepared to assume landscaping costs beyond that needed for its right-of-way, nor were company executives willing to give any time frame commitment for development. Because the railway had been denied access to Mewata Park, the CPR also expected the city to bear the costs for any land needed west of 14th Street. The one concession gained by the city was the removal of the provision for a convention centre on CPR land.

The August 30 draft was exactly that: a draft. Details had to be worked out before a final agreement could be put to City Council for approval. As negotiations proceeded through September, October, and November, the city continued to buckle under CPR pressure. And if that was not enough, significant problems emerged with the areas east and west of the agreement area. With these problems still unresolved, a final draft was put to an uninformed City Council in early December, one that mirrored the August version but reflected added concessions by the city. Confronted with an agreement that seemed to mock what they had expected, city aldermen reacted angrily and negatively. CPR managers were taken aback, given the agreement they thought they had achieved in August.

One should not discount the several minor issues to be resolved; it is a tribute to the negotiators that, in general, these were carried through successfully. One of the most difficult concerned the purchase of land by the city for both the new right-of-way and the parkway.[56] This land had to be acquired with careful phasing to meet timely construction of the parkway, rails, and bridges. Aside from difficulties involving the ownership of mineral versus surface rights, multiple landowners of individual parcels, and encumbrances that could not be overridden, problems arose with designating the parcels of land to be purchased without driving up the price by making this information public. The percentage of cost to be borne by each party was another issue, since the amount of land needed for the right-of-way and the parkway was too imprecise to enable an equitable division of cost. Two additional matters concerned cost sharing for the relocation of utilities and the conditions of easement when they passed under the new right-of-way. These and many other details related to the project were so complex that the city assigned its capable deputy director of planning, Geoffrey Greenhalgh, to work as a full-time coordinator.[57]

Several legal issues were involved. With regard to the land purchases, any action the city took in buying or expropriating land for the CPR contravened the City Act and the Expropriation Procedure Act. Similarly, once the main line was removed from the existing right-of-way, the land would be taxable under the City Act since the contract of 1881 would no longer apply. This presented a potential stalemate since the city had no power to exempt railways from taxes under the City Act, and the CPR would not agree to move its main line if the existing right-of-way would then be taxable.[58] A third legal issue concerned the agreement to designate the existing right-of-way a special development area, which contravened both the Planning Act and the regulations made under provisions of the City Act. Because of these legal matters, any agreement reached between the two parties required provincial approval. The Heads of Arrangement had anticipated this by referring to approval by the province. However, the insertion of the term "provincial approval" in the Heads of Arrangement tended to obscure the role of the public and the place of the plebiscite as a deciding factor.

THE PLEBISCITE

At first glance, the matter of public approval via a plebiscite was not a major issue in that it was procedural. The proposal required the city to borrow substantial sums for land acquisition, bridges, and construction of the parkway. Under the City Act, any money bylaw covering borrowing that could not be repaid in the current year required a two-thirds majority of ratepayers in a plebiscite. City Council recognized this responsibility early. The June 27, 1963, motion instructing the commissioners "to prepare a money bylaw to cover proposed borrowings for the CP project for presentation to the ratepayers at the earliest possible date" was carried by a 10-1 majority.[59]

Recognizing the company's less-than-stellar image in the city, CPR executives were not happy with the prospect of any plebiscite, let alone one that required a two-thirds majority. On August 29, Ian Sinclair told the commissioners that "the money bylaw was a bad idea."[60] He was more specific a few days later. Blustering that "if the city voters turn down the project they would be making a terrible mistake," Sinclair threw in what was to become a familiar refrain. If Calgary wasn't interested in a project of such grand design, he warned, then there were plenty of other cities that were.[61]

Sinclair's sentiments struck a chord. City administrators were also not keen on the plebiscite, doubtless for the same reason. So they delayed it.[62] Acting on advice from the city's Solicitor's Office that certain clauses in the City Act allowed for two-thirds of City Council to approve a debt not payable within the current year without submitting the same to the ratepayers, the commissioners asked the Provincial Local Authorities Board for a decision.[63] The response was favourable. On November 14, the commissioners happily reported to City Council: "It is clear therefore that Council may proceed to borrow the money for this project under the section of the City Act without reference to the proprietary electors."[64]

Although the need for a plebiscite on the money bylaw had been avoided, the option to hold one remained a City Council prerogative. The idea of consulting citizens on a matter of general importance was common in local government. For instance, Calgarians had resisted the city's proposal to add fluoride to their water supply in a number of plebiscites. As an instrument of direct democracy, plebiscites had their supporters and detractors. The city councils of 1963 and 1964 were no different. Populists like Grant MacEwan believed that on major issues with wide-ranging and significant impact, the people ought to be the final arbiters. Indeed, on June 10, he had moved a motion "that the principle involved in the city's obligation in the proposed program will be presented in a plebiscite at the earliest possible date."[65] Other members of City Council, such as Ted Duncan, believed that general plebiscites violated the principles of representative democracy. This view held that the role of aldermen was to make reasoned decisions for the people who had elected them. So while the need to ratify the necessary money bylaw in a plebiscite had been removed, the question of soliciting citizen opinion had not. Thus, the issue of the plebiscite continued to simmer. Would one be held? If so, when? To what degree would it be an approval (or an escape) mechanism?

On September 12, 1963, the *South Side Mirror* referred to the upcoming municipal election as "the most important in the city's history."[66] It had a point. Given the CPR's historic unpopularity in the city and the nature of the project, one might have anticipated a heated fall election with victories and defeats hinging on the CPR's downtown project. Surprisingly, it was anything but. In the election's aftermath, it was no wonder that the CPR refused to budge on the one remaining issue. The news that a plebiscite might not be necessary was good enough. But to have an election in which the company had not been attacked and the CPR project had been just one of several campaign issues put to an apathetic electorate was icing on the cake. When the results were in, a low 36 percent of eligible voters had elected a mayor sympathetic to the project. Of the six aldermen elected, three were returnees, and none of the six had campaigned against the CPR project.[67] Only Jack Leslie remained as a consistent critic among the six incumbent aldermen.

The mayoralty election was a gentlemanly affair with no name calling and little personal animosity between two front-running candidates, who described themselves as friends. Grant MacEwan's opponent was a native Calgarian, Arthur (Art) Smith — a well-known name in local political and business circles. The son of a former local member of Parliament and a decorated wartime pilot in the Royal Canadian Air Force, Smith had been a city alderman in the early 1950s, a Conservative MLA from 1955 to 1957, and an MP in the Diefenbaker government for six years before resigning to seek the mayoralty. Highly popular and a well-respected businessman, Smith went into the election an overwhelming favourite and was clearly relying on his personal popularity to carry him to victory. Although concerned about "the cloud of mystery" that blanketed the CPR project, he left it out of his campaign and focused instead on MacEwan's capacity to carry it forward.[68]

Grant MacEwan paid more attention to the CPR project, giving it high priority in his seven-point campaign platform.[69] There was no impassioned rhetoric, however: only an acknowledgement that since he had been associated with the issue from the start, it was his responsibility to see it through to completion.[70] His personal popularity with the working public ensured the support of the influential Calgary Labour Council, while his straightforward manner brought the support of a powerful moneyed group — mostly Liberals who unequivocally endorsed the project and who felt that their best chance lay with the popular, laconic, money-conscious figure who shared both their vision and their political beliefs.[71] When the votes were in on October 16, MacEwan had outpolled Smith by a margin of 37,371 to 24,084. Although Smith had also favoured the project, there can be little doubt that MacEwan's victory was seen as a clear endorsement. Certainly, the *Financial Post* thought so, noting that MacEwan now had "a Council without outright opponents of the plan."[72]

The aldermanic races were lacklustre. The three new aldermen elected were Mark Tennant, Dave Russell, and Roy Deyell. It was the third time on City Council for decorated war veteran Mark Tennant, who supported the project, even though it had not figured in his campaign. He was also a business associate of Carl Nickle, one of the project's most ardent supporters. Architect Dave Russell had served as an alderman in 1960–61. Although he was later to emerge as a major opponent to the project, he supported it in principle during his campaign. Roy Deyell, a lawyer who had run unsuccessfully in the 1959 provincial election as a Conservative, was known to support the project but made little mention of it during his campaign.[73] For example, his profile published in *The Albertan* on October 7, 1963, contained nothing about his attitude toward the issue. The closest he came to taking a position was a statement he made to the *North Hill News* to the effect that he was in favour of any development that would benefit the city but needed to know the cost.[74]

In summary, it could be argued that the election, while evincing a general approval of the project, was marked by a lack of vitality and low voter turnout. On October 18, *The Albertan* editorialized on "The Campaign That Wasn't." In contending that the campaign "failed abysmally in dealing with the issues before it," the editorial noted that while all mayoralty candidates recognized its advantages, the CPR project "cannot be said to have been treated as an issue." This should not have been surprising. The CPR redevelopment project was not a major issue because no candidate — nor anyone else, for that matter, aside from the commissioners and the CPR negotiating team — was aware of what had been decided, what had been rejected, and by whom.

With the elections confirming the CP project, albeit by default, the ongoing negotiations seemed destined for success, at least from the CPR's viewpoint. The terms of the August 30 draft remained in place, with a CPR rider added in October acknowledging the city as the initiator of the project. The city commissioners' refusal to go along with this is puzzling, given the credit they could claim as initiators.[75] It may have indicated nervousness over what was transpiring in the negotiations, since, for the most part, city administrators continued to give in to CPR demands. In fact, in October, the commissioners yielded to the CPR's insistence that the agreement be worded to disallow the city any expropriation rights on the existing right-of-way.[76] This was to prove a major point of contention.

In November, the city's negotiators lost on a final major issue, one that seemed to grab public attention in the heated debates that were to follow in the spring of 1964.[77] It concerned traffic crossings on the existing right-of-way. The city had always considered any agreement to be contingent on providing better traffic access to the downtown from the south. Originally, city negotiators had assumed — and, indeed, had been led to believe — that all crossings between 6th Street East and 14th Street West (twenty-one in all) were eligible to be opened to north-south traffic and that the city had the right to decide whether they would be level crossings or subways under the tracks. As negotiations proceeded, it became clear that the CPR had other plans. Against the city administrators' wishes, the company favoured the existing subways rather than conversion to level crossings and wanted them to remain at 2nd Street East, 1st Street East, 1st Street West, 4th Street West, 8th Street West, and 14th Street West. Moreover, they were not to be widened. The only concession granted by the CPR was to allow the city to remove the centre spans and to use the subway sidewalks to secure added traffic capability. As for additional crossings, the CPR allocated 3.5 acres of land for three more crossings but stipulated that they must not "preclude commercial development" in two-block units. Specific prohibitions were inserted into the draft agreement. Centre Street was to remain closed to north-south traffic. More significantly, so was 2nd Street West, the crossing most desired by the city. The CPR wanted the city to use 3rd Street West instead, an option unacceptable to the city since, aside from being blocked by the Robin Hood Flour Mill, there was no linking street on the south side of the tracks, thus necessitating a connection to 4th Street, an undertaking that would cost the city $1 million.[78] The CPR also refused to allow the city any land along the right-of-way to allow the widening of 9th and 10th Avenues. Although the city's negotiators bargained long and hard during several meetings in November, the CPR refused to budge.

By the end of November, a final draft was ready for submission to City Council. To summarize the main points, this draft called for track relocation with tax exemptions along both rights-of-way. It did not commit the CPR to any time frame for or details of development. It specified special zoning status for the existing right-of-way and released the company from the normal 10 percent recreational land requirements. It prevented any expropriation of land along the existing right-of-way and denied the city the crossing it most desired at 2nd Street West while restricting options elsewhere.

That the CPR's will had prevailed is undeniable. Equally undeniable, however, is the fact that the November draft was the result of a negotiating process. Whether the city's negotiators had been out-bargained or intimidated, or were simply intent on securing an agreement at any cost is of no consequence. The fact of the matter is that they had reached this agreement with the CPR through a prolonged negotiating process.

City administrators erred in not keeping City Council abreast of the negotiations. This was due to prevailing executive practice in local government, which tended to exclude council input until necessary. Furthermore, the commissioners may have felt that nothing was written in stone as long as negotiations continued and that it was inadvisable to publicize or politicize details before absolutely necessary.[79] Given the magnitude of the project, the abysmal lack of communication between the city's executive and legislative arms was poor politics, poor practice, and poor government.

Once the city's negotiators learned of the CPR's position in August, they should have either abandoned the project or brought it to City Council for guidance. They did not. Then, when they saw that they were making few inroads in September and October, they should have advised City Council through interim reports. They did not do that either. On September 24, a commissioners' report referred to a general draft under preparation.[80] The authors stated that they hoped that the draft would be ready for submission to City Council by the end of October, but they also noted that considerable negotiations were still necessary.[81] On October 23, the commissioners argued that more time was needed and that a special meeting of City Council would be arranged after November 11, "at which time a comprehensive report on all matters relative to this scheme will be submitted."[82]

The only indication that all might not be well with the negotiations was in a qualified commissioners' report to City Council on November 14.[83] Aldermen were told that the agreement was based substantially on the Heads of Arrangement that they had approved. The commissioners stressed that while they were not entirely happy with certain parts of the agreement, neither was the CPR. No details of the points of issue were given. Instead, the report passed on positive news. The city's bill for the project had been reduced from $8.787 million to $6.606 million because of a $400,000 contribution from the federal Grade Crossing Fund and a CPR share of $182,250 for alterations to the Louise Bridge. A further $1 million had been saved in reduced land acquisition costs thanks to a decision by the provincial Water Resources Branch to allow part of the new CPR right-of-way to extend into the channel of the Bow River. Another piece of good news was an assurance that the city could complete its obligations in four years within the normal capital budget. Better still, a saving of almost $1 million could be realized in reduced interest on the $6 million borrowing debt because of the Provincial Municipal Development and Loan Fund, which allowed a quarter-percent discount and possible forgiveness on up to two-thirds of an incurred municipal debt. There the matter rested until November 25, when Mayor MacEwan advised aldermen that a special meeting with the commissioners was in the offing in which they "would be brought up to date on the negotiations with the CPR."[84]

City Council was lax in its oversight. Recall that in June 1963 it had appointed a three-man coordinating committee with the admittedly vague mandate to work with the CPR to assure the accomplishment of the plan. Council minutes show no reports from this group after negotiations began in August. When two members of the committee, Clarence Mack and Peter (P.N.R.) Morrison, declined to run for election in the fall, the incoming council disbanded the committee, advising that "matters be left in hands of Commissioners to call on the aldermen when required."[85] It was not the smartest of moves.

As anticipated, the commissioners requested a special City Council meeting on Friday, December 6, for consideration and approval of a final draft of the agreement. It was showtime at last. The draft was given to the aldermen on Tuesday, December 3, three days before the meeting. At first, no problems were anticipated. In a front-page article on December 4, *The Albertan* referred to the $35 million plan being the city's Christmas present and noted that CPR officials in Montréal were very happy with an agreement that waited only on a few minor points of contention.[86]

It was the lull before the storm. The draft agreement was clearly not what the aldermen expected, and a day before the meeting, several made their opinions public. Alderman Ted Duncan told *The Albertan* that he couldn't approve it to save his life.[87] Walter Boote said it was one-sided and loaded against the city.[88] Jack Leslie expressed his opinion in a Thursday address at the Al San Club, where he told 150 geologists that the city had been out-bluffed, out-negotiated, and double-crossed, angrily adding, "They must think we are so stupid we'll sign anything."[89] Although other aldermen were more non-committal, none expressed his support of the draft.

The December 6 special meeting of City Council commenced at 8:40 a.m. All twelve aldermen were in attendance, as were the mayor and the three commissioners. It opened with the Commissioners' Report and recommendations. It was a remarkable document with clear underpinnings of embarrassment about what the negotiations had produced — an admission of defeat, if you will.

Although it recommended acceptance, the tone stressed doubt as much as conviction:

> Although we are of the opinion that the overall conception of the scheme is advantageous to the City, we must frankly admit that there are singular aspects on which we are unhappy and regarding which we have been unable to secure the agreement of the C.P.R.
>
> We are of the opinion that there are some physical and economic features of the scheme which viewed singularly are unacceptable. . . . However we are still of the opinion that the overall conception of the scheme will produce benefit to the city, and within this broad generalization, we are prepared to recommend the scheme and the accompanying agreement.[90]

In a surprising turnaround, the commissioners also recommended that the agreement be put to a plebiscite. They offered no details as to why they now favoured an action they had taken such pains to avoid less than a month earlier beyond pointing out that the electors could force a plebiscite by means of a petition signed by 5 percent of ratepayers.[91] It was a lame excuse.[92] Probably, they were mindful of the rocky road ahead and were suggesting a way out for City Council, and for themselves. In any case, the issue of the plebiscite was back in the aldermen's court. Ultimately, it was to prove crucial.

City Council received the report more calmly than might be expected. No recriminations were directed at the commissioners. The draft was rejected, but no vote was taken. Jack Leslie wanted to go back to the drawing board and challenged the need for depressing the tracks and the special zoning status. Although his objections were overruled, the aldermen opted for a last-ditch attempt, voting 9-4 to direct the commissioners to reopen negotiations on five points: taxation, development time commitment, the 2nd Street crossing, the expropriation issue, and the merits of filling in the subways to allow level crossings.[93] Later that day, the CPR's Calgary-based team met with the commissioners, but no details were divulged. As far as the CPR was concerned, this was the extent of the discussions: Vice-President Fred Stone was dispatched from Montréal to deliver the official message.

In private meetings with the commissioners and City Council, Stone focused on the August 30 agreement and, in short, said that a deal was a deal. Affable as ever, he tried to downplay this take-it-or-leave-it ultimatum. He did not want the scheme to end as a bad dream and stressed the fact that the CPR had no intention of trying "to push it down your throat." His company certainly did not want to involve itself in something the city did not want.[94] However, speaking from Montréal, Vice-President Ian Sinclair was more aggressive. His warning was clear. Wondering whether "we should spend all that money in Calgary," he told the press that he was waiting on Stone's assessment "to see if we are interested or not in staying around any longer."[95] As for the five points of contention, his position left little room for optimism. The taxation, development time commitment, and 2nd Street crossing points were dismissed as non-negotiable. He laughed at the idea of filling in subways when cities everywhere else were constructing them. The only gleam of hope he gave was an admission that while extra land for road widening on 9th Avenue was out, some consideration would be given to 10th Avenue. But technically, Sinclair's utterances were unofficial. The city had to wait for a formal response from the CPR.

It was the project's darkest hour. In the aftermath of Sinclair's comments, a poll of the aldermen indicated that most intended to vote down the agreement.[96] Not surprisingly, the strongest comment came from Jack Leslie: "I can't accept this agreement. I don't see how anybody can."[97] Yet no special meeting of City Council was set to vote the draft down.

Surprisingly, given their bluff and bluster, CPR executives blinked. On December 20, Ian Sinclair announced that the CPR would not be making a decision until the New Year, albeit accompanied by an insensitive aside: "We don't want to give out any bad news for the holiday."[98] On January 3, 1964, the city received the official response in a letter from President N.R. (Buck) Crump. Dismissing opposition to the draft agreement as the work of naysayers and noting concessions already made, other projects left in abeyance, and weakening investor confidence in the city, Crump advised that he was not prepared to wait any longer:

> We cannot afford to let the project drag on much longer. . . . If this proposal is not carried out, we are not prepared to spend further time and money in considering alternatives as you suggest. . . . I think CP has given Calgary every opportunity to join with us in this redevelopment and your administration must be the judges as to whether they want to forego the opportunity.[99]

In a masterful stroke, Crump closed with a ray of hope and a final ultimatum. Omitting any details, he advised that Stone and Sinclair intended to meet, not with the commissioners but with City Council, "to see if an agreement can be worked out." However, "if they are unable to do this," he warned, "then CP must use the funds available for redevelopment in other cities."[100] Mollified and still desiring a project that meant so many good things for the city, the aldermen consented to the CPR's face-to-face offer. A new game had begun. While the CPR was playing its usual hardball, the discourse had shifted away from the commissioners. It was now up to an unprepared City Council to debate what was becoming a highly emotional public issue.

THE PUBLIC DEBATE BEGINS

The release of the draft agreement marked the beginning of the public controversy that was to dominate the press, coffee shop discussions, and public consciousness for the next six months. In fact, on December 21, City Hall received three bomb threats, although the record is silent as to at whom the threats were directed and why.[101] On one side were those who felt that despite its deficiencies, the project was too good to pass up. Both daily newspapers fell into this category. So did the vast majority of the business community, and it was this group that supplied the initiative and force to promote the merits of the project. Opposing interests, being more diffuse and against the project for a variety of reasons, were less coordinated. However, they had outrage on their side, as well as a "big, bad enemy," and this combination represented a potent force. As for the average citizen, it was hard to get a read. Both sides attributed citizen ignorance of the scheme to a lack of reliable information. It was to the filling of this information gap that both groups addressed their energy, although it was the pro-project group that took the initiative.

Pro-Project

The release of the Hanson Report in November had been music to the ears of the business community. Already on record as favouring the project, the Chamber of Commerce went public on November 27 in a press release in which it unanimously lent its support and exhorted the commissioners to make the best deal possible.[102] The Real Estate Board followed suit on December 9, noting that without the project, "the constant threat of a decaying central business district will remain."[103]

Following City Council's refusal to endorse the draft agreement, the business community coalesced. On December 30, representatives from the Chamber of Commerce, the Downtown Businessmen's Association, and the Calgary Real Estate Board combined forces to create the Calgary Development Committee (CDC). Ostensibly neutral and upset that "some of the citizens of our community — and indeed some of our civic officials — are criticizing points upon which their information is in error, [and which] in actual terms are more favourable to the city than the critics imply," the CDC sought to "get the show back on the road" via a six-man executive committee chaired by the Chamber's Carl Nickle.[104] The formation of the CDC resonated well with the CPR. In fact, on January 2, Rod Sykes wrote to the Chamber of Commerce. After referring to "widespread misunderstanding or ignorance of the facts which if not corrected will be sufficient to destroy a project that is as good for Calgary as it ever was," Sykes called on the business community "to get the facts out and create a climate in which it [the project] will be evaluated on its merits."[105] Four days later, the CDC told the city that it would "do its best to prevent narrower views or relatively minor issues from destroying the reality that should come from the vision."[106] That the CDC and the CPR were on the same page was evidenced in a statement made by Steel on January 7 to the effect that the CDC had given him a tip that the CPR might be willing to make some concessions.[107] City Council was not pleased that a private organization apparently had the ear of the CPR before it did.[108] Not surprisingly, the CPR was quick to deny the insinuation.

The CDC went on the offensive in several press releases in January that showed the project in a very favourable light. Using statistics, persuasion, and the Hanson Report, the CDC emphasized the economic advantages of the proposal. The loss of the required 10 percent community reserve was explained away by noting that the CPR had made adequate open space available under the plan and that the maintenance of that space would be a financial burden on the railway company and not on the city.[109] The CDC dismissed the contentious 2nd Street crossing by citing the absence of city reports supporting the need for it and referring instead to two undated and anonymous documents, one of which used statistics on traffic flows to show that a crossing at 2nd Street was not necessary; the other made the opposite case for 3rd Street.[110] On January 17, the eve of the intensive last-ditch discussions, the CDC came down on the side of a healthy financial climate when it solemnly announced that "Calgary's business climate for years to come is being decided." In the opinion of CDC members, the project represented the kind of "big thinking and unique planning which would ensure that Calgary's financial climate would be sound far into the future."[111] Otherwise, they warned, Calgary "would become just another western city." No criticisms of the project or the CPR were ever offered. So much for neutrality!

In fairness, the CDC's claim to neutrality was based on the assumption that the project's advantages so far outweighed the negatives that approval should be a foregone conclusion. As such, the organization's task was to stress the positives and ignore or ameliorate the negatives. This view was supported by the daily press, especially the *Herald*. On December 12, the newspaper editorialized that "it would be folly of the first order to allow this great project to founder [on trivialities]. It's too big for either side to lose."[112] On January 7, the same message was repeated: "There can be no resigned folding of hands on this matter — no losing of this golden opportunity for downtown revitalization by default."[113] Even the *Herald*'s publisher, Frank Swanson, entered the fray when he announced in a "Memo from the Publisher" that the loss of the plan represented "a great tragedy for the City of Calgary." In a biting reference to the growing voice of opposition, he added, "The scuttlers did their work well."[114] The city's other daily, *The Albertan*, though less effusive than the *Herald*, supported the project. In December, for example, it ran a series of three articles outlining advantages to the public if an agreement was reached. However, its focus was more on City Council, which it charged to exercise due diligence and professionalism to secure a positive outcome. On December 5, just before discussion of the draft, *The Albertan* urged City Council not to put forward unreasonable demands but to arrive at a good agreement as quickly as possible.[115] An editorial supporting the CDC on January 9 referred to "the fog of ignorance, confusion and misconception which enveloped the project" and to the CDC as "a vital factor in the achievement of an agreement."[116] At no point did either paper charge the CPR with its obligations.

The weight of the CDC's influence and the steady portrayal of the project in positive terms by the press combined to force City Council's hand. As the *North Hill News* wrote, "City Council is under tremendous pressure to accept the CPR agreement at any price."[117] On the one hand, the rhetoric of economic prosperity inherent in the agreement appealed to the business instincts — and, in some cases, interests — of most of the aldermen. On the other hand, it was impossible to ignore the rising wave of public opposition.

Anti-Project
Before the submission of the draft agreement to City Council in December, the redevelopment plan had not stirred the public consciousness. Certainly, there were those who opposed it. The Local Council of Women worried about the loss of the riverbank. Some Calgarians were suspicious of CPR motives; others felt threatened by the project. A good example of the latter was outspoken geologist, J. C. Sproule, whose office building was on the proposed new right-of-way.[118] On September 30, Sproule told a local Kiwanis Club

that the project was detrimental to the city and that citizens were being brainwashed by commissioned reports to City Council that were biased and not based on independent feasibility studies. He also claimed to have information from aldermen that garbage was being intentionally left along the riverbank to reduce property values for speculative purposes.[119] A likely reason for his disquiet emerged a few weeks later, when he complained to the Chamber of Commerce that the city was offering $100,000 below its appraised value for his own property.[120] He may have had a point. Certainly, property owners in the forty blocks between the Bow River and 4th Avenue along the route of the new right-of-way and the parkway thought so. Their lawyer, Hugh John MacDonald, announced in late January that the city's under-market-value price could lead to a thousand legal claims and cost the city about $12 million in the courts.[121]

With the release of the draft agreement in December, opposition to the project took a wider and more critical focus. The city's 1967 Centennial Committee had doubts, while the Calgary Labour Council, an advertised supporter of the project, also expressed reservations.[122] Letters to the editor against the project began appearing with greater frequency. However, two responses deserve discussion. The first focused on planning principles and came in the form of the so-called Coulson Report, mentioned earlier. Referring to "a history of mismanagement," the report's stated aim was "to show that this series of agreements was arrived at through faulty planning procedures."[123] Essentially, the authors argued that the agreement violated sound planning practices by accepting the project at face value and failing to consider other alternatives: "The C.P.R. scheme is only one approach to downtown re-development in Calgary, and its attempted introduction shows lack of appreciation of proper procedure and of the many conflicts of influence involved."[124] Regarding the choice of the riverbank route, for example, the report had the following to say:

> Although the south bank route has been tentatively selected as the best route, all alternatives possible to track movement have not been properly evaluated from the economic, aesthetic or

other standpoints. . . . The City approach seems to have been to negotiate on re-location of the tracks with the CPR, accept the idea of the south bank route and proceed to justify this route for reasons other than the C.P.R. negotiations, which actually caused the acceptance of the south bank alternative in the first place. [125]

The report took exception to the findings of the recently released Hanson Report and concluded by stating, "Our study indicates that, as now constituted and understood, the C.P.R. scheme should not be approved by Council." Although not stated in the report, one of the authors, J. G. Nelson, later told *The Albertan* that more study was needed and that as it stood now, the riverbank would continue to be defiled under the project, which Nelson believed would proceed at a pace known only to the CPR.[126]

With its stamp of academic legitimacy, the Coulson Report, combined with the public statements by the authors, reinforced the confidence of other local like-minded groups upset with the agreement on planning grounds. The most significant was the Calgary chapter of the Community Planning Association of Canada. By the New Year, it was ready to move. On January 8, 1964, the association initiated a meeting of about fifty professionals, including planners, architects, lawyers, academics, and representatives from the Local Council of Women.[127] When the meeting was over, Calgary had its second citizens' group. The Citizens' Committee for Community Development (CCCD) initially saw itself as a sounding board for public opinion with a primary focus on planning in the downtown area. At this first meeting, the defeat of the redevelopment plan was not an issue, although it was realized that in its present state, the project represented a businessman's view of planning. However, in stressing the importance of the Downtown Master Plan as a prerequisite for any long-range planning decisions, the CCCD set itself on a collision course with proponents of the CPR-city redevelopment project.

While the CDC was welcomed by the press, the CCCD was not so well received. *The Albertan* warned the new group that it was on "thin ice" and that it had to "skate carefully lest it not only fall through the ice itself but also muddy waters which are already murky enough."[128] City Hall was no more enthusiastic. Mayor Grant MacEwan said that planning in the city was already in good hands. Some aldermen were not so restrained: one likened the CCCD to a "ginger group," another feared that it had an axe to grind, and yet another hoped that it wasn't simply a pressure group. No such reservations had accompanied the formation of the CDC.[129]

Opposition on another front emerged a week later in the form of a lengthy letter to the mayor and commissioners and the press by J. B. Barron, a long-time and highly respected city lawyer.[130] Barron blasted the agreement, arguing that in denying the street crossings and developing an extensive retail and commercial complex more than a block long, the CPR was not removing but preserving "a monstrous barrier." According to Barron, the agreement had no advantage to the city and was inconceivable in its one-sidedness: "Never before in the history of any city on this continent," he raged, "has any private corporation ever had the temerity to put forward such a demand." In what was easily the most scathing criticism of the project to date, Barron upped the bar: "In my opinion and I am quite prepared to back this opinion up in any plebiscite or in any court of this land, the proposal of the CPR is an attempt to perpetrate a brutal and unprecedented rape on an unsuspecting public. . . . It is illegal and will not be permitted to stand in the courts." In closing, he called on the public to support him in his intention to secure an injunction "against the carrying out of this agreement if City Council has the audacity to attempt to bring it into force without a plebiscite of the citizens."

Barron was far from finished. In early January, *The Albertan* ran an article comparing his views with those of Rod Sykes on several points of issue.[131] He followed this up on January 15 with another letter to the city criticizing the riverbank route and the lack of information regarding the CPR's timeline for removing the spur lines from the existing right-of-way. He lambasted the CDC, calling its chair, Carl Nickle, a "hand maiden" of the CPR. As for the plebiscite, Barron believed that a clause should be added to the draft agreement making it conditional "upon it [the agreement] receiving the assent of the ratepayers at a plebiscite to be held either before or after the agreement has been duly approved by the Legislature."[132] In light of what transpired, this was a most interesting observation.

The only newspaper to offer critical comments on the project was the weekly *North Hill News*, which was owned by former alderman Roy Farran. In December 1963, in obvious reference to the support extended by the two dailies and the CDC, the *News* wrote: "While we, along with the daily platitudes and Big Guns of business, agree to the value of the proposed CPR scheme, we cannot agree that it should be a lopsided agreement for the ratepayers of this city."[133] The weekly newspapers offered a more reasoned assessment of the project than did the major dailies. In fact, an outside interested party wanting a more accurate and unbiased assessment of the issue would have been better served consulting the *North Hill News* and the other city weekly, the *South Side Mirror*.

Coulson's indictment of the project on planning grounds and Barron's emergence as an articulate highly respected private citizen well able to counter the CDC helped to provide the points of coalescence around which public anger toward the project began to mount. All it required was a catalyst.

AN EMBATTLED CITY COUNCIL SURRENDERS, JANUARY 1964

The final phase of the negotiations began quietly. On January 6, 1964, City Council passed a motion to meet with the commissioners and the CPR. Ian Sinclair and Fred Stone arrived in the city, and both sides began formulating their points for debate and discussion. The final negotiations began in earnest on January 16. Six days later, on January 22, the deal was sealed when City Council endorsed the project by an 8-3 majority. It was an amazing two weeks, characterized by the most sustained, intensive, acrimonious, and emotional debates in the city's civic history. Given the tones of rejection that had resonated through City Hall when the project first faced the aldermen in early December, the decision to approve it seemed an unlikely turnaround. But it was not, for several reasons. First, the aldermen, most of whom had had a lingering predisposition toward the project, had been under immense pressure to see it through. Second, the CPR was willing to yield, however marginally. The final and most significant reason was the way in which the project was approved.

In the first half of January, city administrators tried to prepare the aldermen for the final go-around. The CDC continued to infuse the press with rhetoric about a fine future with the project and a descent into urban anonymity without it. The CPR held to its ultimatum: "We settle this now or we walk" — ostensibly to a more appreciative urban centre.[134] In a gripping atmosphere of tension and public apprehension, the two sides met on Thursday, January 16, in the first of four daily special meetings that were to total over thirteen hours. The sessions, already in camera, were further shrouded in secrecy when the council chamber doors were locked and uniformed guards were placed by the doors following a death threat to the mayor and nine aldermen. On January 20, Mayor Grant MacEwan received a letter lavishly smeared with human excrement and depicting where each victim would be shot and by how many .303 bullets. "I'm slated for three," MacEwan wryly noted.[135]

City Council records show no transcripts of the marathon meetings on January 16, 17, 20, and 21. Press coverage referred to weary, tight-lipped aldermen emerging from council chambers and to official comments that hinted of stalemate or progress, depending on interpretation: "The toughest set of sessions I have ever attended" was how Ted Duncan described it.[136] However, some idea of the dynamics is captured by the writings of Rod Sykes. While it is unfortunate that his personal observations were directed at City Council only, the jottings that he recorded over the four-day period provide an eyewitness glimpse into the actions of a group of people under tremendous pressure and tasked with making what was believed to be the most important decision in the city's history. In his neat handwriting and unequivocal language, Sykes gave testament to an emotional, circuitous four-session dialogue between Sinclair and the city, a dialogue in which detailed questions on all aspects of the project were phrased, rephrased, re-presented, and countered. His notes show the aldermen and administration in various guises: what they had to say, how they said it, how they disagreed with each other, and how they attacked Sinclair.[137]

Using words like "aggressive," "rude," "pugnacious," "shuffling us around," "lots of hooey," and "not here to listen; want answers," and identifying histrionic behaviour that saw CPR reports being thrown in the wastepaper basket and aldermen walking out in disgust, Sykes underscored the frustration, anger, and intensity that never made it to the press or to the official minutes that later sealed the deal.

On Tuesday, January 21, City Council held a final question-and-answer session with Sinclair, who went through the agreement clause by clause. While queries were still being fired at the resolute big man who led the CPR team, it was clear that the tone had changed. There appeared to be a consensus that the city had received all that it could. Late that evening, an Agreement of Intent was hammered out and a special meeting called for the next day at which City Council would announce its decision.[138] The meeting ended with a tribute by one alderman, who noted Sinclair's "Daniel in the lion's den" role and lauded him as an exceptional Canadian. The much-vilified Sinclair must have been amazed, or amused.[139] Sykes did not record the reactions of other aldermen to this far-from-unanimous sentiment.

Not surprisingly, the Agreement of Intent had not moved the CPR far from its previous position. The big contentious issues remained in place. There would be no level crossing at 2nd Street. Nor was there any long-term time commitment for developing the entire existing right-of-way. The tax-free regime remained in place. The 10 percent reserve exemption was maintained and the city was permanently denied the right to expropriate CPR land on the existing right-of-way.

But concessions had been secured, and, though minor, they were sufficient to grind a weary council down. The CPR negotiators had bargained well. First, they backed off of demands that were probably made in anticipation of their rejection. For example, their request for a half-share of the proceeds from the sale of excess land acquired by the city for the new right-of-way was weak. So was their claim to share the $400,000 that the city received from the federal government for alterations to the Louise Bridge.[140] A second concession involved the proposed convention centre, which the CPR had put back on the negotiating table by resurrecting the original stipulation that it be built on railway land. However, the negotiators acquiesced to a statement of intent by the city that included the stipulation that the final choice of site would devolve on a two-thirds majority vote in City Council. Third, the company executives consented to the existing right-of-way being put under "direct control," a zoning option that increased the city's power and that was not in the original agreement. They also softened their stance on the contentious 2nd Street crossing by hinting that a future subway under the tracks at the city's expense might be possible pending engineering feasibility and other considerations. Fourth, the company allowed the city a one-time expropriation of a strip of land seven feet wide along the right-of-way along 10th Avenue and agreed that leased land on the existing right-of-way would be permanently taxable if the lease extended beyond ten years. (The city had wanted seven.) Finally, the CPR made a concession to short-term development by agreeing to spend a minimum of $10 million on the existing right-of-way within seven years.

Late in the afternoon of Wednesday, January 22, City Council met once again, this time to render a final decision on the Agreement of Intent reached the day before.[141] All of the aldermen had spent a private hour with the agreement before the meeting except for Ernie Starr, the newly elected president of the Alberta Tourist Association, who was in Edmonton attending the association's annual convention.[142] It was a bizarre meeting in that it really had nothing to do with the Agreement of Intent, which was apparently seen as a given. Instead, the meeting was about who had the right to approve or reject it. The plebiscite was back on the table, a fitting new twist in an issue that had had more turns than a CPR mountain route full of switchbacks.

In short, City Council was divided about whether to put the proposal to the ratepayers immediately and be guided by their decision or to make the decision unilaterally, without a plebiscite. The first motion was pro-plebiscite, with a preamble that underscored the contentious nature of the proposal and the division among the aldermen. Moved by Mark Tennant and seconded by Walter Boote, it read as follows:

WHEREAS Calgary City Council and its officers have displayed enthusiasm and eagerness to obtain the many benefits of the City-CPR Redevelopment Proposals, and

WHEREAS the present Agreement represents the maximum benefit which City Council can achieve with the approval of the CPR, and

WHEREAS the present Agreement contains features with which individual Aldermen are not in agreement, and

WHEREAS City Council can, therefore, only give qualified approval to the Agreement, and

WHEREAS there are strong and conflicting views now existing in the City of Calgary respecting such agreement, and

WHEREAS such Agreement must receive the consent of the Provincial government, and

WHEREAS all matters pertaining to expropriation and litigation should have the support of City Council,

BE IT RESOLVED THAT this Council's final approval be determined by the outcome of a plebiscite to be held as soon as possible.

The prevailing ambivalence was reflected in the vote on the motion, which was lost on a 6-6 tie.

Then it was the turn of those who wanted City Council to make a decision. It was a short motion, put forward by Bill Dickie and seconded by Ted Duncan: "That we approve the Letter of Intent and the agreement that has been placed before us between the City of Calgary and the Canadian Pacific Railway dated January 22, 1964."

Again the divide prevailed. The motion was rejected in a 7-5 vote.

After discussing and voting down two additional peripheral motions, the council brought the original motion back via mover

Harold Runions and seconder Mark Tennant.[143] It was defeated by the same count as before. The meeting was then adjourned with a provision to reassemble at "the call of the chairman," whatever that meant. It was enough to disperse the crowded gallery. A sombre Ian Sinclair faced the television cameras and admitted defeat: "This was a great opportunity but apparently you didn't want it. I am sorry. At least we tried."[144] Jack Leslie and Roy Deyell left for other engagements, but the rest of the aldermen hung around, waiting, and in numbers sufficient for an energized Ted Duncan to draft another motion and then ask Mayor MacEwan to reconvene the meeting in an eleventh-hour effort to save the project. Leslie was notified in time to return via a police car; Deyell was not.

Soon after 8:00 p.m., the compromise motion was moved and seconded by anti-plebiscite supporters Ted Duncan and George Ho Lem. It was a clever compromise in that it called for City Council to "execute the contract as before us and approve the signing by his worship the Mayor of the Letter of Intent, and That the documents be sent to the legislature after signature by the CPR, for ratification and validation provided that before the agreement become binding on either party it is approved at a plebiscite by the majority of the proprietary electors of the City of Calgary." Council autonomy was preserved and the principle of the plebiscite was honoured. It was enough to bring the divide together. The motion carried 8-3 with Jack Leslie, Dave Russell, and Runo Berglund voting against.

Jubilation reigned; resentment lurked. And all was not what it seemed.

THE FORGOTTEN ISSUES: EAST AND WEST OF THE RIGHT-OF-WAY

In the nail-biting and posturing that marked the frenzied and closely watched negotiations in that momentous third week of January, no thought was given to two seemingly peripheral issues. They weren't even on the table. The public was ignorant of them; the city administration knew about them, of course, but had adopted a head-in-the-sand attitude. That, as soon become clear, was a big mistake!

The fall negotiations that had led to the disputed final draft in December had focused on the rights-of-way for the railway and the parkway between 6th Street East and 14th Street West. Not being within the parameters defined by these negotiations, the potential rights-of-way to the east and west were of lesser significance. In fact, there was no specification of responsibility for these acquisitions. In the east, city-CPR co-operation seemed accepted. In the west, the situation was not so clear. However, both negotiating parties initially assumed that these rights-of-way to accommodate the parkway and the railway tracks beyond the 6th Street East and 14th Street West could be acquired without difficulty. As it turned out, nothing could be further from the truth. The failure to resolve problems that arose in both areas did more to destroy the project than the issues that had been made public in December. A bewildering sequence of events that eventually led nowhere clearly demonstrate the confusion, lack of communication, and misconceptions that plagued the project from the outset.

East of 6th Street

Initially, neither participant foresaw any problem with the rights-of-way east of 6th Street East. Both needed to cross land owned by the CNR and currently in use as a freight yard. This freight yard blocked the CPR's proposed diverted route to the Bow River and also prevented the parkway from continuing east of the Elbow River to join Blackfoot Trail at 15th Street East.

It is true that the city tried to open negotiations with the CNR early. Beginning in February 1963 and continuing through the summer, Commissioner John Steel carried on extensive correspondence with Norman J. MacMillan, the CNR's executive vice-president. Using maps and plans, Steel acquainted MacMillan with details of the project and apprised him of his hopes to secure joint rights-of-way through the CNR land.[145] MacMillan, however, was non-committal. After all their correspondence, it must have come as a surprise to Steel when MacMillan informed him in July that the city's request had been put on hold and, furthermore, that MacMillan preferred to deal with the CPR rather than the city on the matter.[146] No doubt puzzled but comfortable with the idea, Steel agreed to let Ian Sinclair take over the direct negotiations with the CNR and was encouraged when Sinclair promised to deal not with MacMillan but with CNR President Donald Gordon directly. But Steel had made an understandable mistake. Believing that matters were now in capable hands and that a satisfactory resolution could be expected on both rights-of-way, the city removed itself from negotiations. Initially, all seemed well. On September 25, the commissioners were sufficiently encouraged to tell City Council that the negotiations were proceeding satisfactorily and that it was expected "that a satisfactory outcome will shortly be reached."[147]

Then, on October 9, Mayor Grant MacEwan received an interesting letter from Rod Sykes, in which Sykes referred to the successful negotiations between the two railway companies that had led to an understanding in principle for the release of 9.8 acres needed for the CPR's new station and right-of-way.[148] This "understanding in principle" indicated that the CNR was not going to give anything away for nothing. In return for the right-of-way, the CNR expected the CPR to use the CNR's bridge across the Elbow River. In compensation, the CPR would build another bridge for the CNR upstream and pay for the costs of relocating rail lines and customers.[149] Sykes made no reference to the right-of-way for the parkway but indicated that the CNR was interested in securing further information from the city regarding its plans for the parkway.

Although puzzled by Sykes's remarks, since the information which the CNR was requesting from the city had already been forwarded, MacEwan wrote to MacMillan the next day stressing the need for CNR co-operation if the city was to secure the parkway and its vital east-west transportation link.[150] MacMillan continued to stall, noting in correspondence to MacEwan eleven days later that he would be prepared to comment in the near future.[151] Two months later, the CNR announced its decision. From a letter by MacMillan to MacEwan dated December 20, the city was shocked to learn that there was no way the parkway was going to pass through the CNR freight yards east of 6th Street.[152] Almost in judicial fashion, MacMillan gave his judgement: the CNR "could release a strip of land sufficient for the purposes of *either* a new Canadian Pacific main line or a parkway of modest width but not for both. However," he went on, "having in mind interest of both the Canadian Pacific and the City in redeveloping the present Canadian Pacific main line, the devoting of any available area in the Canadian National yard to right-of-way for the Canadian Pacific would seem to have priority over use for highway purposes." In other words, no parkway.

City officials were astounded. No parkway! The parkway had been used to justify the project in the first place. What had happened? Had Sinclair not bargained hard enough for the parkway? Why would the CNR be so recalcitrant over a seemingly minor issue and in an area that clearly had no great future as a revenue producer? It was a double blow for the city. Not only were there significant points of disagreement in the draft agreement, but to learn five days before Christmas that the parkway was not possible was enough to put a pall of doom over the whole project. Yet following MacMillan's bombshell, the city commissioners announced blithely that they would again be approaching the CNR.[153] All was not what it seemed. The rejection of the parkway probably had nothing to do with Sinclair's bargaining efforts or his willingness to put the CPR's interests before the city's. The CNR was simply playing hardball over another, unrelated issue.

The CNR rails entered the city from the southeast and diverged into two separate sets of tracks at the Valleyfield subdivision. One line went straight north and veered northwest before crossing the Elbow River and terminating in the freight yards under discussion at 6th Street East. The other passed to the west and north, crossing Macleod Trail at about 26th Avenue and terminating in freight facilities, as well as a small passenger station, on 18th Avenue and 1st Street West that serviced passengers to Edmonton. These facilities comprised well over twenty acres of underused industrial land plus spur lines that served major customers, including Massey Ferguson, Kraft Foods, and McLellan Coal and Wood. With the opening of its modern industrial park in Highfield, the CNR saw this area in terms of diminishing importance. Hence, when the city began making overtures to purchase the land in 1962, the CNR was very receptive. The city's interest was twofold. The CNR land stood in the way of planning needs regarding the reconfiguration of Macleod Trail, the city's main south artery. The Calgary

Exhibition and Stampede, which operated on nearby city-owned land under a lease, was also interested in the area for expansion purposes.[154]

Although negotiations began as early as 1960, it was not until July 1962 that the CNR and the city got together to discuss the possibility of lifting the rail tracks, moving the Communication and Freight Sales building from 17th Avenue, rebuilding the passenger station east of 2nd Street East on 25th Avenue, and relocating Massey Ferguson.[155] In January 1963, Commissioner Steel took the next step and asked the CNR to name its price for the entire area.[156] The CNR responded in May with a $1.8 million price tag that included $152,000 for track removal, $357,000 for the new station, $175,000 to move the Communication and Freight Sales building, and $758,000 for acquisition of about twenty-four acres presently taken up with sidings and spur lines (now Lindsay Park).[157] In an interesting sidelight, a day after the city's formal offer was received in July, MacMillan offered a subtle compromise, one that the city either chose not to pursue or else simply ignored. Referring to current dialogue over the 6th Street East site, MacMillan wrote to Steel: "I agree completely that the proposal looking to the relocation of our passenger station is a separate and distinct project from your project to relocate the CP."[158] It was double talk. In other words, "Give us what we want and we'll give you what you want."

The city thought that the price was too high and, in October, produced its proof in an appraisal by its land manager, Bob Leitch, that reduced the CNR's asking price of $1,867,800 to $1,018,600 million.[159] The biggest reduction concerned the twenty-four acres. According to the CNR, the land was worth $32,000 an acre. Bob Leitch's figure was $3,000 an acre, which he said was the going rate for unserviced industrial land. But Leitch was wrong. The location alone gave the land a much higher premium, and the CNR knew it. The *quid pro quo* intimated by MacMillan five months earlier had gone by the board. In response, the CNR gave fair warning of what to expect: "We wish to carry the possibility of our vacating certain CNR properties in this area through to conclusion prior to considering the possibility of releasing certain properties in the vicinity of 6th Street East."[160] On October 11, the Board of

Commissioners' secretary, Jack Wilson, referred to the $800,000 differential and to the CNR as "being difficult" in not wanting to deal until plans for its new station were settled.[161] But Steel appeared not to get the message. Instead, he remonstrated with MacMillan over his breach of faith and intimated that it all had to do with the unsettled Lindsay Park issue.[162] The matter was left in limbo while both sides secured independent appraisals of the land costs. They were still waiting for these appraisals when MacMillan seized the initiative on December 20 — whether his refusal to release land for the parkway was a bombshell or a wake-up call was for the city to decide.

Thus, in the context of the wider issues involving the city and the CNR, the flat refusal to allow the right-of-way might not have come as a total surprise. However, the implications for the redevelopment plan were inescapable. As of December 20, 1963, when the details of the agreement for redevelopment of the designated area were the subject of intense debate, the city was being told by a third party that its projected parkway, its justification for the riverbank route, and the agreement itself was no longer possible. And not just across the freight yards. According to city plans, once the parkway had crossed the CNR freight yards, it was to continue along the CNR right-of-way east to Blackfoot Trail. Yet nothing had been discussed, let alone settled, with the CNR regarding this route. The "road to nowhere" was still exactly that. Furthermore, one wonders what the commissioners were thinking when they balked at the price the CNR had set on its land in the south. It was an added complication to what was already a monster in the making.

West of 14th Street

Although ultimately the area west of 14th Street West was to prove as big an obstacle to the agreement as that east of 6th Street East, only the possibility of problems had emerged by the end of December. But as with the east issue, the city was assuming too much.

The first problem concerned the CPR right-of-way for the rerouted rails west of 14th Street: more specifically, where was it to be and who was to secure it? The issue arose when the CPR had to abandon its original plan to rejoin the main line near or at 14th Street by traversing Mewata Park. The city solicitor had advised the commissioners that since Mewata Park was a grant from the federal government, any change in land use necessitated provincial approval and probably a plebiscite.[163] Forced to change their plans, CPR officials had to consider continuing the rerouted tracks beyond 14th Street before rejoining the main line. A problem immediately presented itself. Under the Heads of Arrangement, the city was to secure the right-of-way for the CPR in the area covered by the agreement, with recompense to follow. Beyond this area, the responsibility for securing rights-of-way for the rails and the parkway was unclear, although it seemed to be understood that the primary role fell to the city if the two routes were to parallel each other. At a meeting on August 29, 1963, the CPR stressed that the removal of Mewata Park from right-of-way considerations obligated the city to secure the entire new right-of-way west of 14th Street. Over the next two months, the city and the CPR were at odds over this point.[164]

As with the issue in the east end, matters were further complicated by a third party. This time it was a British-based developer, Canbritam Development Corporation Ltd. Formed in 1960 by Eagle Star Insurance Company, Second Covent Gardens Property Company, and Philip Hill Higginson and Erlanger Merchants and Bankers, Canbritam concentrated on North American real estate and developing what it called "fully integrated communities."[165] Attracted to Calgary by a promising investment climate, Canbritam, shortly after its formation, secured several properties in the city and, in 1962, began focusing on the forty-acre area west of 14th Street up to 22nd Street, between the Bow River and the CPR main line. Although options to purchase were secured from major landowners like Dominion Tar, Canbritam had not yet secured title to all of the properties it needed when it began putting forward its Bow Village proposal to the city.

Canbritam proposed to develop the forty acres in a $30 million high-rise residential, commercial, and retail complex.[166] The city welcomed the high-rise residential component, which promised to house three thousand families within ten years, and was further encouraged by projections of $846,543 in annual tax income from the area compared to the $24,934 it was currently receiving. However, city administrators were not as impressed with Canbritam's proposed zoning for commercial and retail facilities, arguing that their size and scope detracted from downtown development.[167] Aware of the city's positive attitude toward the project, however, Canbritam was not discouraged. As the development company scrambled to complete its land assembly, the waiting game continued. In October 1962, City Council gave first and second readings to a bylaw approving rezoning for Bow Village.[168]

This was the situation when, following the removal of Mewata Park from the CPR–City of Calgary project, the parties involved had to consider the option of acquiring rights-of-way for both the railway and the westbound fork of the parkway from Canbritam. A major issue for Canbritam was the lack of traffic access to its Bow Village project, a situation that company executives hoped would be alleviated by the proposed parkway. Their transparent attempt to force the city's hand in this regard was evidenced in the fall of 1963, when they rejected no fewer than six possible routes submitted by the city for the two rights-of-way, none of which allowed access to the Bow Village development. Faced with a problem that had the potential to derail the entire project, the city sought a pragmatic solution. In a tentative agreement reached with Canbritam on November 28, 1963, the city agreed to provide direct north and south access to the parkway from Bow Village. In return, Canbritam agreed to release sufficient land for rights-of-way for both the CPR and the westbound parkway along the riverbank. Moreover, land for the parkway was promised at no cost to the city.[169]

With this agreement, it seemed that a major obstacle had been overcome. Both rights-of-way west of 14th Street had been assured. The city had secured land for its westbound parkway at no cost. Although CPR executives had not made anything public, they had also ensured reasonable costs for the right-of-way through Canbritam's land. Unlike city administrators, Rod Sykes believed from the outset that the Bow Village proposal was more speculative than real. To protect his company from the inflated land prices he was sure Canbritam had anticipated and would demand for releasing land for the railway right-of-way, Sykes had convinced his superiors to allow him to purchase a strip of land from Imperial Oil before Canbritam did, land that just happened to be in the centre of the Bow Village residential component. It was a bargaining chip par excellence. His satisfaction is evident in a letter he wrote to Canbritam's president, Brian Showell, in December 1963. In referring to a recent meeting with Canbritam officials, Sykes noted, "We indicated our willingness to assist you to obtain the land you need while you showed willingness to facilitate our obtaining a new right-of-way along the riverbank, part of which would impinge on property you now own."[170]

The first indication that all might not be well emerged only a week after the November agreement between the city and Canbritam was drafted. As the two proposed rights-of-way passed under 14th Street and continued along the riverbank toward the Canbritam properties farther west, they had to traverse city-owned land. This piece of land was, however, too narrow to accommodate both rights-of-way because of the presence of a warehouse belonging to the Hudson's Bay Company. On December 6, city officials indicated that since they had secured the right-of-way for the CPR across the city's own land, the CPR should be prepared to discuss sharing the costs of relocating the warehouse to accommodate the parkway.[171] The CPR negotiators were not convinced. This was the situation at the end of 1963.

To summarize, in addition to the debate over the redevelopment area, the project also faced serious threats east of 6th Street East and west of 14th Street West. The city-CPR redevelopment project was a complex issue in itself and was to be the focus of intensive debate during the emotional roller coaster that would follow its ratification by City Council on January 22. However, the other two threats remained relatively hidden from the public until the very end. Given the histrionics over CPR greed versus a vision for a better downtown, it is ironic that a project of such grand design was to flounder on two peripheral issues that were allowed to wend their own fatal paths. More astounding is the fact that both parties actually negotiated an agreement while realizing that crucial areas of dispute still remained outside the area covered by the agreement.

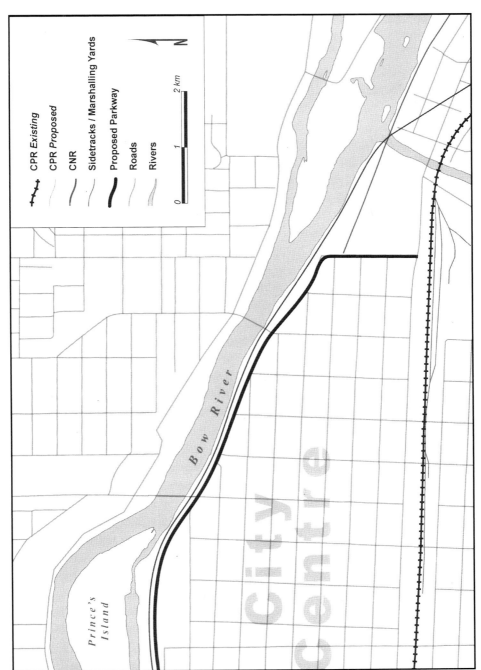

Map 4. Route of parkway as presented to City Council, December 1963

Legend:
- CPR Existing
- CPR Proposed
- CNR
- Sidetracks / Marshalling Yards
- Proposed Parkway
- Roads
- Rivers

0   1   2 km

N

Bow River

Prince's Island

City Centre

Several questions arise from this discussion. While the CPR's behaviour was questionable given its faith in the project, in a way it was also predictable. The city's actions, though, seem more difficult to understand.

The first and most important question concerns the Heads of Arrangement signed by Mayor Harry Hays in April 1963. As has been shown, the CPR considered it an ironclad agreement, whereas the city saw it as a base for negotiations. It was on this point that the city surrendered the initiative to the CPR. After the city had taken such a strong stand on August 6, its meek acquiescence the next day is hard to fathom. One can only conclude that the city negotiators were well and truly blinded by dollar signs and bright visions of prosperity.

The parkway question is equally problematic. The thoroughfare was supposed to link Blackfoot Trail with the proposed bridge at 22nd Street, but land was being bought for its passage through the redevelopment zone before any arrangements to secure the right-of-way east of the Elbow River had been made. In fact, as late as December 1963, maps depicting the route of the parkway did not show it going through the CNR grounds — or farther east, for that matter. Rather, they showed it turning south at 6th Street to join with 9th Avenue. Essentially, this meant that negotiations were stalled over a road whose ultimate route was still at the conceptual stage.

Yet regardless of plans to the contrary, it was also clear that the commissioners wanted the parkway eventually to extend to Blackfoot Trail. In order for this to happen, the parkway would have to traverse CNR land. CNR officials, however, had made it plain that they would not co-operate until the city had settled the issue of the railway's land in Lindsay Park. Yet the city did nothing, and when the Agreement of Intent was ratified on January 22, City Council had no idea of this stumbling block. The point is that although the east end issue was resolvable, the city commissioners were continuing to stall. Evidence suggests, though, that an east-west freeway along the south bank of the Bow River, although ostensibly a dead issue, continued to linger in the minds of more than one commissioner. In all the debate that surrounded the project during this period, the practical need for the road to nowhere was never called into question.

One must also question the decision to put the redevelopment proposal ahead of the city's first downtown plan. In fact, it was the city's intention to base the downtown plan on the achievement of an agreement with the CPR. This backwards approach to planning is difficult to understand, especially given the fact that the CPR had no plans for redevelopment beyond its announced two-block project. One wonders what the Planning Department must have thought of all this, particularly because it had largely been kept in the dark during negotiations.

Despite their belief that the Heads of Arrangement was a binding document, the CPR negotiators' intransigent bargaining strategy is surprising: after all, they purportedly wanted the project as much as the city did. As bargainers, CPR managers were out of touch with the reality of the times. Rod Sykes said as much in an impassioned plea begging the company leaders to explain their position and to put on a more transparent face:

> We have to convince them that we will do our best to minimize disadvantages and that we will give them something much better somewhere else — we can't just *say* this — we must *show* them, too. This is not hard to do and if we hope to succeed we can't avoid it. We must play the game according to the rules. We can't expect to win the race without running in it.
>
> If you take a "take it or leave it" attitude — what we do with our land is our business — we run serious risk not only of wilfully and unnecessarily destroying the whole project, but of proving what one speaker told council on Thursday is true — "CP is arrogant, don't give a damn for the public, attempt to railroad things through without giving chance for examination, can't do business with CP and shouldn't try." You cut the ground right out from under us. . . . As I mentioned, I am interested only in doing a successful job, and if in my best judgment I can't do that then I must make place for someone who can because I am not cut out for a puppet or a yoyo. It is in your hands and yours alone whether we win or lose.[172]

One possible explanation for the company's intransigence might be that history got in the way. It seems that the company's bargaining tactics were the same in 1963–64 as they had been fifty years earlier when negotiating the Palliser Hotel and the Ogden Shops Agreements with the city. In those negotiations, the CPR offered the city a covetous prize, the benefits of which were too good to resist. As the dispenser of this discretionary largesse to a grateful supplicant, CPR leadership viewed negotiations as a vehicle to iron out minor details. That nothing had changed in 1963 was evident as much from the surprise evinced by CPR officials when the city proved reluctant simply to accept their assurances that all would be well in the long run as from their concerns about crossings, taxes, and cost-sharing. All of these issues invited some level of compromise, and given the city's enthusiasm for the project, the compromise would not have had to be great: two good examples are the 2nd Street crossing and a willingness to pay some taxes early. Yet in typical fashion, the CPR took the hard line approach and, in so doing, gave its several opponents all the ammunition they needed.

Finally, there is the question of the way in which the proposal was ratified. The first vote to accept the Agreement of Intent subject to a plebiscite was lost. The second — to accept it without a plebiscite — was also lost. The final vote called for immediate acceptance *and* a plebiscite. With its face-saving, win-win undertones, it was a brilliant motion, one that allowed all in favour of the project to go home with clear consciences. But questions remain. Technically, the final vote accepted the agreement subject to conditions linked to a plebiscite. However, the question as to when City Council actually decided to accept the agreement on its own terms remains unanswered. Also, did City Council honour or abrogate its responsibility? Was this politics at its best or at its worst? For, after all the months of negotiations and diatribe, the final onus would fall neither on the commissioners who had negotiated the deal nor on a hesitant City Council that was at last grappling with the issue, but on an uninformed public.

4

Temperature Rising

The Project Under Public Scrutiny,
February to June 1964

Following the signing of the Agreement of Intent on January 27, 1964, the CPR–City of Calgary redevelopment plan was launched into the public spotlight. It did not fare well. Defenders of the project were assailed by a mounting tide of opposition. The plan came under critical scrutiny by the provincial government. By April, plan supporters who had confidently expected a favourable outcome in the plebiscite were not so optimistic. But as it turned out, the major forces that mattered in the long run were hovering on the periphery, unmentioned in the public debate that swirled around the issue. It is fitting, perhaps, that a project with so much at stake but with poor management from the beginning should perish on two minor issues, both removed from the public eye, both resolvable, and with both sides equally culpable.

The relief and joy that had accompanied the signing of the agreement did not last. In the ensuing days, a more sober reaction reflected the uncertainty that surrounded the document. The agreement was not seen as a victory for the project but as a prelude to provincial approval and the plebiscite. No alderman emerged to deliver self-congratulatory comments. One of the three dissentients, Jack Leslie, hoped he would be proven wrong for the sake of the city.[1] At least four who had voted for the plan expressed reservations. The mayor said there were aspects he did not like, Walter Boote did not approve of the riverbank route, Roy Deyell intimated that the city had not done its homework, and one of the staunchest supporters, Ted Duncan, implied that the city had wanted much more from the CPR.[2] Ernie Starr, who had been absent from the January 22 meeting, wanted more concessions from the CPR prior to the plebiscite.

With a plebiscite now certain, the project became a major public issue for the first time. On January 24, *The Albertan* blamed "uninformed prejudice" for almost pushing the project into the "jaws of defeat" and urged supporters to coalesce and work toward helping "the public reach a decision on the project as it really is."[3] Even the staunchly supportive *Herald* noted that "City Council will have to do a terrific selling job."[4] This muted reaction by a pro-project press and its concerns over the way City Council had opted to let the public decide indicated a resident unease that the project might not fare well on voting day.

Although one ardent letter to the *Herald* suggested that critics of the project be sterilized, it was clear that the business community knew it could not leave public education to the city.[5] After announcing its disbandment on January 24, the Calgary Development Committee emerged three days later in a new guise. Comprising the same groups, with the important addition of labour interests, and with the same chair (Carl Nickle), Calgarians for Progress described itself as an "association of citizens who believe that the Agreement is beneficial to Calgary and to the City's future." It pledged itself to "urge approval of the Agreement in the coming plebiscite" — or, as Carl Nickle later stated, "a large part of Calgary's future is wrapped up in plebiscite day."[6] Operating from a permanent downtown office supplied by a supporter, the new group released its first brochure on January 27.[7] In addition to maps explaining the alternative routes and why they were rejected (plus three more routes that had not even been considered in the first place), the brochure used three model photographs and cross-section views to show future downtown development between 4th Street West and 1st Street East that included grand modern designs for a transportation centre, three office towers, a motor hotel, a major department store, and a communication centre. The brochure listed the main provisions of the agreement and detailed its advantages in terms of tax revenues, investment climate, and employment opportunities. All in all, the brochure reasoned, to be a New Look City in a New Look Age, Calgary could not afford to be faint-hearted.

Although Calgarians for Progress did not ask the city for money to promote the project, the organization was welcomed at City

Hall by Deputy Mayor Ted Duncan, who praised its campaign on behalf of the city. Sensibly, however, the city did not endorse Calgarians for Progress as its official mouthpiece. Over the ensuing weeks, the organization continued its promotional activities in a series of reports, all designed to show citizens that the agreement meant only good things for the city. One report, for example, by showing how land prices near the new right-of-way had actually risen, tried to balance the negative viewpoints of those holding land in that area who were threatening legal action.[8] The organization also tapped into support elsewhere. The magazine *Western Business and Industry* noted in its February 1964 issue, "If the scheme clears remaining hurdles Calgary is virtually assured of one of the greatest commercial booms of any western city." On February 13, support for the project came from an unlikely source. The *North Hill News*, the only media holdout on the merits of the proposal, decided to lend its support with the statement that the project was "sound enough to justify a Yes vote at the plebiscite."[9]

A HAIL OF OPPOSITION

By January 31, a group that had formed just three weeks earlier as an information-gathering watchdog had changed direction and focus. Recall that on January 8, an assorted group of planners, academics, architects, and representatives from the Local Council of Women had formed the Citizens' Committee for Community Development (CCCD) as a sounding board for public opinion with a primary focus on planning in the downtown area. However, at a meeting at the Allied Arts Centre on January 30, the group decided to leave publicizing on planning matters to the Calgary Planning Association and to concentrate its efforts instead on the CPR plan. Although the project was not condemned outright, misgivings were several and included the two rights-of-way, the vagueness of construction time commitments, the lack of a traffic study validating the need for a parkway along the river, the inconclusiveness of the Hanson Report, and the impact of the rerouted rails and parkway on Chinatown.[10] According to a map in the Sykes papers, six

Chinese-owned properties priced collectively at $257,000 were on the CPR purchase list, as were several other buildings in Chinatown valued at a total of $310,000.[11]

The CCCD called for additional professional planning advice and mass public debate. It also urged the publication of the Agreement of Intent in the press; although this suggestion was initially opposed by Commissioner John Steel on the grounds that no one would understand it, the text of the agreement appeared in The Albertan on February 12.[12] The CCCD acted as a catalyst, attracting other disenchanted groups. For example, in a spirited meeting organized by the CCCD for February 5 at the Allied Arts Centre, speakers against the project included academics from the University of Calgary Geography Department and representatives from a local architectural association.[13] When the CCCD refused to join Calgarians for Progress and later criticized that organization for displaying inaccurate and misleading models of the project in its downtown office, it cemented its public image as anti-project.[14]

Rumblings of opposition came from another direction as well. On January 25, Ruth Gorman, an outspoken social activist who once likened attendance at a City Council meeting to a prison sentence, blasted the agreement in a letter to The Albertan. Under the heading "Time to Call a Spade a Spade," Gorman wondered about "the air of mystery" clouding the issue and accused the city of favouritism in allowing the CPR far too much in terms of tax breaks and development leeway, noting that crucial specifics had been concealed from City Council.[15] In calling for answers showing "where the taxpayer would not lose by this deal," Gorman laid out the issue as she saw it:

> Considering the future cost of supporting four blocks of tax-free land through the middle of the city, losing for all time our river front property for either lucrative tax property or pleasant parks, and the future concessions we will have to in all fairness give other owners of buildings and houses, this beautifying of our city is being done at a ridiculous price.

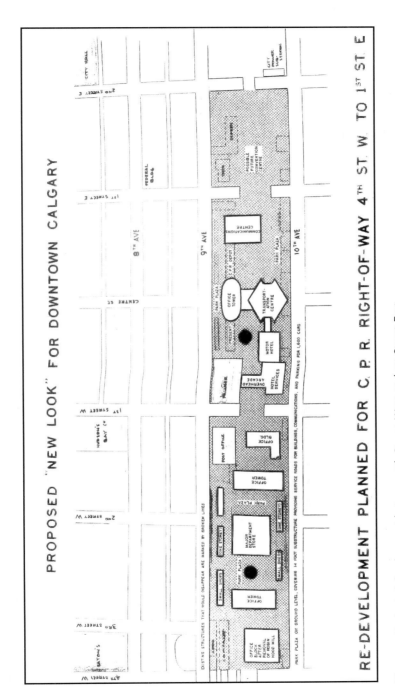

Figure 5. Projected development between 4th Street West and 1st Street East.
Source: City of Calgary Archives.

In terms of tone and focus, this letter was no different from dozens of others that had been written to the editors of both daily presses.[16] There was a difference, though. Ruth Gorman was no ordinary private citizen. A fiery, articulate, and socially active lawyer, she was also representing the thirty-four organizations and sixteen thousand women who made up the Local Council of Women, a group that had already gone on record as opposing the riverbank route. As such, her letter made the opposition sit up and take notice. Carl Nickle, the chair of Calgarians for Progress, challenged Gorman's claims in his own letter to the editor three days later, arguing that taxpayers would ultimately be far better off if the proposal went ahead.[17]

Gorman's entry into the fray also caught the attention of Rod Sykes, who was concerned enough to write her on January 29. In polite tones, Sykes commended Gorman for her "good sense and moderation" but attributed her remarks to misinformation. As the following comment attests, it is clear that he, too, perceived Gorman as a force to be reckoned with: "I believe, in view of your letter, that you owe it to yourself and to the many people who respect and who are influenced by your judgment to explore this matter both further and a little more thoroughly and I look forward to hearing from you soon."[18] As Sykes recalls, Gorman did not reply. The point is that Gorman's influence was clearly recognized. It reached out to female voters and was probably perceived as a more neutral and persuasive general voice than that of either Calgarians for Progress or the CCCD.

Others also began questioning, not the project itself but the fact that it had been prepared without sufficient planning. The February issue of the *Home Buyers' Guide* quoted Jack Leslie, who felt that the agreement did not protect the best interests of the city and that it should have been either rejected or tabled pending further negotiation. Leslie's view was supported on February 10 by a citizens' petition, which, after listing twelve negative aspects of the agreement, asked the provincial legislature to withhold approval pending an impartial cost analysis and further engineering studies.[19] But probably the most damaging commentary came from an expert and former supporter, Daniel van Ginkel. Recall that Van Ginkel Associates had authored one of the three favourable reports on the proposal back in June 1963 but that, three months later, van Ginkel had qualified the report's recommendations in a letter to the commissioners, the contents of which apparently never reached City Council. On January 3, 1964, he wrote another letter to Chief Commissioner John Steel, in which he criticized Robert Dowling's vision for development. What was needed, according to van Ginkel, was a comprehensive (lengthy and expensive) study by professionals from several disciplines, including architecture, planning, engineering, transportation, and economics.[20] Unlike his first letter, this one was leaked and a copy fell into the hands of ardent critic J.C. Sproule, whose offices occupied land on the new right-of-way.[21] With Sproule going public with the letter during an address to the Alberta Old Age Pensioners Society on February 12, fresh and potentially damaging seeds were planted. The editor of *The Albertan* probably never made a truer statement when he noted three days later, "The public must be fast coming to conclusions that the more that is said about the CPR redevelopment project the more confusing it becomes."[22]

Van Ginkel agreed to address City Council on the matter on February 17. Arguing that despite what the press had intimated, he had not changed his opinion that the project was good for the city, van Ginkel explained that his objections were purely "technical." However, his statements that the massive size of the project could prejudice the community's best interests and that his own professionalism demanded revisiting a report that had originally been prepared in too short a time only served to muddy the waters further.[23]

The project was further undermined by an article prepared by Demetrius Styliaras, an associate professor of architecture and planning at the University of Manitoba, following a visit to Calgary. The article, titled "CPR Redevelopment Proposal" and published in the *Royal Architectural Institute of Canada Journal*, argued that the redevelopment project would ruin the riverbank and result in a city core that would remain "fragmented, aimless and spotty with no true urbanity."[24] Styliaras felt that the city downtown should preserve its northern orientation and suggested that the proposed parkway be relocated and elevated just south of the existing CPR tracks. Although Styliaras's solution would only have strengthened the existing barrier, his academic credentials and his contentions about an integrated downtown with an unspoiled riverbank appealed to planners and designers. It was thus another unwelcome voice of opposition to the project.

As for the CPR, although the prospects of a plebiscite were dismaying, its leadership decided to keep a low profile. Always adamantly against the notion of voters deciding an issue in a city where its popularity had long been on the decline, the CPR must have signed the agreement with a great deal of misgiving. For example, three days after the signing, the city's deputy solicitor, John DeWolfe, told Commissioner Steel that the railway company did not feel that the agreement was delivered to the CPR "on any understanding that the documents were subject to ratification by electors."[25] Then, on February 19, President Crump rehashed old and familiar rhetoric when he told the press that the company was not interested in a publicity campaign to sell the project: "If the people here don't want it, fine. We'll pull out. There are other cities and towns that do."[26] Yet a week earlier, the company had assembled its one thousand employees at its Ogden maintenance plant and, via speeches and a handout, portrayed the agreement in a very positive light. As one worker commented, "You almost had to go. . . . They started out by telling you they weren't telling you how to vote but I'm sure they mean you to vote yes."[27]

The City of Calgary was proactive in preparing the public for the plebiscite with a "Yes" vote in mind. The most vociferous aldermen lauded the agreement at meetings of clubs and organizations.[28] Ted Duncan told the *Home Buyers' Guide* that the agreement exemplified the city's motto, "Onward," and was proof positive of the city's growing international reputation. Bill Dickie informed the South Calgary Businessmen's Association that the agreement meant millions of investment dollars to the city.[29] City administrators went about it more quietly.[30] By the end of January, Steel had decided to assign city staff permanently to the project, partly to disseminate "factual information" to the public. He followed this up with a trip to New York with Sykes, where they visited with the CPR's high-powered consultant, Robert Dowling, to discuss the project.[31] Dowling wanted to court popular favour by invoking the city's motto and naming the vacated right-of-way "Onward Plaza," a suggestion supported by the commissioners but tabled by City Council until after the plebiscite.[32] The aldermen accepted the conclusion of a commissioners' report that because "many of the public are still endeavouring to fairly and factually assess the matter," a publicity campaign was necessary. Accordingly, they recommended spending $10,000 in a series of releases detailing aspects of the physical plan, financial and economic impact, communication and traffic, and development and expenditure. These releases were to begin three to four weeks in advance of the plebiscite.[33] A three-man committee made up of aldermen Harold Runions (chair and supporter), Jack Leslie (opponent), and Ernest Starr (undecided) was subsequently appointed to coordinate the campaign.

PREPARING FOR THE LEGISLATIVE HEARINGS

On February 22, the city was advised that the requisite provincial hearings on the project were to be held on March 3–5 at the Legislative Building before the entire legislature. Technically, these hearings were to establish valid reasons for the statutory amendments necessary to proceed with the project. These amendments included special expropriation powers on land required for the new right-of-way, relief from provisions in the Planning Act regarding roads and recreational areas on the existing right-of-way, a simple majority plebiscite, and exemption for the new right-of-way from the Municipal Assessment and Equalization Act. But because the three western premiers were currently preparing a federal challenge to the CPR's 1881 contractual tax exemptions on rights-of-way through prairie municipal areas, it was more than likely that the wily Ernest Manning also wanted closer scrutiny over a project with implications for the larger concessions he and his colleagues were seeking.

The provincial hearings were to take the form of briefs for and against the project, followed by questioning. It would appear that despite the growing concern over the project, city leaders — initially, at least — did not anticipate any great problem securing provincial approval. One has only to note its draft legislation just days after the Agreement of Intent was signed. Set up in form and language to replicate an actual statute, the draft sent to Edmonton asked for only two amendments related to the agreement: the right to expropriate land for the new right-of-way and relief for said right-of-way from the provisions of the Municipal Assessment and Equalization Act.[34] Another reason for city officials' optimism was that Premier Manning was known to be supportive of such bold municipal initiatives.[35] And then there was the city's brief: long, stacked with sound and persuasive statistics, and reinforced by expert opinion in the form of the Hanson Report. The articulate and persuasive Ian Sinclair, now an ally, would present the CPR's case, and, having faced his forcible presence across the table, city officials knew the power of his words and the body language with which he delivered them. Another ace in the hole was the "great man" himself: Robert Dowling had agreed to speak for the proposal. Other supportive briefs had been prepared, including one from Calgarians for Progress, or to be more accurate, Calgary's business community.[36] Furthermore, City Council had the appearance of being a bastion of unity. Opposing aldermen had chosen to remain silent. As Jack Leslie said, "Council is on record as favouring the plan. There is no need for any other view to be presented."[37] Although opposing briefs were on the agenda, they were not expected to represent "sound" research or sizable cross-sections of public opinion.

There were warnings, though, that this optimism might be misplaced. In the middle of February, a local MLA raised some questions about the project.[38] *The Albertan* was nervous that the legislature might overstep its powers and damn the project without due thought.[39] However, the most serious indication that the city might be in for a rough ride came on the afternoon of February 24, when the city's deputy planner, Geoff Greenhalgh, and deputy solicitor, John DeWolfe, met with provincial officials: Planning Director Noel Dant, Deputy Minister of Municipal Affairs A. W. Morrison, Deputy Attorney General John Hart, and Assessment Commissioner J. B. Laidlaw. In a three-hour meeting, these four officials bombarded Greenhalgh and DeWolfe with a volley of questions about the project, which they described as "vague," especially in its terms of CPR development on the existing right-of-way.[40] For the most part, Greenhalgh and DeWolfe were on the defensive. For example, when asked why the agreement specified that the CPR's promised expenditure of $10 million was to be on real estate in Calgary rather than specifically on the right-of-way, DeWolfe could only reply, "Council was satisfied with it." Similarly, when the provincial officials questioned the absence of a time limit placed on tax exemptions, all DeWolfe and Greenhalgh could say was that that was how the CPR wanted it. Yet despite this defensiveness, DeWolfe and Greenhalgh ended the meeting on an aggressive note, advising their interlocutors that in their opinion, the province had the power to approve or reject but not to modify the agreement, noting that "it might exceed the jurisdiction of the province to compel the railway company to comply with the legislation." In light of what transpired, it was a very interesting comment and arguably one that just might have thrown down the gauntlet to the province. Two days later, DeWolfe wrote to Steel summarizing the meeting "in order to form a proper background of the Alberta Government to the proposed validating statute."[41] There is no record of Steel's reaction.

One wonders how much these dark clouds on the horizon diminished the optimism of the city delegation, which arrived in Edmonton on the evening of March 2. Nothing, though, could have prepared them for the events that were to follow, events that left them reeling amid the crumbling integrity of their cherished project.

THE LEGISLATIVE HEARINGS, MARCH 3–5, 1964

In all, eleven briefs were heard under oath over the three-day period of March 3–5, 1964. Only three of those briefs had a significant impact, and of these, two were heard on the first day. Proceedings opened on Tuesday, March 3, amid a flurry of back-door lobbying. At the last minute, Walter Boote, a City Council alderman, had broken ranks by contacting all Social Credit MLAs and asking them to block the project.[42] This was no mean feat in a pre-email era, since sixty of the sixty-three members of the legislature were Social Credit. According to Jean Leslie, one anti-project presenter was warned by an unnamed MLA not to go ahead with his brief.[43]

One wonders, though, how much it all mattered. Over the three days, notwithstanding several members who asked questions from the floor, three senior cabinet ministers stood out: Premier Ernest Manning, Municipal Affairs Minister Alfred Hooke, and Highways Minister Gordon Taylor. Of these three, the very astute Ernest Manning was the most dominant.

Premier Manning opened proceedings around 9:00 a.m. by flexing the provincial muscle, warning the CPR of the pending challenge to their right-of-way tax exemptions and of what this might mean for projects like the one under review.[44] He made the official position clearer when he stressed that it was not the province's role to decide if the project was good or bad for the city but rather to weigh the wider implications of the statutory changes being requested.[45] He then called on Mayor Grant MacEwan to present the first brief on behalf of the city. Supporting MacEwan were Chief Commissioner John Steel; Finance Commissioner Ian Forbes; Deputy Solicitor John DeWolfe; representatives of the Assessor's, Planning, and Transportation Departments; and three aldermen, including Walter Boote.

Days One and Two: Briefs in Support and Opposition

The fifty-nine-page brief, the first official public statement made by the city on the project, took MacEwan an hour and a half to read, and even then, he did not cover it all.[46] In many ways, it followed predictable lines. Replete with general statistics derived mainly from the Hanson Report and based on projections that reached seventeen years into the future, the brief argued that for an expenditure of only $6.6 million, the city would gain a reconfigured downtown with added traffic access, a significant increase in investment capital, a surfeit of jobs to support a fast-growing population, and, by 1981, $4 million more in annual tax revenues.[47] There was no mention of planning implications: how the project would integrate with the ongoing downtown plan or how the projected block-by-block development would help to remove the existing barrier. The brief was, at best, an optimistic statement about anticipated gains in taxation revenue and investment.

On another level, the brief was overly cautious. It stressed that neither partner was satisfied with the agreement, that it was a document of compromise, and that the city shared the fears and forebodings of those who opposed it.[48] These fears were reiterated in the summary comments, which noted that the agreement had ignited vociferous opposition and an intensifying atmosphere of confusion.[49] In essence, though, the brief favoured the project because "the pluses . . . most definitely outweigh the minuses."[50] Probably the closest the city came to delivering a strong endorsement was in MacEwan's hopeful call to arms that drew an analogy to the province's pioneer heritage: "This is no time to be timid. On the contrary this is the time to take on the mantle of our forefathers, the pioneers who exercised vision, faith and vigour."[51] This rhetoric, however, was mocked in the simple comment that ended the brief: "There is no better alternative."[52] Such was the city's last word. Honest, perhaps, but hardly a statement of confidence.

The subsequent questioning period did not help matters.[53] MacEwan had to admit his mistake in telling the legislative assembly that the CPR's spending commitment was on the existing right-of-way rather than on the city at large. He had also omitted the statutory changes being asked from the province and was forced to call on DeWolfe to present them. Questions about bridge costs had the city officials huddling with Sinclair to get answers. Responses to tough questions were no different from those given a week earlier by the city delegation to senior provincial civil servants. To a question from Manning on the reason for the agreement's lack of a time commitment for development, John Steel's only answer was that the CPR could not entertain a time factor in its obligation.[54] And on the question of the relocated right-of-way, MacEwan offered the following assessment:

> Eventually it was made clear by the CPR that the re-location of the mainline to the south bank of the Bow River was the only alternative they would entertain. We have been satisfied throughout all our negotiations that this is their position and one from which they would not deviate. Accordingly, we have not assumed the responsibility of either criticizing this decision or studying any feasible alternative.[55]

All in all, the city's presentation was too unconvincing to rouse much confidence. *The Albertan* did not see it as damaging but was right on the mark when it offered the comment that the city's brief "didn't seem to go down well with the government front bench."[56]

Two other briefs were heard in the afternoon of that first day.[57] The first, by the South Bank Bow River Property Association, opposed the agreement, arguing that it penalized landowners along the new right-of-way by removing their full rights of compensation. The second brief, by the Calgary Real Estate Association, supported the agreement largely by virtue of the association's knowledge of the land business and a survey that showed majority member support. It was not until 8:25 that evening that Ian Sinclair was sworn in to present the CPR's case.

An energetic Sinclair took the floor, spoke for half an hour, and fielded questions for another three and a half.[58] Overall, he defended his company's position by balancing it against the benefits to the city, while deflecting criticism by arguing that scheme was originally the city's idea.[59] Any rejection, he told the assembly, would be Calgary's "irrevocable mistake."[60] He handled questions deftly. For example, when he was asked to specify those city requests that the CPR had rejected, he replied that he could more easily enumerate what the city had refused to do.[61] To one reporter watching Sinclair finger stabbing and "bearishly prowling the floor," it was "a magical performance."[62] Even Robert Dowling, no stranger to rhetoric himself, remarked that Sinclair's performance was grand theatrics and later sent him a membership card in a professional actors' union.[63] Sykes, who was sitting beside Dowling, was of the opinion that Sinclair did a superb job of demolishing the opposition.

Observers also felt that the exchanges between Sinclair and Manning were a joy to watch.[64] But if anyone blinked, it was Sinclair. Manning's weight bore sway when Sinclair was forced to agree that the province's right to expropriate extended to the agreement. He also accepted Manning's argument that the present right-of-way would be taxable under the agreement if the tax exemption clause were to be removed from the 1881 contract.[65] Sinclair probably knew he had no choice, in that provincial sovereignty and not the agreement was at stake in both instances. These two capitulations by the CPR were, in all likelihood, crucial in influencing Manning's later decision.

Several more briefs were presented on March 4, including those supporting the project from Robert Dowling, the Calgary Labour Council, and Calgarians for Progress.[66] Focusing on exhibits showing planned development, Dowling pleaded for "the tender loving care" and the imaginative design that would make Calgary the "most distinguished on the continent." Leo Chikinda, president of the Calgary Labour Council, stressed the powerful support wielded by sixty-three unions and 13,500 workers, the importance of the added jobs created by the project, and the property tax reductions that the average homeowner would enjoy. Carl Nickle, presenting for Calgarians for Progress, saw the project in terms of its potential for unbounded entrepreneurship and wooed the province by stressing that the project would benefit not only Calgary but all of Alberta.

Five opposing briefs were heard that day, including one from the North Calgary Businessmen's Association and two from private groups who felt that the value of their land on the new right-of-way was threatened.[67] The remaining two were the only briefs presented that day that focused on broad deficiencies in the agreement. One was by Martin Kernahan, a local engineer and a long-time critic of the project. In calling the agreement "a masterpiece of evasion," Kernahan castigated the commissioners for misleading the public about the total costs of the project.[68] He also questioned the CPR's engineering studies that had rejected the possibility of depressing the tracks on the existing right-of-way. He claimed that track depression was feasible economically and that he had actually offered to do it for them. Edmonton lawyer W. G. Morrow read a twenty-two-page brief on behalf of fifty local Calgary businessmen, one of whom was J. C. Sproule. In reference to its many defects, Morrow told the legislature, "If you are minded to approve this projected scheme, we suggest that you first appoint a Royal Commission to investigate, hear evidence and carry out research and appropriate studies."[69]

The first two days of the hearings had given the proponents of the project no real cause for alarm. Although the city had not covered itself with glory, neither had it self-destructed. The CPR representatives had given their assurance of success and Robert Dowling had equated the project with international urban greatness, while the Calgary Labour Council, the Calgary Real Estate Association, and Calgarians for Progress had thrown the weight of business and labour behind the project. By comparison, many of the opposing briefs had hinted of personal axes to grind. Although the Morrow presentation was a solid critique, it was weakened when MLA and Alderman Bill Dickie refuted some of Morrow's claims about City Council behaviour. Set against these predictable proceedings, the events of the next day were as surprising as they were significant.

Day Three: The City's Shaky Legal Ground Exposed

Members of the Barron family were highly respected long-time residents of the city. Mention has already been made of J. B. Barron, a Calgary lawyer, entrepreneur, and real estate investor. The son of Jewish immigrants, Barron and his brother formed the first Jewish law firm in Calgary in the 1920s. He later diversified his interests, buying the Grand Theatre in 1937 and constructing what came to be known as the Barron Building on 8th Avenue in 1949–51. Eleven storeys high and described very loosely as the city's first postwar skyscraper, the Barron Building attracted so many oil companies that it has been credited with physically anchoring the fledgling oil and gas industry in the city. Although Barron had openly expressed his opposition to the project, it was his son Robert who carried the family concerns to Edmonton and who delivered the brief that sparked the events that rocked the legislature.

At 10:32 on the morning of March 5, Robert H. Barron QC was sworn in. In his opening statement, he referred to his brief as a legal analysis of the agreement, one made on his own behalf but with benefit to all Calgarians. His aim was to show that the agreement was worded carefully to give the CPR enormous discretionary powers while leaving the city defenceless in many areas. In his own words, "At almost every step of the way the vital interests of the City have been disregarded and extraordinary and unprecedented concessions have been obtained from it."[70] For the next half hour, Barron laid out his case. He charged that the term "railway operations" was "not worth the paper it was written on," being worded so loosely that it covered anything implicit in the Railway Act.[71] Barron further contended that the conditions stipulating responsibility for expropriating land along the new right-of-way left the city, not the CPR, liable for any injurious legal claim.[72] In what he called "a forcible illustration of how the agreement has been carefully worded not to fetter the CPR," Barron argued that the insertion of specified clearance heights of bridges above the rail tracks left the city solely liable for the costs of raising them should the CPR ever decide to elevate its tracks.[73] In like vein, Barron kept working his way through the agreement. In his opinion, the terms governing the new transportation centre obliged the city to operate it in a CPR facility in perpetuity. Amazed that the full implications of the clause were not appreciated by City Council, Barron hammered home his conclusion: "The obligation is unlimited in time. Five hundred years from now it will still bind the City."[74] As to the clause that compelled the city "to co-operate to its fullest extent in facilitating the specific development plans of Canadian Pacific," Barron felt that it warranted "the closest scrutiny" since its interpretation "was bound to be the subject of litigation for generations to come."[75] Calling the taxation provisions "one of the most disturbing features of the agreement," Barron felt that the wording prejudiced the city's ability to collect any contestable taxes on lands on the existing right-of-way. It was, said Barron, "a clear invitation to all succeeding generations of railway lawyers to invent devices by which non-railway operations can be carried on without coming within the express terms of the taxing clauses."[76] In his concluding remarks, Barron challenged the legislature. Referring to the clause that prohibited the city from ever petitioning the legislature for changes to the taxation clauses, Barron scathingly asked, "Has any legislature ever before ratified a provision of this kind?"[77]

Yet for all its persuasiveness, the brief was less damaging than one might imagine. As far as the legislature was concerned, many of Barron's arguments were those that the members of the assembly had already raised, while others were certainly not as cut and dried legally as he had made them out to be. But Barron had ably demonstrated that the CPR held far more discretionary powers under the agreement than did the city. In effect, he had argued that the city's belief that the CPR would always honour the intent of the agreement was naïve and probably misplaced. It was enough for the premier to raise his eyebrows and turn to the city delegation for a response.

In response to Manning's request, Mayor Grant MacEwan called Deputy Solicitor John DeWolfe forward. Manning retorted by asking why the city's chief solicitor was not present. MacEwan countered by referring to DeWolfe's primary role in negotiating the agreement with the CPR. Manning was not satisfied and insisted that the chief solicitor be present. Following a vote by the MLAs, the hearings were adjourned until the chief solicitor could fly to Edmonton. Carson MacWilliams arrived in the capital in the late afternoon and was in the legislature by 4:30.

The son of a Presbyterian minister, A. Carson MacWilliams was born in Hamilton in 1896 but had lived in Calgary since 1907. He saw service in both world wars and achieved distinction as a golfer when he won both the Alberta Amateur and Open Championships in 1923. He was called to the bar in 1920 and practised law first in Winnipeg and then in Calgary with Lougheed, McLaws, Sinclair, and Redman. He was elevated to Queen's Counsel in 1951 and was near the end of his career when he became the city's solicitor in 1961, on "a short-term appointment," according to *The Albertan*.[78] At 4:50 p.m., the silver-haired MacWilliams was sworn in and proceeded to give the testimony that no one expected: certainly not the MLAs, the CPR, and, most of all, his employers.

MacWilliams dropped his bombshell early in the questioning. When asked his opinion of the agreement, MacWilliams replied that it was the most one-sided agreement he had ever seen and one he would never have written himself.[79] He proceeded to exonerate his department through a neutral interpretation of the role of the Solicitor's Office. According to MacWilliams, "although you might hate every word," legal documents were drafted to be consistent with the position of City Council. In MacWilliams's opinion, it was not the role of the Solicitor's Office to advise the city on the content of an agreement reached but rather to attend to its form, a process that he equated to "making sure the 'i's' are dotted, the 't's' crossed and the signatures are on."[80] When questioned further, he said he agreed with Barron for the most part, calling the expropriation clause "most fearsome" and the term *railway operations* "most elastic." Yet he also admitted that he was well aware of the negotiations that had taken place and that the agreement was in line with what the city wanted.[81] When he was finished, the city delegation sat in stunned silence. According to an account by Jean Leslie, "Mayor MacEwan and the council delegation looked like they wanted to crawl into a hole pulling the Canadian Pacific Railway behind them."[82]

Even as reporters rushed to write up the details of a startling turn of events, the hearings wound up. It was doubtful that either Barron or MacWilliams had damaged the chances of securing the enabling legislation. To be sure, they had shown that the agreement might have reflected city officials' naïveté, negligence, or ineptitude. However, as Manning had already stated, the legislature was not interested in whether the agreement was good or bad for the city but rather whether it reflected City Council policy and support from the right people, and therefore warranted the enabling legislation.

MacWilliams's testimony, however, dealt the city and the project a blow from which they never recovered. Confusion and divisiveness began breaking down the fragile consensus reached on January 22. Most aldermen registered surprise at MacWilliams's revelations.[83] As for Mayor MacEwan, it was the first time he became aware that MacWilliams was against the plan, a sentiment echoed by aldermen Ray Ballard and George Ho Lem and by Commissioner John Steel. Other aldermen held differing opinions. Dave Russell was not surprised. Neither was Roy Deyell, who said he knew about MacWilliams's opposition to the plan. Ernie Starr felt that MacWilliams had done "a marvellous job," and Walter Boote expressed his delight. Then there was Ted Duncan, who saw a conspiracy, or, as he phrased it, "a carefully contrived scheme by someone on Council and several Social Credit MLAs" to destroy the plan.[84] According to *The Albertan*, a closed meeting of the aldermen and Steel on March 9 "erupted in charges and counter charges, fireworks, lost tempers and a storm." A day later, the same paper reported that the aldermanic count favouring the project had gone from 8-3 to 7-6.[85]

The city's Law Department polarized the issue further, especially after rumours began swirling that MacWilliams was about to be fired for his indiscretion.[86] On March 11, John DeWolfe, probably on MacWilliams's instructions, sent a letter accompanied by several attachments to John Steel. Dating from September 1963 to January 1964, eighteen pieces of correspondence showed how Steel had been kept apprised of the principal unresolved matters of the agreement right up to the eve of its approval on January 22. In terms of responsibility, DeWolfe left little doubt onto whom it devolved:

> At no time did we ever indicate that the Agreement as a whole was desirable or otherwise since it was assumed by the writer at that time that council was substantially in accord with the general approach of the Agreement as it was indicated in the minutes of the special meeting of August 30, 1963, at which the mayor, all commissioners except yourself, and five persons from the CPR including Mr Sinclair were present. The minutes of this meeting which covered five and a half single-spaced typed pages set out the points which were discussed and on which agreement was either reached or not by the negotiating parties.[87]

City Council attempted to resolve the MacWilliams issue internally. On March 11, the mayor asked MacWilliams to inform City Council in writing of his reasons for believing that the plan was detrimental to the city. MacWilliams's response was received by the city on March 12. In it, he reiterated several of Barron's points and, in thirteen instances, demonstrated legal deficiencies in the agreement.[88] Taking another tack, the aldermen then asked MacWilliams to go beyond merely legal aspects of the agreement and to provide his opinion as to whether it "is so detrimental to the city that the scheme should be abandoned having regard to the intent and the Agreement taken *together*."[89]

MacWilliams's written response was short, to the point, and damning.[90] His opening sentence said it all: "My opinion is, and I have not the slightest hesitation in saying, that the scheme in its present form should be abandoned." After suggesting that negotiations should continue but not on the present one-sided playing field, he closed by hitting at the heart of what he thought was at stake in the agreement: "In spite of all the window dressing," the agreement was nothing but "an attempt to perpetuate tax exemptions presently held not only to the C.P.R. but to its subsidiaries and into commercial operations." Given this response, one wonders what would have transpired had City Council received the same information before the crucial August 30, 1963, meeting referred to above by DeWolfe.

The commissioners responded to this unwelcome news by trying to get MacWilliams to change his mind. It was a desperate gesture. MacWilliams was told that his opinions were probably based on "a misunderstanding of some of the technical features of the scheme," whatever that meant! Then, furnished with various departmental comments that purportedly cleared up these "misunderstandings," MacWilliams was given a few days to consider and possibly "revise his thinking."[91] It didn't work. MacWilliams refused to budge and informed the commissioners that he had nothing further to say.[92] Faced with nowhere else to go, the commissioners hastily prepared a rebuttal to MacWilliams and presented it to City Council on March 30. It was a poor attempt, being a qualification of some of the criticisms and not even addressing crucial elements of the agreement that had been challenged by MacWilliams.[93] The issue was quietly laid to rest when the aldermen agreed to a recommendation by the commissioners to table the chief solicitor's concerns until after the plebiscite. Put simply, the city had gone too far to turn back.

MacWilliams's revelations sowed the seeds of mistrust in the public eye. In its April 12 issue, the *North Hill News,* often critical of the project, praised his courage and ranked him as "the citizen of the year." Letters poured in calling for the resignation of the mayor and several aldermen.[94] A public survey called for an investigation of City Hall.[95] This negative press encouraged opposition to the project. Ruth Gorman tore into the agreement, which was so convoluted it took her a day and a half to digest it.[96] A letter to *The Albertan* raised concerns about a forgotten aspect of the agreement: the spur tracks. Technically, there was no time limit on their removal regardless of how quickly the new main line was constructed.[97] The writer had a point. Robert Dowling later inadvertently reinforced this criticism, but not his credibility, when he told the *Herald* that even if the spur tracks "did remain for a while . . . they could be hidden by greenery and a woven wooden fence."[98] City representatives were heckled, hissed at, and howled down at a public meeting organized by the Local Council of Women on March 9. Even the usually unflappable MacEwan described it as "a loaded meeting with things being made extremely rough for those supporting the plan." Opponents of the project received a better reception. University of Calgary geographer Mike Coulson's comments undermined the city's judgement and wisdom. Noting that cities across North America were depressing and building over railway tracks and not despoiling their riverbanks, Coulson referred to City Council as "a bunch of amateurs against a group of professionals."[99]

Through March and early April, the battle for public support continued. On April 2, Jack Leslie and Carl Nickle took part in a forum sponsored by the Advertisement and Sales Bureau of the Chamber of Commerce.[100] The rhetoric went back and forth: one condemned the concessions given to the CPR; the other anticipated increased investment and lower taxes. But Leslie's comments were sufficient to induce the Junior Chamber of Commerce to break from its senior counterpart and later vote to oppose the agreement. However, William O'Reilly, the regional manager for the Central Mortgage and Housing Corporation, praised the project, saying that "it would generate a tremendous amount of construction over a relatively short period of years."[101] The real estate journal *Alberta Homes* delivered a huge endorsement of the project and referred to opponents as demonstrating "a lack of understanding, narrow thinking and prejudice."[102] The Calgary Jaycees were not as convinced; they came out against the project.[103] On April 8, Mannix Company, a major Calgary business heavyweight, entered the fray. In a letter to MacEwan, which was copied to Manning, Crump, and Sinclair, the company equated its own history and future with Calgary's, saying that it "wished to make known our unqualified endorsement of the City of Calgary–C.P.R. plan, and urge every citizen of Alberta and particularly Calgarians to support the scheme not only at the polls but afterwards also to ensure that the fullest possible development will take place at the earliest possible time."[104] A day later, Ruth Gorman went on the attack again, using her favourite argument that with all the fuss over the main line, no one seemed to be asking the CPR about the array of freight lines on the existing right-of-way, which, in her opinion, might be there forever.[105] A few days later, a voice from the past emerged. Writing from Phoenix, Arizona, former mayor Don Mackay dismissed the relevance of rail lines through urban downtowns and argued that if the main line was rerouted through Balzac north of the city, "it would 'fuse' all the objecting groups into an army of 100 percent supporters."[106] He had a point, but nobody was listening.

Figure 6. Spur line in warehouse district, 1955. Although most of the discussion surrounding the redevelopment plan focused on the CPR's main line, the plan also called for the removal of spur lines, such as those in the foreground of this photograph. Critics of the proposal, among them Ruth Gorman, were skeptical, arguing that tracks such as these might remain in place far longer than anticipated. Source: Glenbow Archives, NA 5600-7137a.

As for the CPR, its executives avoided the public spotlight by refusing to take part in public forums. On declining to participate in the stormy meeting on March 9, Sykes took a more prudent stand by noting that he did not think that "a brawl got anything settled."[107] However, by the beginning of the second week in April, CPR officials had more on their minds than "brawling." On April 7, the legislature released a draft of its proposed legislation to the city and the CPR. The latter was not happy.

The Enabling Legislation

Much of the proposed legislation that passed first reading was predictable.[108] The city was granted the necessary expropriation powers for land acquisitions along the new right-of-way. The enabling plebiscite was to be decided by a simple majority, and City Council was authorized to expedite the necessary money bylaw on a two-thirds vote without ratepayer approval. The province applied its powers of expropriation to land covered by the agreement and gave the city taxing powers should the federal government change the terms of the 1881 contract. The province also added two provisions to the agreement. A formula was applied that negated two taxation-free rights-of-way by transferring the amount normally payable on the new to the existing right-of-way. Most important, the provision that had removed the CPR's obligation under the Planning Act to provide 10 percent of the development area for recreational requirements was struck down. Under the draft, this meant a donation of approximately 11.4 acres, or alternatively, if the CPR wished, a financial contribution of $500,000.

The city was pleased. The CPR was not. The city saw the draft legislation as a green light. On April 9, City Council's Special Coordinating Committee met with MacEwan, Steel, and Greenhalgh to discuss preparations for the plebiscite. A total of $6,000 was set aside to cover the costs of renting the Jubilee Auditorium for the requisite public meeting and of printing and distributing information brochures. A plebiscite date of May 4 was set, with the brochures to be delivered door to door by May 1, at the latest.[109]

The withdrawal of the 10 percent clause did not sit well with CPR executives, who argued that they had already met this requirement in their open plaza design. It was a weak argument, since the 10 percent recreational requirement was intended to balance private development by redirecting 10 percent into the public domain.[110] Be that as it may, the reinstatement of the requirement was enough to infuriate Sinclair. He could live with the other provisions in the draft but not with the one that would deprive the company of over eleven acres worth potentially $10 million. In typical fashion, he commented: "They know how they can save this project and how they can destroy it."[111] A day later, he told a business group at the Palliser Hotel that the plan was "dead."[112]

As pressure mounted, both dailies took the CPR side.[113] Interestingly, given their prior rhetoric, the CPR negotiators wavered, gambling no doubt on a compromise. The sum of $500,000 was too much, said Sinclair. Not so, argued Manning. Not on a $35 million project.[114] The city seemed content to wait. This passive action upset Manning, who accused city officials of not taking responsibility and of "throwing the ball back to us."[115] His disquiet may have been reflected in his telegram to MacEwan two days later informing him that the province had decided that the monetary compensation would be based on a figure of $40,000 per acre.

In reaching this figure, the province had clearly decided on the compromise. The amount of $40,000 per acre was reached by assessing the value of the ninety acres to be developed at an average of $33,250 an acre and the twenty-four acres of less attractive land to the east and west at an average of $7,500 an acre. From these figures, an overall assessment value of $20,000 per acre and a market value of $40,000 per acre were reached.[116] On eleven-plus acres, this meant that the CPR was liable for about $440,000 in compensation. It takes no mathematical wizardry to figure out that this amount was skewed in the CPR's favour. An average over ninety acres cannot be set equally against an average over twenty-four acres to reach a mean figure. If this differential had been factored in, the amount the CPR would have had to pay for the 11.4 acres was $63,450 per acre, or $723,330 in all — an amount greater than the original suggested figure of $500,000.[117]

On April 15, the enabling legislation was enacted. The act, titled An Act Respecting the Calgary–Canadian Pacific Agreement, generally mirrored the draft but with important additions.[118] It allowed flexibility not contained in the agreement in that the dates for the plebiscite and for the completion of land assembly on the new right-of-way were left to the two parties to decide. The CPR was allowed to allocate land for its 10 percent requirement anywhere along the existing right-of-way. However, if said land had a market value of less than $40,000 an acre, the railway company had to pay the difference. Also, the province was not going to allow the CPR the luxury of two tax-exempt rights-of-way. Any present land taxes being paid by the CPR on the existing right-of-way had to be increased by the assessable taxation on the new right-of-way. These increased taxation levies would cease when the amount payable on the existing right-of-way had dropped to a level below that payable on the new.

Naturally, the *Herald* was pleased with the legislation, calling it "the most important item to come before this session" and further declaring "that the project's survival has been the ultimate aim of almost everyone."[119] City Council was satisfied as well. At a meeting the day after the legislation was passed, council members wanted to move ahead, and they asked if the CPR was as happy as they were. They received a typically aggrieved response: "We will consider the matter," grumbled Crump. "We're not tied to the Calgary project. We're involved in other projects and we're not spending much time on this."[120] A week later, he carried his ire to City Council via a letter to the mayor. Crump complained that the CPR could not be expected to commit itself when "it is met from time to time by attempts to secure concessions beyond the terms of the agreement."[121] Probably as a result of a long meeting between Sinclair and City Council, Crump relented. On April 27, he wired Mayor MacEwan, informing him that the CPR had agreed to execute the agreement with the modifications required by legislature.[122] All that remained now was the plebiscite and the enabling money bylaw. It was the closest the project would come to fruition. The *Herald* breathed a sigh of relief at a successful ending of two weeks of uncertainty, referring to the project's turbulent history and to its near collapse in December 1963.[123] The paper's tone was obvious: all was well at long last. Unfortunately, even as the media champion of the project was printing its cheerful news, the unravelling process had already begun.

The agreement signed on January 27 covered only the area between 6th Street East and 14th Street West. It was this area that was the focus of the debate that had raged in February and March and on which the Edmonton hearings and the subsequent legislation had focused. The parallel issues of the two rights-of-way east and west were lost to the public eye.[124] They were not discussed in City Council. And their pursuit at the administrative level by John Steel was unhurried. At least at first.

The East-West Issues Emerge

In December, the city had been shocked to learn that the CNR would not release any land east of 6th Street East for the extension of the parkway, having stipulated earlier that it was not prepared to entertain the matter until the pending sale to the city of its properties south of 17th Avenue was finalized. Worried but not dissuaded, John Steel travelled to Montréal in January to reopen the matter with the CNR's executive vice-president, N.J. MacMillan. Steel came back reassured by the promise of further study and "optimistic that all difficulties can be overcome."[125] Nothing happened, and Steel waited over a month before inquiring as to progress. Two weeks later, he received an oblique reply in which he was told that MacMillan would "bear in mind the City's primary interest in the parkway."[126] By this time, Steel was getting worried but he waited another two weeks before trying again. On March 18, Steel laid it all on the line when he informed MacMillan that "the entire scheme cannot be proceeded with until we have a clear understanding with the C.N.R. that this is possible."[127] MacMillan made him wait over a month. After a phone call from the city to nudge him into action, his frustrating reply was received on April 27. "Quite frankly," wrote MacMillan, "I have felt somewhat reluctant to go too far into specifics so long as your arrangements with Canadian Pacific have continued in the negotiating and legislative stages. . . . Our interests must remain at the academic level until we know exactly what it is that has been authorized." He concluded by offering hope: "I can assure you that Canadian National would not be slow to give evidence of its full and sympathetic co-operation once the matter has been sufficiently crystallized."[128]

MacMillan's actions are difficult to understand. One possible explanation is that he felt that until the agreement was re-executed, he had better sit tight. Yet he had been willing to reach a tentative agreement with the CPR months before to cross CNR land and, on that basis, had informed the city that the parkway was not possible. So why temporize and offer vague allusions to positive support? Another possibility is that he was stalling. Although he did not mention it, he could have been holding out until the ongoing negotiations for the land sale south of 17th Avenue were settled to his satisfaction.[129] Here, negotiations were not going well: the city was still hedging on the prices the CNR was asking for the land.[130] Either way, Steel was faced with a very real dilemma. And if that was not enough to haunt him, there remained the issue of the right-of-way west of 14th Street. It was just as bad, or worse.

The right-of-way issue to the west was another jumble of misconceptions. It was accepted that negotiations for securing the rights-of-way west of 14th Street fell to the city, even though it was not spelled out specifically in the agreement. In fact, any specific reference to the acquisition of land for the parkway was restricted to the area between 6th Street East and 14th Street West.[131] CPR officials certainly felt that the onus fell on the city since they believed that they had been forced to reroute the new river route to join with the main line west of the development area. But the city was obligated to secure a right-of-way for the CPR only when it ran parallel to the parkway. Costs were to be shared in these instances. Otherwise, each was responsible for its own right-of-way and, of course, the associated costs.

Originally, there had been no indications that the CPR right-of-way and the parkway would run parallel west of 14th Street. In fact, only the westbound parkway was a factor since 9th Avenue West would accommodate eastbound traffic until east of 14th Street, where it would link up with the main parkway running in both directions. The city intended to run this westward branch along the river. The CPR's specific route was undecided but, regardless of the ultimate route, would have to run southwest toward the main line. The stumbling block here was that this right-of-way had to cross land set aside for Canbritam's Bow Village project. And that posed problems. According to John Steel, "There was little hope of the railway traversing west of 14th Street without being subject to considerable claim by Bow Village for injurious affection."[132] This was misleading since, as mentioned earlier, the CPR had secured a bargaining chip *par excellence* when the company bought a piece of land in the centre of the Bow River project. Regardless, the city solved the problem via its agreement with Canbritam, which enabled both rights-of-way to run through Canbritam's land along the riverbank toward 22nd Street (see chapter 3). It was a win-win situation for both parties. The city received Canbritam land for the westbound parkway free of charge in return for promising linkages with the Bow Village project. The CPR went along with the arrangement. It was a better, easier, and cheaper route, and its bargaining chip was still in play.

The problem arose when it was realized that the city-owned land directly west of 14th street and east of the Canbritam land was not wide enough to accommodate the two rights-of-way. The railway right-of-way was clear, but the parkway to the south was partially blocked by a warehouse owned by the Hudson's Bay Company. The HBC was willing to move its warehouse the requisite fifty feet to the south as long it was not responsible for the $250,000 price tag. The city wanted the CPR to assume this cost even though the move directly involved the parkway and not the rail line. City leaders reasoned that the city deserved compensation since the right-of-way for the CPR had been secured at the expense of its own parkway. The agreement, however, was silent on this issue, only obligating the CPR to pay fair actual value for its own right-of-way needs on city land. The CPR took its stand on this point. It was a touchy issue and the debate that surrounded it was just another example of mistrust, confusion, and misunderstanding.[133]

On the one hand, the City supported its case by contending that the CPR had promised close co-operation in negotiating the area west of 14th Street and that, at one stage, Crump had said that the CPR would take responsibility in said area.[134] John Steel claimed to have reached a "gentleman's agreement" with the CPR on cost sharing for moving the HBC warehouse.[135] On the other hand, the CPR's version of "close co-operation" did not extend to spending $250,000, and any "responsibility" was limited to non-parallel rights-of-way. As to the "gentleman's agreement," Rod Sykes hotly denied this, saying that neither he nor his company would ever make a verbal agreement of this magnitude.[136] In his private notes, he had the following to say:

> This has been unfavourable lately as to tone largely owing to the fact that the only news comment available to print has been critical and negative. The fact that it may be uninformed, biased, and even malicious and inspired by self-interest carries no weight with the general public; the clearly confused impression left is that there is contemplated some kind of land swindle designed to enrich the CP at the taxpayers' expense, that there is in existence a secret agreement requiring the city to make vast expenditures for the sole benefit of CP, and that because no one dares to stand up and answer the charges effectively, apparently there must be some truth in them. Admittedly charges may be a strong word for the kind of innuendo you may detect in clippings but remember that I am speaking for the man on the street and he is important to us because we must have his land for a new right-of-way. If acquisition is long delayed our project may well be at an end.[137]

Following the signing of the agreement, the commissioners began a sequence of correspondences with the CPR trying to resolve the problem of the HBC warehouse.[138] The CPR, via Rod Sykes, first took an indirect approach and contended that inherent complexities in the area west of 14th Street warranted a separate agreement among the three parties involved, something the commissioners might have supported if time had allowed. The wordy dispatches between the city and the CPR came to a head on March 31. With the provincial legislation pending, the need for closure on the issue forced the city's hand. In a long letter to Sykes, the Commissioners' Office delivered an ultimatum: "The Commissioners want it clearly understood at this point that the costs involved in removal of a section of the Hudson's Bay Company warehouse is to be entirely borne by the CPR. Until this understanding is firmly committed we are assuring that City Council will not be prepared to proceed with a plebiscite."[139] Similar letters were sent to Sykes and Joplin by planner Geoff Greenhalgh. Mayor MacEwan said the same thing to Sinclair, albeit in a less adversarial fashion, noting that "the scheme may have a rough passage in Council and certainly with the public in the event that we are unable to give positive indication of our capabilities . . . west of 14th Street."[140]

Rod Sykes was the first to respond for the CPR. Like Mac-Ewan, he did not take the confrontational route, arguing instead that all the fuss was unwarranted and wondering how the issues raised by the commissioners and Greenhalgh "had any bearing on the agreement which specifically does not involve any obligations on the City or Canadian Pacific with respect to extensions of the parkway."[141] Sykes's ameliorative approach would probably have received short shrift given the commissioners' sense of urgency. Buck Crump's response on April 27 was more in line with typical CPR tactics. In a telegram to the city, he closed all doors with the statement: "Canadian Pacific cannot accept any responsibility for any costs of parkway except as set out in the agreement."[142] The president had spoken. The receipt of MacMillan's non-committal attitude on April 24 followed by Crump's flat rejection three days later had a harrowing impact on John Steel. He had gambled and lost. Thus, it was a beleaguered chief commissioner who faced City Council on April 29.

Confusion and Controversy

A special meeting of City Council was held on April 29. It took three and a half hours, and had it not been for the commissioners' report, it would have been a fruitful meeting that moved the project forward. Indeed, those assembled might have passed the bylaw allowing for a plebiscite that asked: "Are you in favour of an agreement with the City of Calgary and the Canadian Pacific Railway Company containing the clauses of an agreement made between parties dated January 27 as was defined and controlled by the statute of the Alberta Legislature validating the agreement?" The Special

Map 5. Location of Hudson's Bay warehouse and the proximity of proposed rail and parkway routes

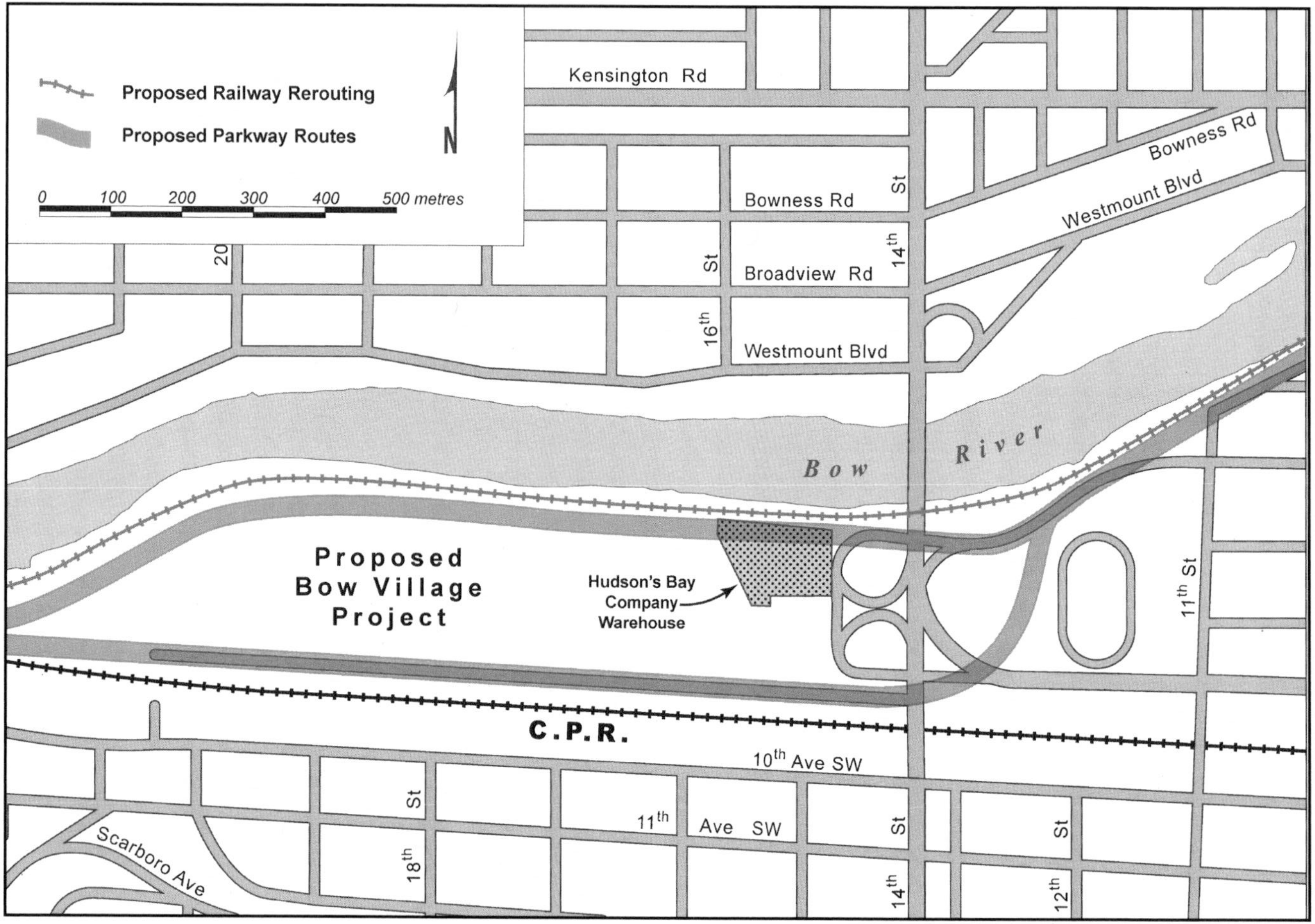

Bowness Rd

Westmount Blvd

11th St

12th St

St

River

14th St

Bowness Rd

Broadview Rd

Westmount Blvd

Bow

16th St

St

14th St

Kensington Rd

Hudson's Bay Company Warehouse

10th Ave SW

11th Ave SW

C.P.R.

18th St

Proposed Bow Village Project

N

Proposed Railway Rerouting

Proposed Parkway Routes

0 100 200 300 400 500 metres

20

Scarboro Ave

Coordinating Committee also reported that all was ready for the printing of eight-page brochures for distribution to the public, with the Jubilee Auditorium having been booked for the requisite public hearing on May 21.[143] Also circulated at the meeting was a copy of the resolution to re-execute the agreement.

Steel's six-page report changed all that.[144] In it, he detailed the failed negotiations west and east of the development area. He expressed his surprise at Crump's rejection, noting, "It is at complete variance with our agreement with the C.P.R. for the total right-of-way acquisition on a cost-sharing basis." As for negotiations in the east, he deferred to MacWilliams's opinion that there were so many unknowns that "it seems completely futile to hold a plebiscite." In his conclusion, Steel reiterated the premise that had governed his original endorsement of the project. Referencing commissioners' reports delivered over a year earlier, Steel reminded the aldermen: "The relocation of the railway in itself cannot be recommended. . . . On the clear and firm basis that the parkway can be built and must be considered an integral part of the entire actions the Commissioners advised the Mayor and Council that the Commissioners were prepared to support the C.P.R.'s proposals." His report ended with his belief that both issues could be settled within weeks and a recommendation that "re-signing of this Agreement should be delayed until matters east of 6th Street and west of 14th Street are resolved."

The recommendation was not received well. Referring to the "gentleman's agreement," Ernie Starr said that members of City Council were fools if they took the CPR at its word; Runions was in shock; Russell blamed a "poor agreement"; and Leslie wanted to get out "while we can." Walter Boote accurately affirmed that if the money bylaw was put here and now, it would not pass.[145] Reason prevailed after a heated discussion in which Steel was criticized and accused of bungling the negotiations. On a 7-6 vote, the Special Coordinating Committee and commissioners were asked to investigate the areas under dispute and report back to the council. The reports of both the Special Coordinating Committee's and the commissioners were tabled pending the results of those investigations. No time frame was set.[146]

The meeting was pivotal in that it demonstrated for the first time a clear distancing between City Council and the commissioners, particularly Chief Commissioner Steel. First, aldermen were now demanding that all relevant documents be made available to them before important matters were discussed. Second, and equally revealing, was the way City Council went after Steel. According to Jean Leslie's account, "Steel took it for two hours. Then he blew up. He had just overcome a nosebleed but shaking a bloodied bundle of documents and letters, he jumped to his feet, and in reference to the 'gentleman's agreement' told Council that 'we're damned if we do and damned if we don't.'"[147] Later, he told the press: "We welcome a committee. The day has passed when everything that goes wrong is laid at our feet."[148]

The press had a field day. The *Herald* wanted City Council "to bow its collective head in shame and apology" for its handling of "this great and important project."[149] *The Albertan* castigated aldermen for their ignorance of events and vilified Steel for criticizing the CPR without substantiation.[150] It was another setback for City Council. Matters got even worse in the middle of May, when the press got what it wanted: a new scandal.

On May 13, anti-plan alderman Dave Russell met with the Calgary branch of the Old Age Pensioners Society. In his address, he accused the CPR of having no conscience. He endorsed remarks made by a fellow architect who said that the CPR's request for concessions was "almost an insult to the intelligence of Calgarians."[151] Five days later, Russell was fired by the prominent architectural firm of Rule Wynn and Rule for mixing his job with politics and for angering too many clients.[152] Another firestorm was ignited. Although the *Herald* was dismissive, calling the firing a private business decision that had been blown out of proportion, *The Albertan* thought differently. Russell's statements might have been "misguided, emotionally based and somewhat immature," but they had also badly damaged the city's reputation.[153] Both papers kept sniping at Russell over the next week.

The predominant reaction, however, was one of outrage. Gordon Atkins, president of the Calgary chapter of the Associated Architects of Alberta, defended Russell's right to speak openly on any issue, adding that when "pressure from clients can affect a professional decision then politics has entered architecture."[154] The *North Hill News* was infuriated. Likening the Russell incident to practices in pre-war Germany, the front-page article raged: "In the Russell case, we can see without exaggeration the end of democracy."[155]

Years later, Dave Russell reflected that he might have been a catalyst.[156] He was probably referring to the persistent calls for an investigation into his dismissal. Alderman Ernie Starr made the first of these when he asked the province to investigate the case; he was informed by the deputy minister for Municipal Affairs that such an inquiry could only be initiated by City Council.[157] On May 29, the Calgary Labour Council formally requested City Council to investigate "all the circumstances of the case."[158] As the controversy grew beyond Russell's dismissal to the agreement itself, the most powerful voice was that of the Local Council of Women, which — through its spokesperson, the redoubtable Ruth Gorman — called for a Royal Commission "to investigate and make public, details of the agreement and to ascertain whether pressure has been exerted on city officials."[159] Predictably, City Council declined to discuss the matter on May 29. However, the idea of an official investigation continued to simmer. In terms of the project, one can understand the fears of pro-project alderman Ted Duncan when, in reference to the Russell issue, he said, "If the CP plan is in need of a death blow this may be it."[160]

The delay occasioned by City Council's call for an investigation on April 29 forced the city to postpone the plebiscite and the preparation of the money bylaw. After consulting the CPR, City Council set the deadline for passage of the bylaw at June 30, with the plebiscite to be held probably a week earlier. The draft of the money bylaw was reviewed on May 12. It called for the borrowing of $8.8 million repayable over twenty-five years at 6 percent.[161] These predictable actions were followed three days later by something far less predictable. On May 14, *The Albertan* told readers that the city administration, after considering reports from planners and engineers, had chosen the route and time frame for the parkway east of 6th Street.[162] It was an amazing disclosure in that it showed that for months, the city had been fruitlessly negotiating with the

CNR for an as-yet unplanned road, one whose construction justified the project.

City Council met on May 29. The meeting was as turbulent as its predecessor exactly one month earlier. According to one critic, it was "the farce of the century," and City Council, "an adult play-pen."[163] The first order of business was the report by the Special Coordinating Committee composed of aldermen Harold Runions, Ernie Starr, and Jack Leslie. However, there was no committee report as ordered. Instead, there were two one-man reports with two vastly different recommendations. The first report was read by the chair, Harold Runions, and was ostensibly on his own volition, since without informing or consulting his fellow committee members, he had consulted with CNR officials in Edmonton and Montréal. His report added a new twist. Runions told City Council that the parkway could be secured by buying the entire CNR freight yard east of 6th Street (the Fort Calgary site). The twenty-eight acres would provide adequate space for both the CPR right-of-way and station, and the parkway. He also indicated that the CNR was receptive. Immediately following Runions, an angry Ernie Starr delivered his own report and recommendation. He began by summarizing Runions's unsanctioned behaviour, and, after reference to several fruitless meetings, he castigated both railway companies and recommended that the scheme be abandoned. Neither report was accepted. Starr's, being a rehashing of old rhetoric and not what the council wanted to hear, was filed. Runions's raised a lot of eyebrows but was defeated on a 6-6 tie.[164]

The rest of the meeting followed in a similar vein with a variety of motions and amendments put forward and lost. Only two warrant mention. The first, which was approved by half the aldermen but lost on a 6-6 tie, showed how a sense of hopelessness had replaced consensus and cohesion. The motion, which would have put the proposal back to square one, called for a new agreement with the CPR following the preparation of the Downtown Master Plan, which would contain the principles of the proposal. The other, which was carried 7-5, directed the mayor "to set up the means to carry out the settling of the matter east of 6th Street East" and suggested that "we do not proceed with the plebiscite until this has been done."[165] It was a desperate motion by a group denied consensus and cohesion. Dave Russell summed up a meeting that had gone nowhere when he said, "I am not going to support this ugly scheme any longer," while Bill Dickie, who would remain stalwart to the end, condemned it as "a stampede to kill the CPR deal."[166] Even the *Herald* saw it as a final clarion call: there can be no equivocation now, it editorialized.[167] In all the debate, there was no mention of the issue to the west of 14th Street: namely, who was to pay the $250,000 required to move the Hudson's Bay Company warehouse. Neither Runions nor Starr had mentioned it. It had disappeared.

The Final Showdown
The difficulty faced by Mayor Grant MacEwan in dealing with the CNR was soon revealed. On May 30, *The Albertan* carried an article in which CNR Vice-President Roger Graham was quoted as saying openly that the CNR would not deal with the city until the issue south of 17th Avenue was settled.[168] Five days later, this had apparently changed. Acting on his mandate from City Council, MacEwan and John Steel met with Graham on June 4 in Edmonton to discuss the stalled negotiations for the parkway east of 6th Street. They found that Runions had been right. Without making any comment on the land south of 17th Avenue, Graham now said that in his board's opinion, the only solution to the existing problem with the parkway east of 6th Street was for the city to buy the CNR out and help it relocate elsewhere. He expanded the proposal a day later in a letter to MacEwan in which he offered to exchange the twenty-eight acres in question for an equal parcel east of Blackfoot Trail in Inglewood from 7th to 9th Avenues along 23rd Street. Graham also gave the city some surprising and disturbing news when he said that the parkway was not the only problem. The CPR right-of-way across CNR land was also uncertain. Contrary to what the city had been told in December 1963, Graham now affirmed that "the proposals presented by the Canadian Pacific Railway to date have been entirely unsatisfactory and unacceptable."[169] Whether this was accurate or not, the city now saw not one problem but two. Seeking to explore the CNR's proposal, the city asked its land manager, Bob Leitch, how much it

would cost. The answer was not good. Over $3 million was needed to purchase 130 land parcels, and another $100,000 to demolish the houses that were on them. Add to that $1.325 million to replace the CNR facilities, and the city was faced with a total bill of $4.542 million.[170] It was just too much, and it made for good press, but none of it favourable to City Council.

Things continued to deteriorate in City Council. On June 8, MacEwan told his frustrated aldermen that Ian Sinclair was not prepared to co-operate on the land east of 6th Street. This precipitated a motion to end the agreement. It was lost 7-5 after a heated debate.[171] Ray Ballard — a former supporter, now an opponent — raged that if the plebiscite went ahead, he would "shout from the roof tops not to vote for it." Roy Deyell wanted the mayor and all the aldermen to resign, himself included, "inasmuch as we have lost the ability to govern the city."[172] To MacEwan, the agreement with the CPR was a moral commitment made by City Council and, as such, he would not "be a party to killing it." But writing in his diary that same evening, he captured the mood among the aldermen in four words: "Everybody sick of it."[173] Of nine motions made during the June 8 meeting, only one passed. It simply added urgency to the one passed ten days earlier. Instead of directing the mayor to "set up the means for the settling of the matter east of 6th Street East," this one called for him to do so "at the earliest possible date."[174] The curtain on the project had dropped a few more inches.

The same urgency did not apply to the CPR. Sinclair seemed unconcerned and failed to notify Crump of City Council's decision. When he was informed, Crump set the suggested date back, ostensibly because he needed time to assemble key personnel. MacEwan made his formal request on June 12. In a carefully phrased letter by one well versed in the art, MacEwan threw the onus back on the CPR.[175] He asked for a meeting "to arrive at some acceptable formula which would enable the plebiscite to take place." This formula, he felt, devolved on the capacity of the CPR to reach an agreement with the CNR that allowed the parkway. If this could be achieved, MacEwan was confident that City Council would re-sign the agreement and go straight to the plebiscite. If not, he was at a loss. "I don't know what will happen," he confessed.

In closing, MacEwan referred to a presently divided council and, indirectly, to the CNR for raising "new, quite formidable difficulties." It was a good letter: a forewarning couched as a plea. As such, it was also a big gamble. Thus, with the die probably cast, the city delegation set off for Montréal for what MacEwan called a "show down visit" with CNR and CPR officials on June 18.

Even as the city was preparing for its final stand, events were unfolding that moved the public focus away from the merits of the project to the morality of those promoting it. On June 10, the Local Council of Women convened a public meeting at Central High School to "consider ethics, morals and civic government in our city" and to determine "whether democratic and moral principles in this city have been seriously harmed."[176] Attended by approximately 250 people including representatives from religious groups, both school boards, and labour, and chaired by University of Calgary chaplain Reverend John Patterson, the meeting opened the podium to individuals and groups alike. They did not fail to deliver on accusations: MacWilliams was kept out of the negotiations because it was known he was against it. Russell lost his job because of CPR pressure. Two community planners were asked to resign when they came out against the project. Aldermen were corrupted by private interests. The democratic process was being violated and Calgary was in danger of developing a political climate akin to Nazi Germany . . . and so on.[177] Innuendo, verbal licence, or fact, it did not matter. In the public eye, City Council members and city administrators were not only incompetent; they were self-seeking and dishonest.

At the public meeting, two motions were passed to be presented to City Council and the provincial government. One resurrected sentiments voiced weeks earlier and, in referring to the need to dispel the growing public distrust of local government, demanded that the provincial government "institute an impartial judicial enquiry as to whether civic employees or elected officials have been influenced in their expression of opinion in regard to civic matters over the past two years." The second motion was more surprising. It censured the *Herald* for distorting facts about the redevelopment scheme and for its biased criticism of any who opposed it. It was a strange motion. Although valid in many respects, it was, like the first motion, all about attaching blame.[178] The *Herald* responded by noting that it was a victim, since *The Albertan* held the same view. As for *The Albertan*, it feigned indignation at being left out of the censure and belittled the meeting for its distorted inaccuracies and wild histrionics.[179]

Charged by *The Albertan* not to miss the "chance of obtaining a vital east/west artery relatively cheaply," the city delegation arrived in Montréal on June 17.[180] Accompanying MacEwan were John Steel and Aldermen Ray Ballard, Mark Tennant, and Ernie Starr. The choice of aldermen had been the mayor's on the direction of City Council. It was a judicious choice by the scrupulously fair MacEwan. All three had voted for the motion on April 8 to approach both railway companies, but at the same meeting, Starr and Ballard had voted not to re-execute the agreement. Starr was generally against the project while Tennant, like MacEwan, had consistently voted in favour.

The delegation met with both companies on June 18 — with MacMillan of the CNR in the morning and with Crump, Sinclair, Joplin, and Vice-Presidents Emerson and Stone of the CPR in the afternoon. Records of the meeting were kept by MacEwan and show two familiar patterns: the CNR had changed tack yet again while the CPR was predictable right to the end.

The city delegation was encouraged by its 10:00 a.m. meeting with the CNR's "understanding and gentlemanly" executive vice-president, N.J. MacMillan. In MacEwan's words, "there was a thorough examination of the problems presented to taking a parkway through C.N. property east of 6th Street East. Mr MacMillan was most understanding and offered to make parkway requirements available to the City without the necessity of C.N. relocation provided the aggregate C.P. and City needs did not exceed a certain minimum along the riverbank." This accommodation was predicated on the CPR's willingness to adjust its plans for its station and five-track complex to allow the parkway.[181]

The 2:30 p.m. meeting with the CPR shattered the city's hopes. In a series of ultimatums, Sinclair told the delegation what it did not want to hear. Even though MacEwan explained that without the parkway, the plan could not be recommended, Sinclair refused to budge. He contended that the parkway and the railway rights-of-way were separate issues and the sole responsibility of their respective parties. In MacEwan's words, "The Calgary delegates were told that the C.P. would not consider modifying its plans for land east of 6th Street East." Sinclair hammered home his point by referring to the agreement and modifications authorized by the legislature as the last word as far as the CPR was concerned. He also reaffirmed the extended date of September 15 as the absolute deadline for the passage of the money bylaw. The best the CPR could offer, explained Sinclair, was to grant the city air rights over its acquired right-of-way across CNR land for an elevated parkway. It meant a $5 million bill for the city. To this suggestion, the cost-conscious MacEwan could only add: "Having regard to the costs involved, this suggestion, of course, was received by Calgary representatives with surprise."[182]

It was a dispirited group that returned to Calgary to write the report for presentation to City Council. In the interim, MacMillan and Crump followed up with their comments on the meetings. MacMillan reiterated his desire to co-operate but now emphasized City costs not just for the land but for filling in part of the river to accommodate the new right-of-way and for relocating and constructing works and facilities displaced by the proposed parkway.[183] As for Crump, he supported Sinclair and proceeded to justify his company's position further by taking a "no other option" position:

> The additional obligations thus imposed on us (by the province) were of such magnitude that I hesitated to proceed with the project under these conditions. However in view of our long association with the city, the unique opportunities the project gave for future and enduring benefit to the city with an opportunity for CP to participate in the revitalization of the downtown core, I decided that the company should not stand in the way of the project becoming a reality.[184]

His implication was clear and familiar: it was the city's fault.

The historic special meeting of City Council was set for June 22. Signed by the five-man delegation, the report was read by the mayor. It summarized the Montréal meetings and ended with the recommendation to withdraw from the agreement:

> With regards to the absence of anything better than the costly CN re-location, or an elevated parkway through the area east of 6th Street East, and in view of the limits imposed by a deadline date of September 15 which the CP have stated is the positive limit before which the borrowing bylaw must be passed, the Committee unanimously finds itself in the position of concluding and recommending that the agreement be not re-executed.[185]

A discussion on the motion ensued. Faithful to the end, Bill Dickie held out. He was sorry to see the project go and noted that it represented a victory for the killers of the project. Ted Duncan, another supporter, admitted that the CPR might have bargained too rigidly. The mercurial Ernie Starr waxed nostalgic, noting that both parties had really tried and deserved appreciation. Most aldermen were less sanguine. Referring to the obstacles put in their way, Mark Tennant said the scheme should be put to bed. For Jack Leslie, there were too many flaws. Ray Ballard agreed, calling it a one-sided partnership. Dave Russell thought it was a good day for Calgary. Walter Boote was glad it was the end of the trail. As the discussion tapered off, someone called for the vote.[186]

The motion framed by Mark Tennant and seconded by Walter Boote read as follows: "That Council decline to re-execute an agreement containing the clauses in the said agreement made the 27th day of January, 1964, as modified by the Legislature of the Province of Alberta and that all negotiation respecting the said agreement be terminated."[187] It was carried 10-3 with Ted Duncan, Bill Dickie, and Harold Runions voting against. A subsequent motion was then passed to proceed with the completion of the Downtown Master Plan. Tennant and Starr then moved to adjourn. It was all over.

The Aftermath

Immediate reaction included finger pointing and reflection from the press, a renewed interest in urban renewal and the downtown plan, and some self-satisfied comments from the project's opponents. Later comments revealed a lingering bitterness. Most significant was John Steel's revelation.

Carl Nickle blamed City Council for bungling "one of the most important proposals ever presented to it."[188] Martin Kernahan put the blame on Steel for leading the aldermen astray.[189] MacEwan blamed the CPR for its greed and intransigence. Ian Sinclair held the city responsible for rejecting a deal that was better for Calgary than it was for the railway company.[190] Buck Crump sought the last word "for the record," as he phrased it.[191] According to him, excessive caution on the part of the city had damned the project. In his opinion, the city could (and probably should) have saved the day by leaving the issue of the parkway across CNR land for the future when "altered conditions would likely have made more CN land available." If that did not happen, Crump reasoned, there was always the elevated route. Although no doubt sincere, this piece of correspondence underscored the fact that senior CPR management did not really appreciate the city's bottom lines.

A more realistic assessment appeared in both dailies on June 23. A restrained *Herald* hit at the heart of the controversy: the entire project was predicated on unshared assumptions, which probably explained why so many insurmountable obstacles appeared so late.[192] *The Albertan* editorialized that "while the CPR knew from the outset what it wanted, the City did not."[193] It also published the results of a public survey that indicated a "Yes" vote in the plebiscite.[194] Sykes agreed with this prediction and had little doubt of success at the polls. The *South Side Mirror* offered a balanced view, noting that both sides were to blame and that it was neither right nor fair to paint Sinclair and Crump as the sole villains.[195]

Some hoped that City Council's decision simply meant a delay and that the project would be resurrected in a new and better form. Others took quick advantage of the project's demise. Exactly one week after the vote, a local group of investors announced the construction of Eau Claire Place. The $40 million project on thirty-five acres between Centre Street and 6th Street West, directly south of Prince's Island, involved eight twenty-six-storey apartments. Noting that the project had long been on the books, a spokesman for the investors expressed satisfaction that it could go ahead now that city-CPR project had been abandoned.[196]

Opponents of the project were elated and took far more credit than they deserved. As W. G. Morrow noted to Robert Barron, "It shows what a few determined citizens can do even against newspapers and the combined weight of large corporations and an overpowering combination of important businessmen, pressure groups and politicians."[197] Robert Barron was equally self-congratulatory: citing the crucial role played by Ruth Gorman, he wrote, "We will always be able to look back on these past few months with a good deal of satisfaction because there were many times when we thought it was hopeless to continue the fight."[198] One wonders how much they were caught up in their own rhetoric over a final decision that had nothing to do with them or over a "victory" that never went to a plebiscite.

The bitterness resurfaced months later amid the municipal election campaign and the resignation of John Steel. In October, in response to a critical article in the *Herald*, an angry MacEwan defended the June decision. Noting that "editorial writers can file away their mistakes but we have to live with ours," he defended his council as "the best he had ever worked with," adding, "The aldermen refused to be pushed into a hasty decision or browbeaten and had the courage to turn down the deal because it didn't look good for the city."[199]

In November, John Steel accepted a position in New Zealand as the general manager of the Auckland Regional Authority. Again, MacEwan lashed out at critics: "It will be a great loss to Calgary but the hounds have been baying for him ever since the C.P.R. deal was under review. In both capacity and integrity he was far above his critics."[200] Then, in January 1965, following a farewell luncheon for the departing chief commissioner hosted by the city at the Holiday Inn, MacEwan recorded in his diary:

Responding to the presentation [of a painting by well-known western artist Roland Gissing], John made something of a "death bed" confession concerning "that thing which was conceived in sin and shaped in iniquity" obviously referring to the late C.P.R. redevelopment scheme. The commissioners had inherited it and tried to make it work but as he looked back now he realized that they should have killed it in its infancy as soon as possible after the former mayor had signed the Heads of Arrangements. The final approval of the scheme, said John, would have been the greatest tragedy that could have befallen Calgary and he wanted to speak out clearly on this before leaving.[201]

It was a powerful lament from the man who had worked the hardest and given his all to a dream that — initially, at least — loomed larger than the above sentiments might indicate. It was also accurate.

With Steel's words on January 6, a final verdict was handed down by the city official who knew the most about the project.

TWO PUZZLES

Although the road to the end had more unexpected turns than a mountain path, two deserve discussion. The first is the MacWilliams issue. How did that happen and what was it all about? The second is the strange behaviour of the CNR. What game was the company playing? Even more puzzling is the city's reaction.

The MacWilliams Issue

On the surface, MacWilliams's testimony in Edmonton is incomprehensible. Here was the city's chief legal officer damning a complex agreement that had been negotiated under the auspices of his office for six months. How could that have happened? Had he been negligent? Was he offering an after-the-fact opinion? Was he distancing himself from an incompetent deputy? Was he an agent of a dark plot to destroy the CPR? Or was it none of the above?

One conclusion is that he had been left out of the negotiations purposely because certain elements in the city administration felt that he was against the project. Which he was. He said as much in 1963 when he warned commissioners to expect many problems with the path they had chosen. He was probably not a fan of the CPR either. Rod Sykes refers to an incident when Crump had snubbed MacWilliams. The pro-project commissioners might have removed him from the negotiations, knowing his opposition to the scheme and feeling that someone more neutral might be more effective. He may have even been advised to say nothing. The trouble with this highly speculative theory is the lack of any shred of supporting evidence. A more valid approach might be to examine MacWilliams's testimony on the stand in Edmonton.

MacWilliams's comment that he "would never have written an agreement like that" implied that he had not been privy to it. Two possible conclusions flow from this. The first is that John DeWolfe was to blame, through either incompetence or collusion. The second is that MacWilliams knew little about the negotiations. Both are unlikely. First of all, if MacWilliams was referring to DeWolfe, he was essentially damning himself. Regardless of what DeWolfe did or did not do, MacWilliams's office held ultimate responsibility. As for DeWolfe, he was an experienced lawyer. A graduate of Dalhousie Law School, he had been with the city's Law Department for over eight years and would remain there for another twenty. Evidence suggests that he was both conscientious and capable. He was the negotiator because City Council felt, and rightly so, that as chief solicitor, MacWilliams could not afford the time. However, this does not mean that MacWilliams was unaware of the negotiations. In his own words, he "lived with them day and night."[202] This suggests that DeWolfe had been reporting to him on a regular basis. So if MacWilliams knew about the agreement, why would he say that he would never have written the one that was passed by City Council, a statement that damned him as much as it did DeWolfe?

The most logical answer is that neither he nor DeWolfe actually wrote the agreement. The CPR did. With no evidence to the contrary, one can speculate that while DeWolfe and the CPR lawyers negotiated the issues in the agreement, it was the CPR's legal team that put them to paper and then tendered the completed document to the city for approval. This could have been what MacWilliams meant when he referred to a document he "would never have written." He did not mean he had been left out of the negotiations, nor was he implying negligence on DeWolfe's part. Instead, he may have been removing his department from responsibility altogether for an agreement that it did not draw up.

Still, this only explains why the agreement gave the CPR an advantage over the city in terms of legal interpretation. It does not exonerate the Solicitor's Office from allowing the city to commit to an agreement that was so stacked against it. In his testimony to the legislature, MacWilliams said it was not the function of his office to advise City Council on the merits of its decisions but rather, when necessary, to give legal form to them. This opinion was also reinforced by DeWolfe. Yet one wonders. Under Alberta law, the designation of the chief solicitor's duties was allocated to City Council.[203] What they were in MacWilliams's case is unknown. It is highly unlikely that City Council would not expect its chief legal officer to advise it on an agreement with the sorts of legal pitfalls pointed out by Barron and later substantiated by MacWilliams himself.

So what is left? Possibly, the entire fiasco was just another example of the breakdown in communication between City Council and city administration that plagued the project from the beginning. Rather than wait until the damage was done, the city's aldermen could have called at any time on MacWilliams — or DeWolfe, for that matter — to provide updates and opinions. Their plea of ignorance about MacWilliams's opinion of the agreement seems more an excuse than a reason. There were enough anti-project aldermen who knew about MacWilliams's feelings to force the matter. The same applied to MacWilliams himself: the Solicitor's Office could have requested a hearing to update City Council on the legal implications of the Heads of Arrangement and of the Agreement of Intent right up to the fateful January 22 council meeting. Neither exercised this option. The end result was that, by accident, a respected Queen's Counsel had to either perjure himself or tell the truth as he saw it. He chose the latter.

The Canadian National Railway

The CNR, a seemingly minor actor in the drama, played a vital role. Company executives' sequence of mixed messages and hidden agendas over the aging and deteriorating facilities east of 6th Street East did as much to destroy the project as any other single issue.

First, the CNR chose to remain disinterested in accommodating the city's request for land pending the settlement of a related issue involving the sale of CNR land in the Lindsay Park area south of 17th Avenue. Then, without any preamble, CNR leaders led the city to believe in December 1963 that they had accommodated the CPR but were unable to do the same for the city, on the ostensible grounds that the former's needs were more important. In the weeks following the signing of the agreement between the city and the CPR, the CNR continued to stall and hold out hope simultaneously. Indeed, the most hopeful indication of co-operation came as late as April 24. Then, on June 4, the company informed the city that negotiations with the CPR had gone nowhere and that the only solution involved a land swap that would cost the city $5 million. No further communication ensued until June 18 when MacEwan, Steel, and three aldermen met with MacMillan. With scarcely a mention of the land swap, MacMillan now gave the impression that all was fine with the CPR, which now had acquired the land necessary for the right-of-way and station. Turning on the charm, he further affirmed that the CNR would be only too happy to grant land for the parkway. But there was a hitch. The CPR had to give a little. With the latter's refusal to budge, the delegation's report to City Council naturally put the blame for the deadlock squarely on the CPR for its intransigence. If anything, the CNR was exonerated.

The only explanation for this strange behaviour is that the CNR was playing a waiting game. It wanted a satisfactory resolution to its Lindsay Park land deal with the city before it would grant access to the parkway. Since price negotiations for the Lindsay Park land were still ongoing and showing no sign of resolution, the CNR was prepared to wait. In the context of doing business, the company's stance was understandable. It had made the city aware of the situation in at least two communications, yet one wonders why the issue did not figure specifically in MacMillan's discussion with the city on June 18. More significantly, there was no evidence that City Council had ever considered the CNR's conditions, if indeed the aldermen even knew about them. Also, why didn't Steel, who had predicated the entire project on securing land for the parkway east of 6th Street, resolve the Lindsay Park land issue? It appears that the deal would have helped the city in its road alignment and possibly the Calgary Stampede, which was considering expanding into the area in question.

The silence on this question is puzzling, so much so that even speculation is difficult. It is possible that the Commissioners' Office was not ready to resolve the Lindsay Park issue. Although the Stampede wanted to expand into the area, the commissioners were less enthusiastic and had another agenda for their major leaseholder.[204] It could have been a matter of cost. Settling the Lindsay Park issue would have cost a lot more than the $250,000 that the city was refusing to pay to move the Hudson's Bay Company warehouse. Maybe there was just too much resident mistrust of the CNR to take the company at its word. Given the dialogue the two had conducted over more than a year, any such skepticism was not misplaced.

A final touch in the bewildering series of events that brought the project down concerned the unresolved issue west of 14th Street — more specifically, the question of who was to pay the $250,000 to move the Hudson's Bay Company warehouse to accommodate the parkway. It is a final irony that even if negotiations on the issue east of 6th Street had succeeded, there was yet another impasse worth a quarter of a million dollars hiding in the wings to the west. It was an ending worthy of the tortuous process that had preceded it.

Conclusion

Had the City of Calgary–Canadian Pacific Railway redevelopment scheme gone to a plebiscite, the outcome would have been close, too close to call. From its hopeful beginning in April 1962 to its sombre end in June 1964, the project had stirred emotions on an unprecedented scale. This unique partnership between the nation's leading corporation and a growing city anticipated a reconfigured, revitalized downtown, ongoing investment, and the promise of a vibrant urban future. Although its vision resonated with the temper of the times, it failed. Several observations present themselves.

The first concerns the very limited parameters within which both parties viewed the project. It was seen purely in economic terms. At stake were investment and the jobs it promised. The CPR pursued an opportunity for diversity and investment in a time of declining railway revenues. The city saw the freed right-of-way in terms of potential tax dollars. All other factors were inconsequential, the most significant being the fact that the pending downtown plan had to be integrated into the project, not the other way round. In the 1960s, urban renewal meant redevelopment, a natural "good" in itself.

Downsides were ignored. For example, given what the CPR negotiated in terms of the number of crossings and constraints placed on the city regarding their enlargement, traffic access to downtown was still severely limited. The parkway would have wrought havoc with Chinatown and Inglewood, areas that remain two of the city's few inner-city jewels. Cut off from the downtown by the railway and the parkway, the riverbank would have been lost as an urban asset, an unimaginable concept today given its enormous popularity with pedestrians and cyclists.

Neither party brought enough to the bargaining table to ensure a successful conclusion. This was compounded by the differing interpretations of the Heads of Arrangement. The tightly compartmentalized CPR may have been new to the field of urban land development, but it had a history of bargaining, and its view of the way things should unfold was firmly rooted in the company's past experiences with negotiation. The city was disadvantaged by the clear disconnect between its legislative and executive arms and by an absence of any clear vision as to what the future downtown should look like.

THE CPR: UNCERTAIN AND INTRANSIGENT

The issue should be set against the immense upheaval within the CPR as a result of its diversification program. Crump likened it to trying to change the direction of a huge ocean liner.[1] Commenting on the changes within the company, one employee equated the situation to a family breakup. Another employee noted, "People got really upset. No one knew what direction we were going in."[2] The least defined of these new directions was urban land development.

The CPR's decision to enter into negotiations was made much too hastily considering the scope of the project. Before 1962, the company had no plans for redeveloping its right-of-way in Calgary. Yet within six months, it was prepared to announce a grand scheme and, within another year, had decided to reroute its main line through the city and enter into an agreement involving the redevelopment of its entire right-of-way through the downtown area.

In refusing to budge from stipulations in the Heads of Arrangement, the CPR negotiators showed that they were not prepared to bargain seriously with the city. Although they claimed to have granted several concessions, they gave away nothing major. Manifesting themselves primarily in a refusal to compromise on major issues and an arrogant "take it or leave it" attitude, they stiffened their relations with city officials and alienated the CPR in the public eye. Rod Sykes, a relative newcomer to the company, attributed this to a specific corporate culture, which included a sense of the company's own importance, a firm belief in a prescribed way of doing business, and an inflexible compartmentalized hierarchical structure. These qualities, working in tandem or individually, combined to polarize the project and ultimately left the city with no more room to manoeuvre.

The CPR might have saved the project had it consented to reroute the tracks via Beddington to the north. It was a feasible solution, one that would have avoided the right-of-way issues to the east and west, and removed the parkway problem. But CPR executives refused to entertain this option, let alone consider it.

This intransigence was also seen in the final days when compromise may have saved the day. The CPR's decision not to yield on the CNR land issue stands as a case in point. Negotiators could have compromised to allow land to enable the parkway. The station site could have been modified or even moved. The same applied in the west end. Even sharing the $250,000 cost for moving the Hudson's Bay Company warehouse would have satisfied the city. One might be excused for thinking that a scheme of such magnitude and importance deserved some compromise.

The CPR officials maintained that they were pushed to the wall too frequently. They felt that the several measures put forward by the city to revisit issues of contention or to return to the drawing board were delaying tactics employed in order to win more concessions. The result of these deliberative measures, they argued, pushed them to the point where they would go no further. In that context, the final confrontation in Montréal was simply the last straw. That the pressure they were facing had everything to do with a document heavily loaded in the company's favour did not seem to matter.

CPR executives' sense of the company's own integrity led them to expect trust from those with whom they did business. With respect to Calgary, they had history on their side. The Palliser Hotel had been a win-win situation, even if the city had had to grant major concessions to secure it. Similarly, although the maintenance facilities in Ogden had made the city a major railway centre, significant concessions had been made for them as well. In short, the CPR was accustomed to securing concessions based on "trust me" promises. In 1963–64, its negotiators brought a similar attitude to the bargaining table, probably without fully realizing that the times had changed and the type of project was different. Unlike the Palliser Hotel or the Ogden shops, which were all about structures with strong ties to railway operations and which promised instant results, this project was about land development across a wide swath of a growing city's downtown. Land development was costly and time consuming and did not align well with CPR's "pay now, gain later" philosophy. Yet, even though the promised benefits clearly were not specific enough to balance the concessions, the CPR managers seemed surprised when city officials began asking for concrete reassurances. Instead of trying to comply, they resorted to ultimatums about going to cities where they would be more appreciated.

The hierarchical chain of command had the volatile Sinclair visiting the city uttering threats even as he dealt with emergent issues. Buck Crump made similar pronouncements from distant Montréal. This tended to fracture ongoing relations with the city. Sinclair was too abrupt and lacked the conciliatory tone that was necessary to move forward. He also did not understand the project well enough to debate its intricacies, and Crump was even less familiar with it. In that context, Sykes thought he was underused. He knew the city personnel. He understood the local business scene and had addressed countless groups on the project's merits. He felt that if he been allowed to deal with contentious issues on his own basis, he could have done a lot more for the CPR without sacrificing any "bottom lines." To Sykes, promotion was key. He felt that the project was being misrepresented by its critics and that the CPR was not doing enough to counter those distortions. As he noted: "Without *very* aggressive promotion this project will fail — on this I will stake my job. *It will not sell itself* now or at any time in the future."[3] Yet, overall, the CPR continued to rely on promotion by city-based business groups. Sykes was right. It was not enough. Unpopular, mistrusted, and feared, the CPR needed to put on a popular friendly face. As it was, it failed to capitalize on the approval signified in the results of the October 1963 municipal election.

The reason for the CPR's lack of specificity about how, where, and when it would develop its right-of-way was due less to a lack of transparency than to uncertainty. When it entered negotiations, the CPR had no idea what it wanted to do on its right-of-way. In retrospect, what it ought to have done was to prepare detailed plans with as much specificity as possible and then bring those plans to the city as a negotiating document. Instead, the company moved too hurriedly and tried to bind the city contractually to what was essentially nothing more than a broad statement of intent. As it turned out, the CPR's spending commitments in the January 1964 agreement embodied no more detail than did their right-of-way development plan announced in June 1962. The reason was simple. The company had not decided on a development plan that balanced its desire for total control with other options.

In summary, the CPR's contribution to the failure of the project was twofold. First, a lack of forethought and planning led to a non-committal attitude and a lack of specifics that served to frustrate city officals and undermine their confidence in the CPR's capacity or willingness to redevelop the right-of-way in a timely manner. Second, regardless of what Harry Hays had signed, the CPR's narrow interpretation of the Heads of Arrangement was too unforgiving. It was simply too one-sided. When this interpretation was accompanied by an intransigent bargaining style that involved very little give and take on major points, the city was left with almost no room to manoeuvre. The negative fallout was inevitable.

THE CITY: ILL-PREPARED AND VISIONLESS

The city, too, embraced the project with undue haste and a lack of forethought. Without consultation with relevant city departments, a growth-oriented mayor personally committed the city to a far-reaching agreement with a private corporation. City Council neglected its responsibilities to the public by endorsing its mayor's arbitrary action without due discussion, deliberation, or consideration of the potential issues and problems involved. As Ernest Manning reflected a few weeks after the project was abandoned, "The whole thing from beginning to end was handled in an almost unbelievable manner."[4]

City negotiators' major mistake was accepting the Heads of Arrangement. Once they learned that the CPR was insisting on the Heads of Arrangement in foundational terms, city administrators should have stood their ground and insisted that the Heads of Arrangement was a negotiating document. In the event of a subsequent unfavourable response from the CPR, the negotiating team should have left the bargaining table and submitted a recommendation to City Council to either abandon the project or redefine the Heads of Arrangement.

When City Council finally entered the fray, it, too, accepted the terms of the Heads of Arrangement. Although there are two later examples, this was best exemplified in December 1963. When confronted with a final draft that put far more onus on the city than on the CPR, angry aldermen railed and protested.[5] Yet they did not vote it down. Instead, they bowed before the CPR's threats to "take it or leave it" and continued to negotiate the agreement based on the Heads of Arrangement.

Even if one accepts the idea that the decision to bargain within the CPR's version of the Heads of Arrangement was linked with a belief that a less-than-satisfactory agreement was better than no agreement at all, the city was remiss in other ways. By inserting an unnecessary component into the mix, by being appallingly ill-prepared, and by failing to align its own departments, the city contributed further to the project's demise.

The insertion of the parkway into the agreement was a major mistake. Recall that it had been promoted as a potential east-west freeway along the south bank of the Bow River, but plans fell through when City Council designated Memorial Drive on the north bank for this purpose. Yet when the CPR decided to move its route to the south bank, the commissioners saved face by resurrecting this dead issue. They convinced City Council that rerouting the rails was a good move because it enabled the construction of a convenient east-west freeway along the south bank. The implications were enormous. The city became complicit in the CPR's decision to use the riverbank despite other options being available. In the east, regardless of the route chosen, the parkway would rip through Chinatown and Inglewood. Furthermore, a twenty-year time frame was projected for completion of the parkway.

The parkway was both unnecessary and unplanned. When the Agreement of Intent was signed on January 27, 1964, the parkway existed on paper as a riverbank road from 14th Street West to 9th Avenue East via 6th Street. The negotiations for taking it across CNR land and continuing across the river east to Blackfoot Trail had not begun. If this still-tenuous plan for the parkway had not been advanced so strenuously by city administrators, the CPR would have traversed the CNR site without difficulty. Similarly, without the parkway, the right-of-way west of 14th Street between the HBC warehouse and the river would not have been an issue. The failed discussion between the city and the CPR in Montréal on June 18, 1964, was primarily about an issue that should never have been considered in the first place.

City officials were ill-prepared and ill-informed. They had not done their homework with respect to other railway relocation and development projects elsewhere. They evinced confusion over the plebiscite and seemed unaware of ambiguities in the agreement. Even more significant was their failure to realize the significance of securing the rights-of-way east and west of the agreement area until it was too late. It was assumed that negotiations with the CNR would present no problem. When problems did arise, the commissioners exacerbated matters by not resolving the Lindsay Park issue. Gross inefficiency and mismanagement plagued the area west of 14th Street. The agreement had been signed for over two months before city officials suddenly realized that there was not enough room for both the parkway and the CPR rails to pass between the river and a warehouse. This issue was still unresolved when City Council voted down the project.

The CPR dealt with the city executive for most of the project; only later did an uninformed City Council become involved. In that context, the lack of communication between city administration and City Council prejudiced the negotiations. Both components were at fault. Aldermen bought into Hays's dream without question and left it to the commissioners to bring it to fruition. With Hays's departure, the commissioners acted alone for far too long, with the result that City Council was ignorant of salient details of the project right up to the final draft presented in December 1963. From that point on, aldermen were heavily involved in a major, controversial agreement that most wanted but knew very little about. The result was friction, fracture, and a lack of direction. Interestingly, the City of Winnipeg was subject to a similar experience in the 1970s when negotiating a downtown development project with Trizec Corporation.[6]

In summary, the city had no idea of what it wanted beyond tax dollars and a glamorous redeveloped right-of-way. The executive was ill-prepared and failed to anticipate and resolve potential problems. A fatal disconnect was evident between City Council and city administration. Finally, since the parkway had not been integrated into the city's transportation policy, its sudden appearance was little more than a pragmatic response to an opportunity. It was also the main factor in dooming the project.

SOME FINAL CONSIDERATIONS

The role of public opposition deserves mention since it has been given much significance in contemporary and later commentary, and in lingering personal memories. Opponents of the project were self-congratulatory following the momentous vote of June 22, 1964. Ruth Gorman said much the same thing forty years later: "I was the legal adviser to the LCW of Calgary for many years. We had taken on the Canadian Pacific Railway when our City Council was going to give the entire south bank of the Bow River to the railway. . . . I legally directed their actions but it was their own dedication that saved the riverbank."[7] There can be no doubt that the energies of the Local Council of Women and other opponents significantly raised public awareness and opposition, possibly sufficient to defeat the proposal in the plebiscite that never took place and certainly enough to influence some aldermen. However, in the absence of the plebiscite, any assertion that public opposition to the project caused its demise is vastly overstated.

Given the suddenness with which the CPR entered the project, the scheme's low priority in the company's diversification program, and the company's tough bargaining stance and persistent threats to go elsewhere, one may well question the CPR's seriousness of intent. Mining, logging, and oil and gas were the company's main areas of interest. Land development was not yet a high priority. The Calgary project might just have been a testing of the waters. If an agreement was reached, then well and good, since it would be primarily on the company's terms. If not, then so be it.

Another related point is worth considering. The negotiations had been long and protracted. Toward the end, it seemed as though the will to continue had disappeared from both sides. There is no doubt that City Council was tired and dispirited. The project just wasn't worth their efforts anymore. The same could be said for the CPR. One of the city's delegates to Montréal in June 1964 believed that the railway company had lost interest and had stipulated terms that gave the city no option.[8] Toward the end, at least, one wonders about the role played by mutual weariness.

Within a few months following its defeat in City Council, the project faded into obscurity. Robert Chodos, in his 1973 study of the CPR's corporate history, makes no mention of it. Neither do David Cruise and Alison Griffiths in their well-researched account of the CPR presidents. Their chapter on Ian Sinclair, "The Buccaneer," documents his fierce personality and his momentous achievements as CPR president in the 1970s. It totally ignores his failure to bring the big Calgary project to fruition. But more surprising is the City of Calgary Planning Department, which is currently revisiting the problem of the continuing barrier posed by the CPR right-of-way. In November 2010, it completed the "Canadian Pacific Railway Corridor Plan (Background Information)," which includes a section titled "Canadian Pacific Railway Corridor — Historical Context." Thomas Mawson receives mention. However, the document contains nothing on the momentous controversy that divided the city in the early 1960s. Apparently, the CPR's first foray into urban land development and the City of Calgary's willingness to negotiate its own urban renewal program did nothing to stir the future.

Epilogue

The project's demise allowed the city's first downtown plan to go ahead. Released in 1966, it recognized the CPR right-of-way as a limiting factor but anticipated redevelopment there. The plan included beautification of the riverbank and provision for automobile traffic via one-way couplets at 2nd and 3rd Avenues and at 11th and 12th Avenues. In the early 1970s, the east-west freeway idea emerged again under a new name. One of the routes for the proposed "Downtown Penetrator" was along 2nd and 3rd Avenues. Opposed by Mayor Rod Sykes, it died on the planning table and was never approved by City Council. The prospective 2nd and 3rd Avenue couplet was seen as detrimental to existing and potential residential expansion in the Eau Claire district as well as in Chinatown. The couplet was transferred to 5th and 6th Avenues in the downtown, and these avenues link up in the west with Bow Trail not far south of the original route of the proposed parkway.

The CNR property that had bedevilled the project suffered a kind fate. On September 23, 1968, Alderman John Ayer moved that the site be acquired for memorial park purposes in time for Calgary's centennial in 1975. The city acted in the early 1970s, buying the twenty-nine-acre site for over $1 million. In 1978, the Fort Calgary Interpretive Centre, now a National Historic Site set amid tranquil open spaces, was opened to the public. To the south of 17th Avenue, the city finally acquired part of the contentious area via a land swap with the CNR. The Talisman Centre, formerly the Lindsay Park Sports Centre, now occupies this site.

The Eau Claire project did not go ahead as planned, and for years, the area remained underdeveloped. The Bow Village project also died. After deciding not to go ahead with the project in 1966, Canbritam asked the city to buy it out, but the city rejected the asking price for the thirty-five acres as too expensive. Following disputes involving expropriation and a threatened lawsuit by Canbritam, the issue was resolved in 1968 when the city acquired the Bow Village land for $1.3 million.[1]

Following the defeat of the project, Rod Sykes remained in place as manager of Marathon Realty, the CPR subsidiary formed in 1963, and was charged with capitalizing all the CPR's non-rail assets west of Fort William. Over the next five years, he began the same process that would have ensued had the project gone ahead, albeit in a different form. In time, this manifested itself in Palliser Square and the Husky (now Calgary) Tower. He was still in the process of attracting investment to the right-of-way when he left the CPR to run for mayor in 1969. He was successful, defeating the incumbent mayor, who just happened to be Jack Leslie, the project's foremost opponent on City Council. Ian Sinclair eventually became president of the CPR in 1969 and was chair and CEO from 1972 to 1981. During that period, he transformed the company into a multinational giant, increasing its assets of $2.14 billion to $16.3 billion.

Leslie himself had become mayor in 1965, possibly on the strength of his outspoken opposition to the project. Grant MacEwan did not contest the 1965 mayoralty election, having been appointed Alberta's lieutenant-governor, a post he held for eight years. Dave Russell entered provincial politics in 1967 and later occupied several cabinet portfolios, including that of Municipal Affairs. As noted, John Steel left the city at the end of 1964. Carson MacWilliams retired in 1966 and died two years later. John DeWolfe remained deputy solicitor until his retirement in 1983. Harry Hays, the man who started it all, served as federal minister of Agriculture until 1965, when he lost his Calgary South seat in the federal elections of 1965. Ironically, the man who defeated him was Ray Ballard, the alderman whose name was on the June 20 report that doomed the project. Hays was appointed to the Senate in 1966 and remained there until his death in 1982.

The Canadian Pacific Railway still runs through Calgary. However, the four-hundred-foot right-of-way is long gone, replaced in part by office blocks and other commercial buildings. The CPR owns very little land along its former right-of-way and now pays taxes on what it does own. Much of the old right-of-way still remains underdeveloped. For example, the entire area between 9th Street and 5th Street West along busy 9th Avenue is devoted to open air parking. The barrier to downtown for traffic from the south remains. Forty-six years later, only two additional crossings have been constructed under the tracks, one at 5th Street West and, in 2011, a second at 4th Street East.

The city is currently revisiting the existing right-of-way. In a preliminary draft (November 2010), reference is made to "exploring creative, bold and innovative approaches to transforming the Corridor into a comprehensive landmark space along a 2.5km spine of downtown Calgary."[2] It is an ambitious plan involving more than thirty public spaces bridging the tracks, and, like its precedent in 1962–64, it will have enormous transformative implications. One hopes it will enjoy a better fate.

HEADS OF ARRANGEMENT

[April 1963]

HEADS OF ARRANGEMENT
BETWEEN
CANADIAN PACIFIC RAILWAY COMPANY (CANADIAN PACIFIC)
AND CITY OF CALGARY (CITY)

1. Canadian Pacific intends to divert its railway to follow the South shore of the Bow River, from 9th Street East to 14th Street West, in order to make available for commercial development the downtown land lying between 6th Street East and 14th Street West now occupied by the railway: Canadian Pacific further intends to prepare a comprehensive Master Plan for the future commercial development of the said area, and, thereafter, to implement that plan.

2. The City considers it in the public interest that the Canadian Pacific plans for relocation of railway trackage and development of downtown property be carried out, and will co-operate to the fullest extent of its powers in assisting Canadian Pacific to further such plans.

3. The City intends to acquire right-of-way land, paralleling the proposed diverted railway to be constructed on the South shore of the Bow River, to provide for the development of a parkway and distributor roadway contiguous to the railway.

In mutual furtherance of the objects stated above, the parties agree that the general principles governing their co-operation shall be as follows:

Taxation:

(a) Land required for the railway diversion will be exempt from taxation on the same basis as the existing right-of-way.

(b) Land in the present right-of-way will retain its present tax status as set out in agreement or statute until any parcel therein is leased or sold for commercial development when it shall become subject to taxation.

Land:

(a) Right-of-way land adequate to provide for the requirements of the City's proposed parkway and for the diversion of the Canadian Pacific Railway main line shall be acquired by the City and transferred, and costs allocated in accordance with the basis set forth in the attached schedules and memorandum, which shall be attached hereto and form part of this document.

(b) It is understood that the valuations set forth in the attached schedules represent estimates only, and that actual costs, when determined, shall be substituted for estimates in the attached schedules.

(c) In the acquisition of land, if the estimated value of a parcel is to be exceeded by 10 percent or more, then the consent of Canadian Pacific must first be obtained. However, throughout the acquisition of each parcel of land, the closest possible liaison between the City authorities and Canadian Pacific will be maintained.

Commercial Development:

(a) Canadian Pacific will lease to the City on a long-term basis, free of rental, land adjacent to the Hotel Palliser for the construction of a convention centre to be built by the City at its cost, and to be operated in conjunction with the Hotel Palliser on a basis subject to further agreement between Canadian Pacific and the City.

(b) The first phase of the development of the present Canadian Pacific railway right-of-way will encompass, in addition to the convention centre referred to in (a) above, a transportation centre and commercial complex as part of an integrated development.

(c) The purpose of the development of the whole area to be freed by the diversion of the main line of the Canadian Pacific is to obtain the maximum economic advantage from development. In accordance with this, the closest possible liaison will be maintained by Canadian Pacific and its consultants with City of Calgary authorities. Specifically, the design and location of the convention centre (which is a City project) shall be subject to Canadian Pacific approval.

(d) The entire area released for commercial development by diversion of the main line of the railway shall be set aside as an "area for special development" in the zoning by-law and shall only be subsequently specifically zoned after general approval by the City has been given to the various developments contained therein as planned and projected by Canadian Pacific. The City will co-operate to the fullest extent in facilitating the specific development plans as they come forward.

(e) The City of Calgary will not require any portion of the area for special development to be set aside as a community and public reserve under the provisions of Alberta Regulation 185/60, Subdivision and Transfer Regulations pursuant to the Surveys and Expropriation Act or under any other legislation, and will use its best efforts to this end.

General:

These Heads of Arrangement are subject to negotiation as to detail and subject to approval by both parties of a formal agreement, which agreement will be validated by the Alberta Legislature.

Allocation of Cost Structures and Works:

It is mutually agreed between the parties that the responsibilities for bearing the cost of works involved in the proposed diversion of railway and in related City structures shall be shared as follows:

Location	Description	Responsibility for Costs
9th Ave. & 9th St. East	1. Rail on bridge over 9th Ave.	1. Canadian Pacific responsible for entire cost.
8th Ave. & 8th St. East and Elbow River	1. Parkway Road over Elbow River and over or under rail, as City may decide.	1. City responsible for entire cost.
Elbow River	1. Rail on bridge over Elbow River.	1. Canadian Pacific responsible for entire cost.
Langevin Bridge, 4th St. East, & Bow River	1. Present Langevin Bridge with rail on road at south approach parkway at ground level. 2. Future bridge either at present site or at some alternative over Bow River, railway and parkway.	1. City responsible for alterations to existing roads. 2. City responsible for entire cost.
Centre St. Bridge, Centre St., & Bow River	1. Centre St. Bridge over parkway and railway.	1. City responsible for entire cost.
Louise Bridge, 10th St. & Bow River	1. Parkway Road over approaches to Louise Bridge. 2. Alterations to existing bridge. 3. Railway bridge over Louise Bridge approach.	1. City responsible for entire cost. 2. City responsible for entire cost. 3. Canadian Pacific responsible for entire cost.
6th Ave. West, parkway to and from 14th St. interchange	1. Railway bridge over parkway. 2. All roadwork.	1. Canadian Pacific responsible for entire cost. 2. City responsible for entire cost.
9th Ave. West road to and from 14th St. interchange	1. Railway bridge over 9th Ave. 2. All roadwork.	1. Canadian Pacific responsible for entire cost. 2. City responsible for entire cost.
14th St. West	1. Modifications to existing rail bridge over 14th St.	1. Canadian Pacific responsible for entire cost.

The City will be allowed to make provision for pedestrians and service vehicle access to Prince's Island Park.

AGREEMENT OF INTENT

January 22, 1964

THIS AGREEMENT made this _____ day of _____ A.D. 1964 between:

THE CITY OF CALGARY, a Municipal Corporation in the Province of Alberta (hereafter in this Agreement called "the City")

OF THE FIRST PART

– and –

CANADIAN PACIFIC RAILWAY COMPANY, a Body Corporate carrying on business in the City of Calgary in the Province of Alberta (hereafter in this Agreement called "Canadian Pacific")

OF THE SECOND PART

WITNESSETH THAT:

WHEREAS Canadian Pacific presently operates its main line of railway, with related buildings, structures and appurtenances, through the City of Calgary and is willing to relocate part of such main line with requisite buildings, structures and appurtenances on a new right-of-way;

AND WHEREAS the purpose of such relocation is to make the present right-of-way, thereby freed of such main line operation, available for commercial development and thus contribute to the re-development of the Downtown Business District of the City;

AND WHEREAS the City proposes to build a parkway contiguous to said new right-of-way to alleviate traffic congestion in said Downtown Business District;

AND WHEREAS the City considers it is in the best interest of the City that all the aforesaid proposals be carried out, and the parties agree to co-operate to the fullest extent in that regard in accordance with the terms of this Agreement;

NOW, THEREFORE, THE PARTIES AGREE EACH WITH THE OTHER AS FOLLOWS:

Article 1: Definitions

1.1   In this Agreement including this Article:

"Avenue" – means a public thoroughfare within the limits of the City running in a more or less easterly and westerly direction.

"Board" – means the Board of Transport Commissioners for Canada.

"Langevin Bridge" – means the bridge by which, at the date of this Agreement,

Fourth Street East spans the Bow River and, where the context requires, includes a new bridge substituted therefor.

"Louise Bridge" – means the bridge which at the date of this Agreement crosses the Bow River and connects Fourth Avenue South and Ninth Street West on the South side thereof with Tenth Street West on the North side thereof and, where the context requires, includes such bridge as it may be reconstructed or altered at such location.

"new main line" – means that portion of the main line of the railway of Canadian Pacific relocated on the new right-of-way pursuant to this Agreement, and all stations and station grounds, workshops, buildings, yards and other property, rolling stock and appurtenances required and used for the construction and working thereof.

"new right-of-way" – means the land for the new main line following generally the route of the new main line as indicated on Plan "A" attached to this Agreement, such land to consist of a continuous strip fifty feet wide except between Fourth Street East and the Elbow River where the width thereof may be, but shall not exceed, four hundred feet for station grounds.

"parkway" – means a roadway located on a right-of-way not less than sixty-six feet nor more than one hundred and fifty feet in width, for the use of motor vehicles and, where the new right-of-way follows the south bank of the Bow River, generally parallel with and contiguous to the south side of the new right-of-way and to extend from approximately Sixth Street East to Fourteenth Street West, as indicated generally on said Plan "A."

"present right-of-way" – means the lands owned by Canadian Pacific at the date of this Agreement within the areas outlined in red on Plan "B" attached to this Agreement and situated between the points where the new main line as constructed pursuant to this Agreement connects with the existing main line of railway of Canadian Pacific, and includes all buildings, structures, properties, facilities and appurtenances, whether related to the operation of the railway or otherwise, within, upon, over or under such lands.

"railway operations" – means all operations which a railway company has authority to carry on pursuant to the *Railway Act*, Revised Statutes of Canada, 1952, chapter 234, and includes the use of all property real and personal required and used for the operation of a railway.

"street" – means a public thoroughfare within the limits of the City running in a more or less northerly and southerly direction.

"utilities" – means those pipes, conduits, wires, poles, cables and other conveyances and structures, whether similar or dissimilar, for supplying water, sewerage, electric energy, natural gas, communications and other services to the users thereof, whether the same are owned or operated by the City, Canadian Pacific or by any other person.

Article 2: Acquisition of Land for Parkway and Railway

2.1 The City shall after the Agreement is validated by the Legislature of the Province of Alberta forthwith proceed to acquire by purchase or expropriation fee simple title to land which it does not now own and which is necessary for the parkway and the new right-of-way along that portion of the route of the new main line where the parkway and the new main line will be more or less parallel with and contiguous to or in the immediate vicinity of each other.

2.2 The land to be acquired by the City pursuant to section 2.1 of this Article 2 shall not exceed those parcels set out in Schedule 1 attached to this agreement.

2.3 Canadian Pacific and the City shall share the amount paid by the City for land acquired pursuant to section 2.1 of this Article 2 in the respective proportions shown in Schedule 1.

2.4 In the acquisition of land by the City pursuant to this Article 2 the City shall acquire title thereto free of all encumbrances if possible and if not possible shall first obtain the written consent of an official of Canadian Pacific in Calgary to the acquisition of land subject to any encumbrance or encumbrances.

2.5 For the purpose of section 2.3 of this Article 2 the amount paid by the City for land acquired by the City pursuant to Article 2 shall include:

(i) the amount paid to the owner for the land,

(ii) any additional amount paid by the City to pay off and remove from the title mortgages, liens and other charges,

(iii) all costs of expropriation proceedings assessed against the City,

(iv) any amount paid by the City to any agent acting by mutual consent of the parties on behalf of the City in purchasing the land if such agent is not an employee of the City,

(v) all fees and disbursements paid to any lawyer engaged or retained by mutual consent of the parties by the City in connection with the acquisition of the land if such lawyer is not the City solicitor or a member of his staff.

2.6 Canadian Pacific shall conduct the negotiations for the acquisition of the land required for that portion of the new right-of-way where the same is not more or less parallel with and contiguous to or in the immediate vicinity of the parkway and if Canadian Pacific is unable to acquire the necessary land at a reasonable price it may request the assistance of the City, whereupon the City shall make such assistance as it is able to supply, including the power of expropriation when the same shall have been obtained, available to Canadian Pacific but the whole cost of such land determined as provided in section 2.5 of this Article 2 shall be borne by Canadian Pacific.

2.7   Before acquiring a parcel of land pursuant to this Article 2 other than by expropria-tion the City shall obtain the written consent of an official of Canadian Pacific in Calgary to the maximum amount proposed to be paid for such parcel; if the City purchase such parcel for an amount exceeding such maximum amount Canadian Pacific's proportion of the amount thereof as shown in Schedule 1 shall be based on such maximum amount.

2.8   Forthwith after acquiring all land required for the new right-of-way pursuant to section 2.1 of this Article 2 the City shall:

(i) provide Canadian Pacific with registerable transfers of all the City's right, title, estate and interest therein except for such easements and rights-of-way as the City may have therein for utilities then within, upon or under the new right-of-way and subject to any encumbrances consented to by Canadian Pacific pursuant to the provisions of section 2.4 of this Article 2, and

(ii) sell and convey to Canadian Pacific fee simple titles to land owned by the City and not acquired pursuant to said section 2.1 which is required for the balance of the new right-of-way, for which land Canadian Pacific shall pay to the City the fair actual value thereof; such fee simple titles shall be subject only to reservations for ease-ments or rights-of-way for utilities then within, upon or under the new right-of-way.

2.9   The easements and rights-of-way of the City referred to in section 2.8 of this Article 2 shall not be transferred or otherwise alienated by the City.

2.10 Upon the City discontinuing for twelve months the use of any utility within, upon, under or over the new right-of-way or the present right-of-way the City shall not thereafter be entitled to the easement or right-of-way therefor, and if such ease-ment or right-of-way is registered or filed in the Land Titles Office, shall withdraw, discharge or remove the same; and at any time or times after such discontinuance Canadian Pacific may remove all or any part of such utility from such right-of-way and shall not be liable in any way to the City for so doing.

2.11 The City and Canadian Pacific shall each own an undivided one-half interest in those portions of the lands set out in said Schedule 1 acquired by the City under section 2.1 of this Article 2 which are not required for the parkway and the new right-of-way, excluding lands acquired for bridge-approach ramps and lands acquired for approaches to Louise Bridge.

2.12 In acquiring land pursuant to this Article 2 neither party shall be required to purchase the mines and minerals within, upon, under the same.

Article 3: Construction of a New Main Line

3.1   Subject to obtaining all requisite approvals and sanctions, which Canadian Pacific shall apply for, Canadian Pacific shall commence construction of the new main line with all reasonable despatch after having obtained the rights to acquire and to enter upon all the land necessary for the new right-of-way and shall there-after diligently continue such construction to completion.

3.2   Except as otherwise provided in this Article 3 the construction of the new main line shall be at the sole cost, risk and expense of Canadian Pacific and, in particular, Canadian Pacific shall:

(i) construct and pay the whole cost of the requisite railway bridge to carry the new main line over Ninth Avenue South at or near the intersection of Ninth Avenue South and Ninth Street East;

(ii) construct and pay the whole cost of the requisite railway bridge to carry the new main line over the Elbow River;

(iii) pay for such alterations as may be necessary to the South approach of the Fourteenth Street West Bridge to enable the new main line to pass under South approach, which alterations the City shall make upon request by Canadian Pacific, provided, however that Canadian Pacific may make such alterations after approval by the City Engineer of the plans therefor.

3.3   For the purposes of the parkway and so that there will be no crossings of the new main line at grade the City shall, at the City's sole cost, risk and expense:

(i) construct a new highway bridge across the Bow River at Fourth Street East to replace the existing Langevin Bridge, such bridge to be so constructed that it will pass over the new main line with the clearances hereafter provided for;

(ii) alter the South approach of the existing highway bridge over the Bow River at Centre Street so that it will pass over the new main line with the clearances hereafter provided for;

(iii) alter the South approach of, or construct a new highway bridge in place of, Louise Bridge so that it will pass over the new main line with the clearances hereafter provided for.

3.4   All bridge construction and alterations shall comply in all respects with the requirements of the Board and, in particular, the City shall provide the following clearances if requested by Canadian Pacific:

(i) not less than twenty-two feet, six inches above the base of rail;

(ii) not less than ten feet from gauge side of nearest rail.

3.5   The City and Canadian Pacific shall coordinate the carrying out of their respective obligations to replace or alter the said bridges and to construct the new main line as provided in this Article 3 so as to facilitate the rapid construction of the new main line in an orderly, efficient and economic manner.

3.6   For the accommodation of passengers and of baggage, mail and other goods carried on its passenger trains Canadian Pacific, at its sole cost, risk and expense, shall construct such buildings, platforms, shelters, other structures and facilities as it deems necessary at a location or locations of its choice on the new right-of-way between Fourth Street East and the Elbow River.

3.7   If any part of the new main line is to be constructed in the existing Bow River channel then the City shall give all possible assistance to Canadian Pacific securing the rights to do so; and the City and Canadian Pacific shall jointly arrange with a Calgary firm for, and shall equally share the cost of, insurance to indemnify and save harmless the City and Canadian Pacific and each of them, and each of their officers, agents and servants from and against all claims and demands, costs, damages, actions, suits or other proceedings whatsoever by whomsoever made, brought or prosecuted in respect of loss of life or personal injury or loss of or damage to property, or obligation to compensate, arising out of or in any way attributable to such construction and the maintenance and use of the new main line in said channel.

3.8   The cost of all reclamation or related work required in or on that portion of the channel between Prince's Island and the South bank of the Bow River which has to be altered for the construction of the new main line shall be shared equally by the City and Canadian Pacific.

3.9   The City shall consent to, and endorse such consent on, all plans and submissions to be made by Canadian Pacific to the Board and any other authority having jurisdiction in respect of the construction of the new main line pursuant to the terms of this Agreement.

3.10 If, in respect of any application made to the Board or other authority having jurisdiction, said Board or other authority orders one of the parties to this Agreement to make any payment or contribution in respect of the cost of any work or works in excess of its responsibility for such cost under the terms of this Agreement then such party shall not be required to make such payment or contribution except to the extent of its said responsibility and the other party to this Agreement shall indemnify and save harmless such party in respect of the excess.

3.11 Notwithstanding the sharing of the costs of land required for the alterations to the South approach of Louise Bridge as provided in Schedule "1" or elsewhere in this Agreement any contribution made to the City by the Board from The Railway Grade Crossing Fund towards the expense of altering the structure of the said bridge shall belong wholly to the City and shall not be shared between the parties hereto or taken into account in determining amounts to be paid between the parties.

Article 4: Removal and Relocation of Utilities

4.1   If, because of the works required by this Agreement, any utility owned or operated by a third party is required to be removed, reconstructed, relocated, modified or protected and such third party is not responsible therefor, the City and Canadian Pacific, except as provided in Article 8 of this Agreement, shall share equally the costs of such removal, reconstruction, relocation, modification or protection.

4.2   Without limiting the generality of section 4.1 at such time as the development of any portion of the present right-of-way requires the removal and relocation of the power lines and related appurtenances of Calgary Power Limited located on Ninth and Tenth Avenues South adjacent to the present right-of-way the City and Canadian Pacific shall arrange with Calgary Power Limited for the removal of the same.

4.3   Except as provided in Article 8 of this Agreement the City and Canadian Pacific shall each do the work of removal, reconstruction, relocation, modification or protection of its own utilities as may be necessary because of the works required by this Agreement but shall share the costs thereof equally; provided, however, that Canadian Pacific shall bear the whole cost of:

(i) removal and relocation of its communications facilities now located on the present right-of-way which are not occasioned by any alterations to subways or by any public thoroughfare works pursuant to this Agreement;

(ii) removal and relocation of its other utilities on the present right-of-way necessitated by the commercial development of such right-of-way after removal of trackage therefrom.

4.4   Except as in this Article provided, all work related to, including reconstruction, repair and maintenance of, utilities owned by the City within, upon, under or over the present right-of-way and the new right-of-way shall be at the sole cost, risk and expense of the City.

Article 5: Crossings of New Main Line

5.1   No public road, pedestrian crossing or other public way shall cross over the new main line at grade, and the City shall not apply, or support any application, for any such crossing to the Board or other authority having jurisdiction.

5.2   Subject to section 3.2 of Article 3 the provisions of the Agreement between the City and Canadian Pacific dated the 13th day of December, A.D. 1911 shall apply *mutatis mutandis* to the new right-of-way and the new main line.

5.3   The City may construct and shall thereafter maintain at its sole cost, risk and expense a public crossing to Prince's Island under or over the new main line.

5.4   Subject to the provisions of sections 5.2 and 5.3 of this Article 5 any public crossings, other than the bridge or bridge approach crossings referred to in sections 3.2(c) and 3.3 of Article 3, which the City may wish to cross the new main line shall either over-pass or under-pass it, the division of costs therefor to be decided by the Board if the parties cannot agree; provided, however, that Canadian Pacific shall consent to the construction and use by the City, at the sole cost, expense and risk of the City, of private crossings of the new main line at grade solely for access by City employees or contractors to City-owned lands situated between the new right-of-way and the Bow River.

5.5 Each private crossing constructed by the City pursuant to section 5.4 of this Article 5 shall be protected at the South boundary of the new right-of-way by a gate with a lock thereon; and the City shall be responsible for ensuring that such gate is kept closed and locked except when such crossing is being used by City employees or contractors.

Article 6: Use of New Main Line

6.1 After completion of construction of the new main line and upon obtaining all requisite sanctions and approvals, Canadian Pacific shall commence to use, and thereafter continue to use, the same for all its through main line trains.

Article 7: Development of Present Right-of-Way

7.1 After Canadian Pacific commences to use the new main line for all its through main line trains Canadian Pacific shall remove as soon as possible all railway trackage and related buildings and facilities on the present right-of-way which are not required for railway operations.

7.2 The present right-of-way shall be an area for special development which development shall be carried out with a view to obtaining the maximum economic advantages for the City and for Canadian Pacific and with the closest possible liaison between the parties in respect of such development, and the City shall co-operate to its fullest extent in facilitating the specific development plans of Canadian Pacific.

7.3 Prior to commencement of railway operations on the new main line the City shall take all steps available to it necessary to amend all City by-laws relating to zoning so as to designate the zoning of the present right-of-way as a Direct Control District as same is presently provided for and described in By-law No. 4916 of the City, and the City shall thereafter retain in its zoning by-laws, applicable to the present right-of-way, such designation and the present provisions relating to a Direct Control District.

7.4 In addition to monies expended for acquiring the new right-of-way and constructing the new main line Canadian Pacific covenants that improvements amounting to a minimum of ten million dollars to and on real estate in Calgary now owned, or hereafter acquired, by Canadian Pacific or any company controlled directly or indirectly by Canadian Pacific will be made during the period between the date of this Agreement and seven years after Canadian Pacific commences to use the new main line for all its through main line trains.

7.5 As one of the first phases of development of the present right-of-way Canadian Pacific shall make all reasonable efforts to arrange for the development of an area of the present right-of-way between the Palliser Hotel and First Street East as a centre primarily for transportation facilities and enterprises associated therewith; and upon the construction of such a centre the City shall use the same as the main downtown terminal of its transit system, the terms of which use shall be on the same basis as those applicable to other similar transportation agencies using such centre.

7.6 *The Planning Act* of Alberta and the Subdivision and Transfer Regulations made pursuant thereto shall apply to the commercial development of the present right-of-way after the removal of railway trackage therefrom except for those provisions thereof relating to public roadways and reserves including payment in lieu of reserves (as "public roadway" and "reserve" are defined in said Act), provided however that all development plans for the present right-of-way shall provide for a minimum of ten per cent allowance for surface space for public enjoyment and use, such as malls, patios, shopping arcades or similar facilities or open space, which may be around or under structures.

7.7 Prior to completion of construction of the new main line Canadian Pacific shall submit to the City a plan showing how Canadian Pacific proposes to develop that portion of the present right-of-way between Second Street East and First Street West; and Canadian Pacific shall make all reasonable efforts so to develop such portion after all trackage, buildings and other facilities presently thereon are removed, subject always to such development being economically feasible.

7.8 The City shall have the right to acquire by expropriation the most southerly seven feet in width of the present right-of-way adjacent to Tenth Avenue for the purpose of widening Tenth Avenue for vehicular traffic but otherwise the City shall not be entitled to acquire for any purpose the present right-of-way or any part thereof by expropriation or any other means of acquisition without the consent of the owner.

7.9 Notwithstanding the provisions of section 7.8 of this Article 7 Canadian Pacific shall not unreasonably withhold its consent for an easement or right-of-way under the present right-of-way requested for a public utility of the City.

Article 8: Existing Subways and Additional Crossings Between Ninth and Tenth Avenues South

8.1 (a) Save as otherwise provided by this Article 8, the subways under the present right-of-way located at Second Street East, First Street East, First Street West, Fourth Street West, Eighth Street West and Fourteenth Street West shall remain and continue to be used for vehicular traffic and for such pedestrian traffic as the City shall determine, and shall be maintained and repaired by the City.

(b) Canadian Pacific shall maintain and keep in repair the deck and span portions of the overpass structures which presently support the railway trackage over said subways as such deck and span portions may be modified or reconstructed pursuant to section 8.2 of this Article 8.

(c) Canadian Pacific may construct or place buildings or other structures or improvements on, over or across said overpass structures, whether so modified or not, and may use the same for any other purposes related to the commercial development of the present right-of-way, but not so as to create a danger that same may collapse by reason thereof.

8.2   (a) After the removal of all railway trackage over the same and upon the written request of the City, Canadian Pacific shall modify at its expense the said deck and span portions over the subways at Second Street East, First Street East and First Street West to allow removal of the centre support piers therefrom; and the City, at the City's expense, shall thereupon remove such piers and do such other related work as may be necessary by reason of such removal.

(b) At any time or times Canadian Pacific may, at its sole cost, risk and expense, modify or reconstruct the deck and span portions of the subways referred to in section 8.1 of this Article 8, provided, however, that such modification or reconstruction shall not reduce the overhead clearance of any subway.

8.3   No alteration, replacement or other work provided for in this Article 8 respecting the said subways shall extend the width of the said subways beyond the existing retaining walls thereof nor affect the existing elevation of the present right-of-way over the said subways.

8.4   When removal of trackage and other facilities and buildings located thereon permits, the City shall have the right to construct crossings at grades:

(a) to connect Fourth Street East, Fifth Street West and Ninth Street West, and

(b) to carry Third Street West across the present right-of-way in a straight line parallel either to the existing vehicular portion thereof or to Fourth Street West, such crossing not to exceed 66 feet in width.

8.5   Canadian Pacific shall grant free of cost to the City the rights-of-way across the present right-of-way necessary for the crossings set out in section 8.4 and for the City-owned utilities within such crossings if the total area of all such rights-of-way does not exceed three and one-half (3.5) acres.

8.6   Canadian Pacific shall retain all rights in the lands granted for such crossings pursuant to this Article 8 other than in that part of the surface and subsurface necessary for utilities and for construction and traffic purposes, and, without limiting the rights so retained, such rights shall include the right to use the space above fourteen feet six inches above the vehicular surface of such crossings when first constructed for such buildings or structures as its plans for development require.

8.7   The City shall at its own sole cost, risk and expense construct, reconstruct, repair and maintain all such crossings and shall be solely responsible for the removal, reconstruction, relocation, modification or installation of any utility affected by such crossings whether such utility is owned by the City, Canadian Pacific or some other person.

8.8   All utilities within such crossings shall be below the surface thereof.

8.9   Save as provided in section 8.4 of this Article 8, the rights-of-way to be granted by Canadian Pacific for such crossings pursuant to this Article 8 shall be of the same width as the streets which they connect or carry across the present right-of-way.

8.10 After Canadian Pacific commences to use the new main line for all its through main line trains Canadian Pacific shall grant to the City, upon written request of the City, said rights-of-way and the City may use same for temporary crossings prior to construction of permanent crossings, provided that such use shall not unduly interfere with or disrupt rail service to industries over trackage not then removed from the present right-of-way.

8.11 If the City discontinues for twelve months the use of any crossing constructed pursuant to this Article 8 the right-of-way therefor granted by Canadian Pacific shall thereupon revert to Canadian Pacific and the City shall have no right, title or estate therein and if such right-of-way is registered or filed in the Land Titles Office the City shall withdraw, discharge or remove the same.

8.12 Canadian Pacific shall have the right at its sole cost, risk and expense to carry under any public thoroughfare crossings of the present right-of-way such passageways, utilities, conveyances and other installations as it deems necessary, providing always that the same shall not be so constructed or installed as to affect the use of such crossings for traffic purposes except during such construction or installation.

Article 9: Parkway

9.1 The City shall proceed with the construction of the initial phases of the parkway after the land has been acquired by for it and after Canadian Pacific commences construction of the new main line, and the City shall open the parkway for public highway use within five years after Canadian Pacific commences to operate its through main line trains on the new main line.

9.2 Except to the extent that Canadian Pacific has agreed to share with the City the price paid by the City for the acquisition of land pursuant to Article 2 of this Agreement the City shall pay all costs of constructing the parkway and related facilities and any extensions to such parkway and facilities.

9.3 The City shall bear all costs of repairs, maintenance and reconstruction excepting any damage (other than damage from vibration or subsidence) resulting from railway operations on the new main line of the parkway and related facilities and extensions thereto.

Article 10: Landscaping of Parkway and Maintenance of New Right-of-Way

10.1 The City shall be responsible for all landscaping within the boundaries of the parkway and for the maintenance of same, all at its sole cost and expense.

10.2 Canadian Pacific shall maintain the new right-of-way in a neat and clean condition so as to present an appearance of a high standard for railway rights-of-way in urban areas in Canada, and shall not allow waste or debris to accumulate thereon.

Article 11: Sanctions and Approvals

11.1   The City and Canadian Pacific shall co-operate and join with each other in obtaining all requisite sanctions and approvals to enable the works contemplated by this Agreement to be carried out.

Article 12: Taxation

12.1   In this Article, including this section:

"development company" - means a body corporate the majority of the issued and outstanding capital shares of which is, or is to be, owned by Marathon and which is or is to be incorporated principally for development of land in the present right-of-way.

"Marathon" - means Marathon Realty Company Limited, a body corporate, the majority of the issued and outstanding capital shares of which at the date of this Agreement is owned by Canadian Pacific Investments Limited, which last mentioned company at the date of this Agreement is controlled by Canadian Pacific.

12.2   The City agrees with Canadian Pacific that the new right-of-way and the new main line shall be part of the "Canadian Pacific Railway" within the meaning of clause 16 of the Contract made between Her Majesty the Queen in right of Canada and George Stephen *et al.*, dated 21st October 1880, approved and ratified by *An Act Respecting the Canadian Pacific Railway*, Statutes of Canada, 1881, chapter 1, and thus to be forever free from taxation pursuant to the terms thereof; and that the City shall not tax or attempt to tax the same or any part thereof while required and used for the construction and working of said Canadian Pacific Railway; it being particularly understood and agreed between the parties that the provisions of said clause 16 and said *Act Respecting the Canadian Pacific Railway* apply to the new right-of-way and the new main line.

12.3   (a) If a part of the present right-of-way is sold such part shall thereafter not be subject to the terms of this Agreement.

(b) If a part of the present right-of-way is the subject of a lease or other right of occupation granted prior to the date of this Agreement such part shall be subject to taxation by the City while subject to such lease or right of occupation.

(c) If part of the present right-of-way is the subject of a lease or either right of occupation granted on or after the date of this Agreement

(i) it shall be subject to taxation by the City during the period that such part is subject to such lease or right of occupation, and

(ii) if the lease or right of occupation is for a term exceeding ten years the portion of the present right-of-way comprised in it shall thereafter remain subject to taxation by the City.

(d) If a part of the present right-of-way is used by Canadian Pacific, Marathon or the development company for earning an income from other than railway operations such part shall be subject to taxation by the City:

(i) if it is a portion of the present right-of-way lying either to the east of First Street East or to the west of Fourth Street West only while it is so used, or

(ii) if it is a portion of the present right-of-way lying anywhere between First Street East and Fourth Street West while it is so used and if it is so used for a period of ten years such portion shall remain taxable thereafter.

12.4 The sale or lease of any part of the present right-of-way

(a) by Canadian Pacific to Marathon or the development company,

(b) by Marathon to the development company

shall not be, or be deemed to be, a sale or lease of such part within the terms of section 12.3 of this Article 12.

12.5 Where Canadian Pacific, Marathon or the development company constructs or maintains a building any portion of which is not to be or is not occupied and used for the railway operations of Canadian Pacific that proportion of such building and the same proportion of the land on which the building is or is to be constructed shall become subject to taxation by the City when the City issues a building permit therefor.

12.6 (a) Except where otherwise provided in this Article 12 the present right-of-way shall be free from taxation by the City.

(b) In this Article 12 any land, buildings or other properties or portions thereof which are free from taxation shall also be free from assessment.

12.7 Sections 12.3 to 12.6 both inclusive of this Article 12 shall only become effective when Canadian Pacific commences to use the new main line for all of its through main line trains pursuant to Article 6 of this agreement.

12.8 Except as the parties hereto shall mutually agree neither party shall at any time seek or request legislation to cancel, alter or otherwise affect the provisions of this Article 12.

12.9 The provision of this Article 12 shall not affect

(i) any agreement or agreements made between the parties hereto respecting the Palliser Hotel;

(ii) any rights of Canadian Pacific under the Contract and the *Act Respecting the Canadian Pacific Railway* which Contract and Act are referred to in section 12.2 of this Article 12.

Article 13: Arbitration

13.1 If any dispute or difference arises between the parties under any of the following portions of this Agreement:

Article	Section(s)	Article	Section(s)
1	All	7	7.5
2	2.1	8	8.1(c)
	2.6		8.10
	2.8(ii)		8.12
	2.11		
		9	9.3
3	3.5		
		10	10.2
4	4.2		
	4.3	17	All

or under any other Article the parties may agree in writing shall be determined by arbitration, such dispute or difference shall be determined by arbitration by a board of arbitration consisting of three arbitrators, as follows:

(i) the Chief Justice of the Trial Division of the Supreme Court of Alberta, or a Judge of said Trial Division nominated by him, and

(ii) a nominee of the City, and

(iii) a nominee of Canadian Pacific,

the said Chief Justice or Judge nominated by him to be the chairman.

13.2 If a majority of said board of arbitration cannot agree, the decision of the chairman shall be the decision of said board of arbitration.

13.3   The decision of said board of arbitration shall be final and binding on the parties.

13.4 Except as in this Article 13 otherwise provided *The Arbitration Act* of Alberta shall apply to such arbitration.

Article 14: Petition of Legislation for Enabling Statute

14.1 The City shall petition the Legislature of the Province of Alberta at the next session thereof after the date of this Agreement for an Act to

(i) validate, ratify and confirm the agreement;

(ii) provide that the City had the power to have executed this Agreement and has had, since the date of this Agreement, the power to carry out all obligations of the City under this Agreement;

(iii) validate all acts of the City done pursuant to this Agreement since the date of this Agreement;

(iv) specifically relieve the City from any liability under, or arising out of *The Municipalities Assessment and Equalization Act* of Alberta or any other related statute to account for and make any payment in respect of the assessment of any part of the present right-of-way which is exempt from taxation by the terms of this Agreement;

(v) specifically authorize the City to borrow such amounts of money as may be required to enable the City to carry out its obligations under this Agreement without submitting a by-law therefor to the proprietary electors of the City if such by-law is passed by two-thirds of the members of the City Council voting thereon;

(vi) specifically empower the City to expropriate land necessary for the new right-of-way and for the parkway or for either of them and thereafter to transfer to Canadian Pacific the land required for the new right-of-way according to the terms of this Agreement without any by-law or resolution of Council or other authorization;

(vii) provide for expropriation by the City of any or all portions of the land required for the parkway and the new right-of-way or either of them

(a) that the provisions of *The Expropriations Procedure Act* shall not apply;

(b) that the validation of this Agreement by the statute shall be sufficient authority to expropriate all of the land set out in the schedules without a by-law or other authorization being required;

(c) that the amount of the compensation for the land so expropriated shall be determined by the award of a judge of the Supreme Court of Alberta or of the District Court of the Judicial District of Calgary or by a barrister appointed by either such judge as arbitrator and the amount so awarded shall be paid to the owner of the land by the party acquiring the same;

(d) such additional procedure with relation to notices, service, tenders, substituted service, use and occupation of the land and other maters necessary and incidental to the exercise of the rights of expropriation granted by the said Act.

(viii) contain such other provisions and relief as the parties may hereafter consider necessary and expedient.

Article 15: When Agreement Null and Void

15.1 This Agreement shall be null and void and of no effect between the parties as if it had not been entered into if prior to the close of the first session of the Legislature of the Province of Alberta after the date of this Agreement or the 15th day of May, A.D. 1964 whichever is later:

(i) the City does not pass such by-law as may be necessary for creating a debt to enable the City to carry out its obligations under this Agreement, or

(ii) this Agreement is not ratified, validated and confirmed by an Act of the said Legislature and the City thereby declared to have had the power to make and execute this Agreement and the power on and from the date of this Agreement to do, perform and carry out all acts, matters and things required by this Agreement to be done, performed and carried out by it, or

(iii) the said Act does not specifically relieve the City from any liability under, or arising out of *The Municipalities Assessment and Equalization Act* of Alberta or any other related statute to account for and make any payment in respect of the assessment of that part of the present right-of-way which is exempt from taxation by the terms of this Agreement;

and the Agreement shall be similarly null and void also if the right to obtain and enter upon all of the land necessary for the new right-of-way has not been acquired by the parties or either of them prior to the expiration of one year after the coming into force of said Act ratifying, validating and confirming the Agreement; provided, however, that until this Agreement becomes so null and void and of no effect all rights and obligations of each of the parties under this Agreement within their present respective powers shall be effective and binding on each of them on and from the date of this Agreement, and if this Agreement becomes so null and void and of no effect neither party shall have any claim or recourse against the other party for anything done by either or both of them pursuant to this Agreement.

Article 16: Waiver

16.1 No waiver on behalf of either party of any breach of any covenant, condition or proviso of this Agreement shall take effect or be binding unless the same be expressed in writing, and any waiver so expressed by one party shall not limit or affect that party's rights with respect to any other or future breach.

Article 17: Suspension

17.1 Either party to this Agreement shall be relieved from performance of such of its obligations and covenants hereunder as are prevented by acts of God, the Queen, and the Queen's enemies or by a casualty or eventuality which is beyond the control and which could not have been foreseen and avoided by the party affected thereby and which renders it impossible for the party to perform its obligations or part of them hereunder. Furthermore either party shall be relieved from performance of its obligation if a court of competent jurisdiction has granted an order, direction or injunction staying anything required to be done in the performance of this Agreement, including but not limited to the expropriation of any land required for the purposes of this Agreement. Lack of finances shall not be deemed to be circumstances beyond the control of either party and shall not excuse performance of any obligation under this Agreement. Either party excused performance pursuant to the provisions of this Article shall only be excused to the extent and for the time that performance of such obligations is prevented by the aforesaid events. The party relieved from performance by this Article shall, as soon as such events allow, resume performance of its obligations hereunder and shall endeavour to rectify any condition which has arisen while it was prevented from performance of the its obligations. Notwithstanding any provision of this Article the City shall not be required to proceed with any portion of its obligations which requires the passage of a money by-law to finance it unless and until the City Council has passed such by-law.

Article 18: Assignment

18.1 In this Article 18 "Marathon" and "development company" have the same respective meanings as in Article 12.

18.2 At any time or times Canadian Pacific may assign to Marathon or the development company its rights and obligations under this Agreement in respect of the present right-of-way or of any portion or portions thereof.

18.3 At any time or times Marathon may assign to the development company such rights and obligations as it has under this Agreement in respect of the present right-of-way or of any portion or portions thereof.

18.4 Any assignment made pursuant to this Article 18 shall be effective only upon an assignment agreement substantially in the form attached to this Agreement as Schedule "2" being entered into between Canadian Pacific and Marathon or the development company and the City, or between Marathon and the development company and the City, which assignment agreement the City shall execute upon the written request of Canadian Pacific or Marathon.

Article 19: Previous Agreements

19.1 This Agreement supersedes and cancels all agreements, letters, memoranda and other writings by and between the parties or any of their agents or representatives previously made relating to negotiations in respect of this Agreement respecting matters affected by this Agreement.

Article 20: Notices

20.1 Every request, notice, statement or bill provided for or to be given or rendered pursuant to this Agreement shall be in writing directed to the party to whom given, and mailed to or delivered at such party's address as follows:

Canadian Pacific	Canadian Pacific Railway Company,
	Calgary Land Project Office,
	202 – 10th Avenue South East,
	CALGARY, Alberta
City	The City of Calgary,
	City Hall,
	CALGARY, Alberta

Any notice mailed by registered mail shall be deemed to have been given to and received by the addressee seventy-two (72) hours after the mailing thereof, and in the event that the same is delivered, as soon as such delivery has been made to the party's said address. Either party may change its address by giving written notice to the other party of the new address, PROVIDED that such new address shall be in the City of Calgary.

IN WITNESS WHEREOF the parties hereto have executed this Agreement as of the day and year first above written.

THE CITY OF CALGARY

_____

Mayor

_____

City Clerk

CANADIAN PACIFIC RAILWAY COMPANY

_____

_____

This is Schedule "2" to the Agreement dated the _____ day of _____, 1964, made between The City of Calgary, of the First Part, and Canadian Pacific Railway Company, of the Second Part.

ASSIGNMENT

THIS ASSIGNMENT made this _____ day of _____, 19____, BETWEEN:

(in this Assignment also called "the Assignor")

OF THE FIRST PART

– and –

(in this Assignment called "the Assignee")

OF THE SECOND PART

– and –

THE CITY OF CALGARY (in this Assignment called "the City")

OF THE THIRD PART

Pursuant to the Agreement between the City and Canadian Pacific Railway Company dated the _____ day of _____, 19____ (in this Assignment called "the said Agreement") THE ASSIGNOR HEREBY ASSIGNS unto the Assignee all the rights and obligations of the Assignor under the said Agreement except as hereafter in this Assignment provided, in respect of the following described lands and premises:

And the Assignee, in consideration of the City entering into this Assignment, hereby covenants and agrees with the City to perform or cause to be performed all the obligations of the Assignor under the said Agreement in respect of the said lands and premises as if the Assignee was the party of the second part in the said Agreement;

And the City, in consideration of the obligations assumed by the Assignee under this Assignment, hereby covenants and agrees with the Assignee to perform all the obligations of the City under the said Agreement in respect of the said lands and premises as if the Assignee was the party of the second part in the said Agreement;

And the City and the Assignor covenant and agree with each other that hereafter neither of them has any obligation to the other under the said Agreement in respect of the said lands and premises, except, however, that

(a) Canadian Pacific Railway Company as well as the Assignee shall be entitled to, and to enforce against the City, all rights of exemption from taxation provided for in the said Agreement in respect of such of the said lands and premises as are used from time to time for railway operations, and

(b) Until the title of said lands is transferred to and registered in the name of the Assignee the City may enforce against the Assignor as well as against the Assignee any liability to taxation provided for in the said Agreement.

And, for the purpose of Article 20 of the said Agreement the address of the Assignee shall be:

IN WITNESS WHEREOF the parties have executed this Assignment effective as of the day and year first above written.

_____

_____

_____

_____

THE CITY OF CALGARY

_____

Mayor

_____

City Clerk

MAJOR PARTICIPANTS

The City

Harry Hays: mayor, October 1959–July 1963

Grant MacEwan: mayor, July 1963–October 1965

Dudley Batchelor, chief commissioner, 1960–63

John Steel: commissioner, Public Works and Utilities, 1960–fall 1963; chief commissioner, fall 1963–1964

Jack Leslie: alderman, 1962–64

David Russell: alderman, 1964

Carson MacWilliams: chief solicitor

John DeWolfe: deputy chief solicitor

The CPR

Roy Norris (Buck) Crump: president

Ian Sinclair: vice-president, Non-Transportation Resources Department

Fred Stone: vice-president, Natural Resources Department

Rod Sykes: project manager, Land Redevelopment Department

Fred Joplin: engineer in charge of track relocation studies

Herb Pickard: legal counsel

Others

Norman MacMillan: CNR vice-president

E.C. Manning: Alberta premier

Ruth Gorman: legal advisor, Calgary Local Council of Women

Carl Nickle: oilman and leading supporter of project

Robert Barron: businessman, lawyer, and leading opponent of project

Eric Hanson: author of report supporting the project

CALGARY CITY COUNCILS, 1962–64

1962
Mayor
Harry Hays

Aldermen
Runo Berglund
Bill Dickie
Ted Duncan
Roy Farran
George Ho Lem
Jack Leslie
Clarence Mack
Grant MacEwan
Don McIntosh
P. N.R. (Peter) Morrison
Ernest Starr
Bruce Watson

1963
Mayor
Harry Hays (to July)
Grant MacEwan

Aldermen
Ray Ballard
Runo Berglund
Bill Dickie
Ted Duncan
Roy Farran
George Ho Lem
Jack Leslie
Grant MacEwan
Clarence Mack
P. N.R. (Peter) Morrison
Harold Runions
Ernest Starr

1964
Mayor
Grant MacEwan

Aldermen
Ray Ballard
Runo Berglund
Walter Boote
Roy Deyell
Bill Dickie
Ted Duncan
George Ho Lem
Jack Leslie
Harold Runions
David Russell
Ernest Starr
Mark Tennant

Introduction

1 On the impact of the CMHC, see John R. Miron, *Housing in Postwar Canada: Demographic Change, Household Formation, and Housing Demand*; Norman Hallendy, *Housing a Nation: Forty Years of Achievement*.

2 Jill Grant, "Shaped by Planning: The Canadian City Through Time." See also L. J. Evenden and G. E. Walker, "From Periphery to Centre: The Changing Geography of the Suburbs."

3 See Charles Clapham's commentary on Wallace Atkinson, "Urban Transportation Problems — Solutions" (also in *Canada: An Urban Agenda,* 225–27).

4 Gerald Hodge and David Gordon, *Planning Canadian Communities: An Introduction to the Principles, Practices and Participants,* 111.

5 City of Calgary Archives (hereafter cited as CCA), Downtown Parking Survey, Summary and Recommendations, December 1963. For a discussion of the forces behind the evacuation of the inner city, see Trudi E. Bunting and Pierre Filion, *The Changing Canadian Inner City,* 2–7.

6 Included in the Toronto plan were provisions for highways 400 and 401, as well as the future location of highways 403, 404, and 407. See John Sewell, *The Shape of the Suburbs: Understanding Toronto's Sprawl,* 64.

7 George A. Nader, *Theoretical, Historical and Planning Perspectives,* 341.

8 Ibid., 340.

9 Stanley H. Pickett, "An Appraisal of the Urban Renewal Programme in Canada."

10 The description is attributed to *Fortune Magazine* in David Cruise and Alison Griffiths, *Lords of the Line: The Men Who Built the CPR,* 394.

11 Cruise and Griffiths, *Lords of the Line,* 394.

12 "News and Views of Investments," *Barron's National Business and Financial Weekly,* February 26, 1962.

13 Cruise and Griffiths credit the phrase "crippled Titan" to the MacPherson Royal Commission, formed in 1959 to investigate national transportation policy and freight rates (*Lords of the Line,* 416).

14 Cruise and Griffiths, *Lords of the Line*, 472.

15 Ibid., 417.

16 Robert Chodos, *The CPR: A Century of Corporate Welfare*, 124.

17 See Joseph S. Clark Jr. and Dennis J. Clark, "Rally and Relapse, 1946–1968"; Edward K. Muller and Joel A. Tarr, "The Interaction of Natural and Built Environments in the Pittsburgh Landscape," 11–40; and Guian McKee, "Blue Sky Boys, Professional Citizens and Knights-in-Shining-Money: Philadelphia's Penn Center Project and the Constraints of Private Development."

18 Track reduction had also occurred in downtown Moncton. In Winnipeg, the Midland Railway intended to move its tracks and locate farther west, and the CNR shops and yards at Osborne Street had been closed and moved to Transcona. An agreement reached in 1952 between the CNR and the City of Edmonton resulted in the removal of forty-five level crossings and a land swap that reduced rail activity in the downtown yards.

19 Thomas H. Mawson, *City of Calgary, Past, Present, and Future: A Preliminary Scheme for Controlling the Economic Growth of the City*.

20 See CCA, Municipal Manuals, 1944 to 1964.

21 Between 1945 and 1964, there were four major annexations (in 1956, 1957, 1962, and 1964), swelling the city's area from 40 square miles to 155 square miles.

22 Eric J. Hanson, "City of Calgary CP Railway Downtown Development Proposals," report submitted to City Council on November 7, 1963, table A-6.

23 Max Foran, *Expansive Discourses: Urban Sprawl in Calgary, 1945–1978*.

24 By the end of the decade and into the early 1960s, a more dynamic element was beginning to appear in city councils.

25 Brahm Wiesman, "A New Agenda for Cities," 12.

26 CCA, Planning Department, "City of Calgary General Plan," August, 1963.

27 CCA, Municipal Manuals, 1944, 1963.

28 Hanson, "City of Calgary CP Railway Downtown Development Proposals," table 2-11.

29 Jack K. Masson, *Alberta's Local Governments and Their Politics*, 214.

30 Hanson, "City of Calgary CP Railway Downtown Development Proposals," 6, tables D2 and D4.

31 "A Face-Lift for Calgary?" *The Albertan*, August 15, 1962; "The Railway Remakes Calgary," *Calgary Herald*, August 15, 1962.

32 "Calgary Welcomes Heart-Rending Plan," *The Globe and Mail*, August 18, 1962.

33 City of Calgary Archives, Board of Commissioners Papers (hereafter cited as CCA, BCP), series 5, box 225, file 6200.4, "CPR Proposed Development — Ivan Robison," August 2, 1963.

34 An Act Respecting the Canadian Pacific Railway Company, 1881 S.C., schedule 1, clause 16. There were two exceptions: the Post Office building and Robin Hood Mills; the land for both had been bought from the CPR.

35 Personal papers of J.R.W. (Rodney) Sykes (used with permission and hereafter cited as Sykes Papers), "Canadian Pacific Interim Report: Calgary Land Use Study," February 1963, "Traffic Study" section.

36 Sykes Papers, Sykes to R.J. Shepp, December 3, 1963.

37 Ibid.

38 Hanson, "City of Calgary CP Railway Downtown Development Proposals," table 2-12.

39 One contemporary source estimated that by 1981, tax revenues from the project would have realized well over $3 million compared to only $451,000 without it.

40 Jean Leslie, *Three Rivers Beckoned: Life and Times with Calgary Mayor Jack Leslie*, 164–218.

41 H.V. Nelles, "How Did Calgary Get Its River Parks?"

42 Marjorie Norris, *A Leaven of Ladies: The History of the Calgary Local Council of Women*, 197–211.

Chapter 1 Setting the Stage

1 Frank Early, "Your City," *Calgary Herald*, August 25, 1962.

2 City of Calgary Archives, City Commissioners Papers (hereafter cited as CCA, CCP), series 4, box 24, file: CPR 1952–59, Commissioners' Report, June 6, 1955.

3 CCA, CCP, series 4, box 24, file: CPR 1952–59, N.J. Fraine, CPR Regional Vice-President, to Chief Commissioner Ivor Strong, June 6, 1955.

4 CCA, CCP, series 4, box 24, file: CPR Ramp 1958, Commissioners' Report, May 23, 1957.

5 CCA, CCP, series 4, box 24, file: CPR 1952–59, Commissioner E. C Thomas to J.L. Hall, CP Superintendent, Calgary District, November 8, 1957.

6 CCA, CCP, series 4, box 24, file: CPR 1952–59, Commissioners' Report, December 5, 1957.

7 CCA, CCP, series 4, box 24, file: CPR 1952–59, Downtown Businessmen's Association to the CPR, June 10, 1958.

8 "Plan Interests CPR," *Calgary Herald*, November 23, 1959.

9 City of Calgary Archives, City Council Minutes (hereafter cited as CCA, CCM), June 4, 1959, report of Downtown Parking Corporation, W.R. Taprell, Superintendent.

10 See CCA, Municipal Manuals, 1960–64.

11 "Plan Interests CPR."

12 It should be added, however, that Hays also enjoyed the support of his veteran and influential chief commissioner, Dudley Batchelor. Indeed, in at least one city report following Batchelor's retirement in the fall of 1963, Batchelor was given credit for initiating the project. Be that as it may, it was Hays, as the chief political executive, who carried the issue forward with the CPR.

13 For further information on Hays's career, see Don Peacock, *Barefoot on the Hill: The Life of Harry Hays*.

14 See CCA, Municipal Manuals, 1960, 1948.

15 For years afterwards, Hays retained his farm house in Haysboro, where, during Stampede week, he hosted the Hays Breakfast, an event as notable for its highly potent brew, called Sillabub, as it was for its exclusive guest list.

16 One wonders about this claim. According to the city's Municipal Manual for the year 1961 (CCA), the debenture debt had in fact risen to $85 million.

17 Unfortunately, details of the negotiations between Hays and Crump are unavailable, although references to them appeared frequently in the press of that time. See, for example, "Rail Firm Maps Huge Development," *The Albertan*, June 25, 1962. The accounts in the press are supported by comments that Sykes made to the author in a number of interviews.

18 Sykes describes his position at the CPR as "rather ambiguous" (personal communication, January 15, 2012). His duties were not very clearly defined, nor was the chain of command. In theory, he was supposed to report to Bob Barnstead, the manager of the CPR's Research Department. In reality, he reported to Fred Stone, vice-president of the Natural Resources Department, and Ian Sinclair, the CPR's vice-president, in collaboration with the CPR's chief economist, Harvey Romoff.

19 Rod Sykes, interview with the author, February 11, 2009.

20 Rod Sykes, personal communication, January 15, 2012.

21 See Jim Stott's column in the *Calgary Herald*, August 30, 1977. In the conversations I have had with numerous individuals, several have been critical of Sykes's personality. None, however, has ever questioned his ability or intellect.

22 John Hopkins, "Sykes May Not Have Been Loved but He Got the Job Done," *Calgary Herald*, October 21, 1977.

23 One of Crump's criticisms of Sinclair was that he treated his staff too harshly. See David Cruise and Alison Griffiths, *Lords of the Line: The Men Who Built the CPR*, 418.

24 *Calgary Herald*, August 30, 1977.

25 Cruise and Griffiths, *Lords of the Line*, 425.

26 Ibid., 427.

27 It is possible, however, that one underlying factor in his trip was Hays's recent correspondence with Crump on the CPR's expansion of its major Alyth switching yards in the city's east end.

28 Robert Chodos, *The CPR: A Century of Corporate Welfare*, 125.

29 Rod Sykes, in discussion with the author, December 22, 2008.

30 Sykes Papers, memorandum dated May 31, 1962.

31 "City Rail Lines Asset in Future," *The Albertan*, October 13, 1961.

32 City of Calgary Archives, City Council Minutes (hereafter cited as CCA, CCM), March 5, 1962.

33 CCA, CCM, March 19, 1962.

34 Jean Leslie, *Three Rivers Beckoned: Life and Times with Calgary Mayor Jack Leslie*, 167.

35 Early, "Your City."

36 "CP-City Plan Backing Indicated by Aldermen," *Calgary Herald*, April 6, 1963; J.C. Leslie, "The CPR Redevelopment Scheme," *Home Buyers' Guide* 2, no. 1 (February 1964): 00–00.

37 Early, "Your City."

38 CCA, CCM, July 27, 1959.

39 All of this information is contained in CCA, City Clerk fonds, box 645, file 4436, "South Bank Parkway — East Extension," City Planning Department Transportation Study, May 1964.

40 CCA, City Clerk fonds, box 557, file 3724, "A Preliminary Report on Urban Renewal in the City of Calgary," August 1959.

41 "City Master Plan Ready Soon," *The Albertan*, October 13, 1961.

42 CCA, CCM, January 8, 1962, in reference to Urban Renewal Report #2, reviewed by Urban Planning Committee, December 14, 1961.

43 See also Ed Grah, "Rail Firm Maps Huge Development," *The Albertan*, June 25, 1962.

44 The CPR's comments about Calgary being a "guinea pig" for projects across the country do appear to indicate some degree of forethought and planning.

45 "Downtown Face-Lifting," *Calgary Herald*, June 23, 1962.

46 Ed Grah, "Rail Firm Maps Huge Development," *The Albertan*, June 25, 1962; "City's Growth Factor in Rail Scheme Choice," *Calgary Herald*, August 17, 1962.

47 "Attack on Mayor Ends in Praise," *The Albertan*, July 7, 1962. See also "Mayor Praised, Criticized," *Calgary Herald*, July 7, 1962.

48 "Mayor Praised, Criticized"; "Attack on Mayor Ends in Praise."

49 This report is not available in the City Council minutes but is contained in CCA, CCP, series 5, box 45, file: CPR 1962, Commissioners' Report, July 3, 1962.

50 Interestingly, the March 5 motion received short shrift in City Council and was only referred to the Commissioners' Office following the defeat of an amendment that would have sidetracked the motion to the less powerful Planning Department. See CCA, CCM, March 5 and 19, 1962.

Chapter 2 Heady Days of Hope

1 Sykes Papers, Calgary Land Use Study, Progress Report #1, June 15–30 1962.

2 Ed Grah, "CP Project Seen as Boon to City's Blighted Areas," *The Albertan*, August 20, 1962.

3 Ibid.

4 "Track Reduction to Provide Land," *Calgary Herald*, August 14, 1962.

5 "CPR Property Plan Seen by Year End," *Calgary Herald*, July 25, 1962; "Track Reduction to Provide Land."

6 "CPR 'New Look' Not Far Off," *Calgary Herald*, August 14, 1962.

7 "The Railway Remakes Calgary," *Calgary Herald*, August 15, 1962; "A Face-Lift for Calgary," *The Albertan*, August 15, 1962.

8 "Ken Liddell's Corner," *Calgary Herald*, August 25, 1962.

9 Sykes Papers, Calgary Land Use Study, Progress Report #5, September 4–25, 1962.

10 Sykes Papers, text of address, untitled and undated [fall 1962].

11 Sykes Papers, text of address to Downtown Businessmen's Association, November 28, 1962.

12 Sykes Papers, Calgary Land Use Study, Progress Report #1, June 15–30, 1962.

13 Sykes Papers, Sykes to Fred Stone, December 4, 1962. The group in question was the Appraisal Institute of Canada.

14 Rod Sykes, written comments to the author, May 2011.

15 Sykes Papers, Calgary Land Use Study, Progress Report #1, June 15–30, 1962.

16 Sykes Papers, outline of Calgary Land Use Study, undated.

17 Sykes Papers, "Canadian Pacific Interim Report: Calgary Land Use Study," February 1963, "Summary of Conclusions" (emphasis in the original).

18 Sykes Papers, Calgary Land Use Study, March 1963, "Office Space in Calgary Central Business District," 1–3.

19 Sykes Papers, Calgary Land Use Study, March 1963, "Introduction," 1–3.

20 Sykes Papers, Calgary Land Use Study, March 1963, "Profit Potential for Development," 4.

21 Sykes Papers, Calgary Land Use Study, Progress Report #3, July 16–31, 1962.

22 Sykes Papers, Calgary Land Use Study, March 1963, "Freight Traffic in Downtown Calgary."

23 Sykes Papers, Calgary Land Use Study, March 1963, "Summary of Conclusions," 1.

24 Sykes Papers, Calgary Land Use Study, March 1963, "Benefits and Costs to the City of Calgary Consequent upon Canadian Pacific Right-of-Way Development," 2.

25 Sykes Papers, draft of Calgary Land Use Study, July 25, 1962, 2.

26 Sykes Papers, Calgary Land Use Study, status as at September 30, 1962.

27 Details of the above are contained in Sykes's various Calgary Land Use Study Progress Reports.

28 Sykes Papers, Sykes to Fred V. Stone, November 6, 1962.

29 Sykes Papers, memorandum to Fred Stone, January 28, 1963.

30 Sykes Papers, Calgary Land Use Study, Progress Report #3, July 16–31, 1962. See also Grah, "CP Project Seen as Boon to City's Blighted Areas."

31 Sykes Papers, "Canadian Pacific Interim Report: Calgary Land Use Study," February 1963, "Profit Potential for Development," 4.

32 Sykes Papers, Calgary Land Use Study, Progress Report #4, August 1–31, 1962, "Summary of Progress: Marwell and the Calgary Inn."

33 Sykes Papers, memorandum dated January 22, 1963, and titled "Western Hotels–Calgary Inn."

34 Ibid.

35 Sykes Papers, Robert W. Dowling, abbreviated biography.

36 Sykes Papers, Calgary Land Use Study, "Robert Dowling's Visit — Summary and Conclusions," November 25, 1962.

37 Sykes Papers, Calgary Land Use Study, memorandum, "Visit to New York," October 9–11, 1962. For more on Sykes's trip to New York and on other contacts made there, see Sykes Papers, Sykes to W.R. Drysdale, October 31, 1962.

38 Sykes Papers, Calgary Land Use Study, "Mr. Dowling's Visit — Arrangements," November 19, 1962. For additional details, see also Sykes Papers, Calgary Land Use Study, "Robert W. Dowling's Visit — Summary and Conclusions," November 25, 1962.

39 Sykes Papers, Calgary Land Use Study, "Robert W. Dowling's Visit — Summary and Conclusions," November 25, 1962.

40 Ibid.

41 The description of this meeting in the paragraphs that follow is from City of Calgary Archives, Board of Commissioners Papers (hereafter cited as CCA, BCP), series 5, box 225, file 6200.4, "Summary of Luncheon Meeting at the Palliser Hotel," September 14, 1962.

42 Sykes Papers, Downtown–C.P. Planning Study, undated.

43 Sykes Papers, City of Calgary document titled "Further Thoughts Regarding City Centre Program," November 2, 1962.

44 Ibid.

45 Sykes Papers, memorandum, "Calgary Land Use Study," attached to "Further Thoughts Regarding City Centre Program," November 19, 1962.

46 Ibid.

47 Ibid.

48 Sykes Papers, text of speech, possibly to the Chamber of Commerce, October 1962.

49 "CPR Unveils Plan," *The Albertan*, August 14, 1962.

50 "City's Growth Factor in Rail Scheme Choice," *Calgary Herald*, August 17, 1962.

51 CCA, BCP, series 5, box 225, file 6200.4, "Summary of Luncheon Meeting at the Palliser Hotel," September 14, 1962.

52 CCA, BCP, series 5, box 225, file 6200.4, CPR Downtown Study, November 1962–December 1963 (file 1 of 3), Progress Report #1, November 9, 1962.

53 CCA, BCP, series 5, box 225, file 6200.4, Downtown Study Group meeting, November 30, 1962.

54 Joplin later went on to become president and CEO of CP (Bermuda) Ltd., a position he held from 1976 to 1984. He was the only man in the history of the company to hold both positions of vice-president of Marketing and Sales and vice-president of Operations and Maintenance.

55 Sykes Papers, "Canadian Pacific Interim Report: Calgary Land Use Study," February 1963, "Engineering Feasibility and Costs."

56 Ibid., 1–9.

57 Sykes Papers, Calgary Project Engineering Appraisal, January 28, 1963.

58 CCA, BCP, series 5, box 283, file: CPR Downtown Development Proposal — Work Papers, 1963–1964 (file 2 of 3), Commissioners' Report, "Diversion of Canadian Pacific Mainline to the South Bank of the Bow River and the Construction of an Associated Parkway Road," undated.

59 Sykes Papers, Sykes to Robert Dowling, January 18, 1963.

60 Sykes Papers, Sykes to Steel, February 1, 1963.

61 Sykes Papers, memorandum dated January 28, 1963.

62 CCA, BCP, series 5, box 283, file: CPR Downtown Development Proposal — Work Papers, 1963–1964 (file 2 of 3), Commissioners' Report, "Diversion of Canadian Pacific Mainline to the South Bank of the Bow River and the Construction of an Associated Parkway Road," undated (emphasis in the original).

63 Sykes Papers, City of Calgary Planning Department, "Objections to Proposed C.P. Right-of-Way on South Side of Bow River, undated [ca. mid-January 1963].

64 Ibid.

65 Some forty-five years later, Sykes admitted that he believed that the Beddington route should have been adopted and that doing so probably would have saved the project (Rod Sykes, in discussion with the author, December 22, 2008).

66 Sykes Papers, Sykes to Stone, January 28, 1963.

67 The description of the meeting in the paragraphs that follow is from CCA, BCP, series 5, box 227, file 6200.4, "Memorandum re: Meeting of Board of Commissioners Held February 19, 1963," undated. Unless otherwise indicated, quotations are from this source.

68 Quoted in F.F. Langan, "Ian Sinclair, Last of the Railway Titans: 1913–2006," obituary in *The Globe and Mail*, April 11, 2006, http://groups.yahoo.com/neo/groups/Tr2000/conversations/topics/3018.

69 Sykes Papers, memorandum dated April 3, 1963. According to Sykes, "Mr. Batchelor stated they were embarrassed in Montreal by their lack of knowledge on this particular subject and they had to get into the picture."

70 "$35 Million Face-Lift for Calgary Revealed," *Calgary Herald*, April 5, 1963; "City-CPR Plan Made Public," *The Albertan*, April 6, 1963.

71 "Hays Win 'Bought,' Claim NDP Losers," *Calgary Herald*, April 9, 1963.

72 "Harry Hays, the 1963 Election Issues," *Calgary Herald*, April 6, 1963.

73 "The Real Issue on Election Day… Party Politics or Stability?" *Calgary Herald*, April 6, 1963.

74 Jean Leslie, *Three Rivers Beckoned: Life and Times with Calgary Mayor Jack Leslie*, 170–75.

75 The vote count was Hays: 20,796; Leslie: 19,496; Social Credit: 8,588; NDP: 3,857.

76 "How the Vote Went in the City," *Calgary Herald*, April 9, 1963.

77 Hays served for two years as minister of Agriculture before being defeated in 1965. During his tenure as minister, he advocated a system of farm marketing boards and a minimum income for farmers. He also oversaw the Dairy Commission Act and the Farm Machinery Syndicate Credit Act. He was appointed to the Senate in 1966 and died in 1982.

78 "A New Calgary Envisioned," *Calgary Herald*, April 5, 1963.

79 "Traffic Snarl Relief Predicted by Steel," *Calgary Herald*, April 6, 1963.

80 CCA, BCP, series 5, box 226, file 6200.4, CPR Downtown Study, Agreement, 1963 (file 1 of 4), "Heads of Arrangement Between Canadian Pacific Railway Company (Canadian Pacific) and City of Calgary (City)," April 5, 1963.

81 In Sykes's words, he raised these rents from "nominal to realistic — for instance, from $30 a year to, say, $1,200 based on current value and going rates — but I often phased increases in over three to five years" (Rod Sykes, in discussion with the author, December 22, 2008).

82 Rod Sykes, in discussion with the author, December 22, 2008.

83 "Hays Spurns Cities in Name of Commons," *The Albertan*, October 15, 1963.

84 "Sad Finale for Council," *North Hill News*, October 3, 1963.

85 City of Calgary Archives, City Council Minutes (hereafter cited as CCA, CCM), May 27, 1963.

86 CCA, CCM, April 15, 1963.

87 Not just "unshared," it appears. Sykes does not remember seeing any official report on the issue of rerouting the tracks (Rod Sykes, in discussion with the author, December 22, 2008).

88 CCA, CCM, June 7, 1963, Ian Sinclair to J.P. Wilson, June 4, 1963. Wilson had asked Sinclair for his opinion on track depression, to which Sinclair responded: "We would not proceed with the project if the tracks were to be depressed in whole or in part at their present location."

89 "Opposition at Meeting," *Calgary Herald*, March 10, 1964.

90 See Sykes Papers, "Canadian Pacific Interim Report: Calgary Land Use Study," February 1963.

91 Sykes Papers, memorandum dated October 4, 1962, attached to "Calgary Land Use Project — Status as at September 30, 1962."

92 Rod Sykes, in discussion with the author, December 22, 2008.

93 For information on these proceedings, see Peter Thurling, "CPR's Presentation Hits Home in House," *The Albertan*, March 4, 1964.

94 Sykes qualified this argument, noting, "In all the discussions I participated in, there was never any understanding of the possibility of two exempt rights-of-ways. It was clearly not possible" (Rod Sykes, in discussion with the author, January 5, 2010).

Chapter 3 From Arrangement to Agreement

1 See Glenbow Archives, Calgary's Grand Story Collection, M 9151, box 5, for a notation in which Alderman Roy Farran said that MacEwan was chosen to be acting mayor on a straw vote taken by City Council, which he (Farran) had rigged. Even if this claim is false, it makes for good apocrypha. If true, it furnishes food for thought as to what might have been. (Calgary's Grand Story Collection was prepared by the noted historian Donald Smith, now professor emeritus at the University of Calgary, as part of his research on the Barron family for his award-winning book, *Calgary's Grand Story*.)

2 "Geographer Urges Study," *The Albertan*, January 8, 1964.

3 "The Plan," Editorial, *Calgary Herald*, May 15, 1964.

4 See "Endorsement in View for CP-City Project" and "CP-City Plan Backing Indicated by Aldermen," *Calgary Herald*, April 6, 1963.

5 City of Calgary, City Council Minutes (hereafter cited as CCA, CCM), June 18, 1963. The aldermen were Clarence Mack, Harold Runions, and Peter Morrison.

6 "CP-City Plan Backing Indicated by Aldermen."

7 CCA, CCM, April 29, 1963.

8 CCA, CCM, July 27, 1963, Commissioners' Report, "City of Calgary CPR Redevelopment Proposals," undated.

9 CCA, CCM, July 22, 1967.

10 City of Calgary Archives, Board of Commissioners Papers (hereafter cited as CCA, BCP), series 5, box 225, file 6200.4, Downtown Study, comment by Harry Boothman, April 26, 1963.

11 "Traffic Snarl Relief Predicted by Steel," *Calgary Herald*, April 6, 1963.

12 CCA, CCM, May 23, 1963, letter from Local Council of Women to City of Calgary, April 14, 1963.

13 "Developers to Press City for Details of Revamping," *Calgary Herald*, April 8, 1963.

14 CCA, CCM, May 23, 1963, letters from Local Council of Women to City of Calgary, April 22 and 26, 1963.

15 CCA, CCM, July 27, 1963, Commissioners' Report, "City of Calgary CPR Redevelopment Proposals," undated. The economist was Eric Hanson.

16 CCA, CCM, May 23, 1963.

17 CCA, CCM, June 27, 1963; Ian MacFee Rogers, *The Law of Canadian Municipal Corporations*, 224.

18 CCA, CCM, July 27, 1963, Commissioners' Report, "City of Calgary CPR Redevelopment Proposals," undated.

19 SRI had also done work for the CPR, having completed a study for Rod Sykes on potential potash markets.

20 CCA, CCM, June 27, 1963, SRI report contained in letter from E.C. Harvey, Stanford Research Institute, to John Steel, June 25, 1963.

21 CCA, CCM, June 27, 1963, Van Ginkel Associates, "Report on the Proposed Central Area Redevelopment Project, City of Calgary," June 24, 1963.

22 According to Rod Sykes, the van Ginkels were also interested in soliciting business from the CPR.

23 CCA, BCP, series 5, box 225, file 6200.4, Downtown Study, A.H. Nicholson to H.P. Daniel van Ginkel, August 26, 1963. See also Jean Leslie, *Three Rivers Beckoned: Life and Times with Calgary Mayor Jack Leslie*, 183.

24 CCA, CCM, June 27, 1963.

25 CCA, BCP, series 5, box 225, file 6200.4, Eric J. Hanson, "Preliminary Report on the Development of Calgary by the Canadian Pacific Railway and the City of Calgary," June 20, 1963. Sykes is of the opinion that Hanson was referring to the CPR's Economic Base Study, which was now in the hands of the city.

26 CCA, CCM, July 22, 1963, Commissioners' Report, July 17, 1963.

27 Eric J. Hanson, "City of Calgary CP Railway Downtown Development Proposals," report submitted to City Council on November 7, 1963, 3–4.

28 Ibid., table 3-e.

29 Ibid., 2.

30 CCA, BCP, series 5, box 225, file 6200.4, Downtown Study, J.C. Sproule to P.N.R. Morrison, July 24, 1963.

31 Letter to the editor, *The Albertan,* March 4, 1964.

32 Glenbow Archives, Local Council of Women Papers, M5841-109, M.R.C. Coulson, D.B. Johnson, and J.G. Nelson, "The C.P.R. Scheme: A Study in Possible Resource and Land Use Mismanagement" (hereafter cited as Coulson Report), December 4, 1963.

33 Ibid., 9.

34 "A New Calgary Envisioned," *Calgary Herald,* April 6, 1963.

35 "Bonanza in Tourism Predicted for City — Sinclair," *Calgary Herald,* April 7, 1963.

36 Sykes Papers, Fred Stone to Fred Kennedy, May 3, 1963.

37 Sykes Papers, jottings, May 1, 1963. In the fall of 1963, Batchelor resigned from the position of chief commissioner; he was succeeded by John Steel.

38 Sykes Papers, Carl Nickle to Rod Sykes, May 29, 1963.

39 CCA, BCP, series 5, box 225, file 6200.4, Downtown Study, John Steel to Rod Sykes, June 3, 1963.

40 CCA, CCM, J.P. Wilson to Ian Sinclair, June 4, 1963.

41 CCA, CCM, Ian Sinclair to J.P. Wilson, June 7, 1963.

42 CCA, BCP, series 5, box 225, file 6200.4, Downtown Study, "Canadian Pacific Railway Company: City of Calgary–Canadian Pacific Redevelopment Project Proposed Relocation of Railroad Tracks," June 10, 1963 (emphasis in the original).

43 CCA, CCM, June 27, 1963.

44 Sykes Papers, details of contract between the CPR and City Investing Company, May 2, 1963. Through Dowling, it was anticipated that financial heavyweights like Met Life, Prudential Life, Sun Life, and Standard Life would be induced to invest.

45 Sykes Papers, Frank Cullen Brophy to Rod Sykes, July 6, 1963.

46 CCA, CCM, October 16, 1963.

47 CCA, CCM, June 24, 1963, Rod Sykes to Dudley Batchelor, June 17, 1963.

48 CCA, BCP, series 5, box 226, file 6200.4, CPR Downtown Study, Agreement, 1963 (file 1 of 4), "Heads of Arrangement Between Canadian Pacific Railway Company (Canadian Pacific) and City of Calgary (City)," April 5, 1963 (emphasis in the original).

49 Mewata Park was a federal land grant with an attached ruling that there could be no change to its status except via plebiscite, something the city was not prepared to undertake. It was also recommended that the federal government be notified if any such change were being considered. See Sykes Papers, A.C. MacWilliams, City Solicitor, to John Steel, March 13, 1962.

50 A city map dated January 1964 showed the parkway parallel to the river and depicted it as a "possible future highway connection to proposed 22nd Street bridge."

51 CCA, CCM, April 29, 1964, Commissioners' Report, April 28, 1964.

52 Grant MacEwan, diary entry, August 6, 1963. (MacEwan's diary, formerly in the possession of the author, was donated to the University of Calgary Archives in the fall of 2012.)

53 CCA, BCP, series 5, box 227, file 6200.4, minutes of meeting of Board of Commissioners with officials of the CPR, Commissioners' Board Room, August 6, 1963.

54 CCA, BCP, series 5, box 227, file 6200.4, minutes of meeting of Board of Commissioners with officials of the CPR, Commissioners' Board Room, August 7, 1963.

55 CCA, BCP, series 5, box 227, file 6200.4, CPR Downtown Study, Commissioners' Report on negotiations to date, August 29, 1963.

56 CCA, BCP, series 5, box 281, file: CPR Downtown Development Report, City Solicitor's Office, "Submission of Matters Requiring Consideration of Board of City Commissioners on Relocation of Canadian Pacific Railway Mainline," September 13, 1963; J.B. DeWolfe, "Re: Changes in City–Canadian Pacific Agreement for Relocation of Trackage," October 4, 1963.

57 Greenhalgh went on to become the director of Planning for Victoria in 1969.

58 CCA, Law Department, series 4, box 92, file 6-C-679, notes on law on taxation in relation to change of Canadian Pacific Railway trackage, September 5, 1963.

59 CCA, CCM, June 27, 1963.

60 CCA, BCP, series 5, box 227, file 6200.4, CP–Downtown Study Agreement, meeting dated August 29, 1963.

61 "Other Cities Seek Same Plan," *South Side Mirror,* September 5, 1963.

62 See Sykes Papers, "Notes on Politics," September 1963.

63 CCA, BCP, series 5, box 281, file: CPR Downtown Development Report, City Solicitor's Office, "Submission of Matters Requiring Consideration of Board of City Commissioners on Relocation of Canadian Pacific Railway Mainline," September 13, 1963. The Local Authorities Board decided on appeals from cities for expansion to their boundaries or any other changes to their status.

64 CCA, CCM, Commissioners' Report to City Council, November 14, 1963. See also Peter Thurling, "Plebiscite Not Needed," *The Albertan,* November 16, 1963.

65 CCA, CCM, June 10, 1963.

66 "Civic Election Most Important in City History," *South Side Mirror,* September 12, 1963.

67 For a good assessment of Farran's views, see his opinion piece, "Inside City Hall . . . CPR Plan," *North Hill News,* October 3, 1963.

68 "Leadership Key Issue — Art Smith," *South Side Mirror*, September 26, 1963.

69 "Mayor MacEwan's Seven-Point Program for a Better Calgary," *South Side Mirror*, September 26, 1963.

70 "MacEwan Endorses City-CPR Project," *South Side Mirror*, September 19 1963.

71 A full-page ad titled "Say Mayor MacEwan, If We Re-elect You, Mayor, What Can You Do for Calgary?" appeared in *The Albertan* on October 11 and gives a good idea of MacEwan's personal style as well as an indication of the level of his financial support.

72 "When CPR Tracks Lifted, New Downtown in Calgary," *Financial Post*, October 26, 1963.

73 For evidence of his support, see *Financial Post*, October 26, 1963.

74 "MacEwan Ducks CPR Plan," *North Hill News*, October 10, 1963.

75 CCA, BCP, series 5, box 26, file 6200.4, meeting of mayor and commissioners, October 23, 1963. To their credit, the commissioners refused, arguing that while the idea may have originated with Harry Hays, the project itself was "more of a joint venture."

76 CCA, BCP, series 5, box 226, file 6200.4: Meeting of Mayor and Commissioners, September 26, 1963. This meeting is referred to in CCA, BCP, series 5, box 281, file: CPR Downtown Development Report, J.B. DeWolfe, "Re: City of Calgary–CP Development Proposals Calgary Development Committee," January 9, 1964.

77 CCA, Engineering and Environmental Services, series 2, box 9, file 2012, negotiating meeting, November 5, 1963.

78 There was no 3rd Street south of the tracks.

79 Here, the behaviour of Grant MacEwan is puzzling. As mayor, he was a member of both the Board of Commissioners and City Council. His failure to keep his aldermen abreast of negotiations was probably linked to a need to keep negotiations under wraps until they were complete. Yet in an ultimately democratic creature like MacEwan, putting the private ahead of the public sphere seems uncharacteristic.

80 Although not stated, the brief was probably drafted by the CPR and reviewed by the city.

81 CCA, CCM, September 25, 1963, Commissioners' Report, September 23, 1063.

82 CCA, CCM, October 23, 1963.

83 CCA, CCM, City of Calgary–Canadian Pacific Railway Downtown Redevelopment Proposal: Report #3, November 14, 1963.

84 CCA, CCM, November 11, 1963.

85 CCA, CCM, October 21, 1963.

86 "CPR Plan May Be Christmas Present," *The Albertan*, December 4, 1963.

87 Peter Thurling, "Showdown Looms for City-CP Redevelopment," *The Albertan*, December 5, 1963.

88 "May Derail 2nd St. Road," *The Albertan*, December 5, 1963.

89 "CPR Double-Crossed City, Alderman Charges," *The Albertan*, December 6, 1963.

90 CCA, CCM, December 6, 1963, Commissioners' Report, December 3, 1963.

91 Thurling, "Showdown Looms for City-CP Redevelopment."

92 It had been hinted that the June 27 motion instructing commissioners to prepare a money bylaw in connection with borrowings for the CPR project had been inspired by news of such a petition.

93 CCA, CCM, December 6, 1963.

94 Peter Thurling, "No Ultimatum — CPR; But Take It or Leave It," *The Albertan*, December 11, 1963.

95 Peter Thurling, "CPR Vice President Pinpoints Issues," *The Albertan*, December 13, 1963.

96 "City-CPR Plan Likely Doomed," *The Albertan*, December 14, 1963. Other comments included: "I'd vote No" (from Ballard); "Broken faith in every way you can break faith" (Boote); "Can't vote for anything like that" (Russell); "CPR takes same attitude every time" (Ho Lem).

97 Ibid.

98 "No CPR Decision Until '64: Sinclair," *The Albertan*, December 20, 1963.

99 CCA, BCP, series 5, box 645, file 4433, Crump to MacEwan, January 3, 1964.

100 According to Sykes, Winnipeg, Toronto, Montréal, and Vancouver were interested parties.

101 "Bomb Threat at City Hall," *Calgary Herald*, December 12, 1963.

102 Sykes Papers, copy of minutes of Chamber of Commerce meeting, November 22, 1963, in Sykes correspondence to President, Calgary Chamber of Commerce, January 2, 1964.

103 CCA, CCM, letter from Frank Johns, President, Calgary Real Estate Board, to City Council, December 9, 1963.

104 CCA, CCM, January 6, 1964, letter from CDC to City Council, December 30, 1963.

105 Sykes Papers, Sykes to the Calgary Chamber of Commerce, January 2, 1964.

106 CCA, CCM, January 6, 1964, letter from CDC to City Council, December 30, 1963.

107 "Aldermen Set Meeting on Plan," *The Albertan*, January 7, 1964; "Changed CPR Stand Discounted," *The Albertan*, January 8, 1964.

108 "Aldermen Set Meeting on Plan."

109 "CDC Suggests Alternative to Planning Act Exemption," *The Albertan*, January 15, 1964.

110 "May Not Require 'Vital' Crossing at 2nd St. W" and "The Report That Never Was," *The Albertan*, January 11, 1964.

111 "Pact Would Foster Favorable Climate," *The Albertan*, January 17, 1964.

112 "Get On with It," Editorial, *Calgary Herald*, December 12, 1963.

113 "New Hope," Editorial, *Calgary Herald*, January 7, 1964.

114 "Memo from the Publisher," *Calgary Herald*, December 28, 1963.

115 "Down to Brass Tacks," Editorial, *The Albertan*, December 5, 1963.

116 "The Third Party," Editorial, *The Albertan*, January 9, 1964.

117 "CPR Pressure," *North Hill News*, January 9, 1964.

118 Sproule was an interesting figure. His survey work on the geology of the Arctic was groundbreaking and paved the way for later development in the oil and gas industry and in the formation of Panarctic Oils.

119 "CPR Plan $40,000 Brainwash — Sproule," *The Albertan*, October 1, 1963.

120 Glenbow Archives, Local Council of Women Papers, M5841-109, J.C. Sproule to J. Lorne Clark, January 10, 1964. In this letter, Sproule referred to an earlier correspondence to Grant Carlyle, president of the Calgary Chamber of Commerce, on December 14, 1963, in which he said that he had had his property independently appraised at $397,000 but had been offered $100,000 less by the city.

121 "City May Face Lawsuits," *The Albertan*, January 20, 1964.

122 "Labour Against CP-City Plan," *Calgary Herald*, December 14, 1963.

123 Coulson Report, 1.

124 Ibid., 13.

125 Ibid., 3.

126 "Geographer Urges Study," *The Albertan*, January 8, 1964.

127 "Fourth Group on CPR: Master Plan First," *The Albertan*, January 11, 1964.

128 "CCCD on Thin Ice," Editorial, *The Albertan*, January 15, 1964.

129 "New Group Welcomed But...," *The Albertan*, January 10, 1964.

130 CCA, BCP, series 5, box 227, file 6200.4, J.B. Barron to Mayor and Commissioners, December 14, 1963.

131 "CPR Mess: Point by Point," *The Albertan*, January 6, 1964.

132 CCA, BCP, series 5, box 226, file 6200.4, J.B. Barron to Commissioner Ian Forbes, January 15, 1964.

133 "Santa Claus and His Trains," Editorial, *North Hill News*, December 1963.

134 "Final CPR Talks," *The Albertan*, January 15, 1964.

135 Grant MacEwan, diary entry, January 20, 1964.

136 "City CPR Strike Pact: Council Decides Today," *The Albertan*, January 22, 1964.

137 Sykes Papers, jottings on the city-CPR negotiations, January 16–21, 1964.

138 "This Is Text of Draft Agreement," *The Albertan*, January 23, 1964.

139 Sykes Papers, jottings, January 21, 1964.

140 CCA, BCP, series 5, box 229, file 6200.4, "CPR Objections to Agreement," January 1964.

141 CCA, CCM, January 22, 1964.

142 "Starr Blasted for Absence from CPR Talks," *The Albertan*, January 23, 1964.

143 One was to delay proceedings until the return of Ernie Starr; the other concerned the removal of the clause pertaining to a crossing at 3rd Street.

144 "Council Warned Grave Mistake to Drop Project," *Calgary Herald,* January 23, 1964.

145 CCA, BCP, series 5, box 229, file 6200.6, Steel to MacMillan, February 28, June 30, and July 16, 1963.

146 CCA, BCP, series 5, box 229, file 6200.6, MacMillan to Steel, July 24, 1963.

147 CCA, CCM, Septenber 25, 1963, Commissioners' Progress Report.

148 CCA, BCP, series 5, box 229, file 6200.6, Sykes to MacEwan, October 9, 1963.

149 CCA, BCP, series 5, box 229, file 6200.6, MacMillan to R.A. Emerson, December 20, 1963.

150 CCA, BCP, series 5, box 229, file 6200.6, MacEwan to MacMillan, October 10, 1963.

151 CCA, BCP, series 5, box 229, file 6200.6, MacMillan to MacEwan, October 21, 1963.

152 CCA, BCP, series 5, box 229, file 6200.6, MacMillan to MacEwan, December 20, 1963.

153 CCA, BCP, series 5, box 282, file: "CPR Downtown Development Proposals (file 1 of 2)," details of meetings with Steel and MacMillan in Montréal, January 10, 1964.

154 CCA, BCP, series 5, box 224, file 6200.2, "CNR, Exhibition Ground Study," May 1963.

155 CCA, BCP, series 5, box 229, file 6200.6, meeting between city and CNR, July 10, 1962.

156 CCA, BCP, series 5, box 224, file 6200.2, Steel to MacMillan, January 30, 1963.

157 CCA, BCP, series 5, box 224, file 6200.2, MacMillan to Steel, May 30, 1963.

158 CCA, BCP, series 5, box 224, file 6200.2, MacMillan to Steel, July 24, 1963.

159 CCA, BCP, series 5, box 224, file 6200.2, R.O. Leitch Estimates, October 9, 1963.

160 CCA, BCP, series 5, box 224, file 6200.2, MacMillan to Steel, October 4, 1963.

161 CCA, BCP, series 5, box 224, file 6200.2, J.P. Wilson, Secretary, Board of

Commissioners, to G.J. Greenhalgh, Deputy Director of Planning, October 11, 1963.

162 CCA, BCP, series 5, box 224, file 6200.2, Steel to MacMillan, October 15, 1963.

163 Sykes Papers, A.C. MacWilliams, City Solicitor, to John Steel, March 13, 1962.

164 CCA, BCP, series 5, box 237, file 6200.4, CPR Downtown Study Agreement meeting, August 24, 1963.

165 CCA, BCP, series 5, box 231, file: Canbritam Developments 1964. The name "Canbritam" was an amalgamation of "Canadian, British, and American."

166 Ibid. The breakdown for the forty acres was as follows: fourteen for residential, seventeen for retail, five for offices, two for motor hotel, and two for gas stations.

167 CCA, BCP, series 5, box 231, file: Canbritam Developments 1964, Al Martin to Steel, April 24, 1962.

168 CCA, CCM, October 1, 1962.

169 CCA, BCP, box 224, file 6230, Statement of Understanding Between City of Calgary and Canbritam, November 28, 1962.

170 CCA, BCP, series 5, box 231, file 6200.2, Rod Sykes to Brian Showell, December 27, 1963.

171 CCA, BCP, series 5, box 252, file: "CPR Downtown Development Proposal Council Minutes, 1963–1964 (file 2 of 2)," notes on discussions between CPR and commissioners, December 6, 1963.

172 Sykes Papers, handwritten draft of letter to CPR vice-president Fred Stone, undated [ca. early 1964]. According to Sykes, a final, typed copy of the letter was sent to Stone, but there is no record of the finished version.

Chapter 4 Temperature Rising

1 "The Reason Why," *Calgary Herald*, January 23, 1964.

2 "The Plan: How They Saw It," *The Albertan*, January 23, 1964; "The Reason Why."

3 "The People's Choice," Editorial, *The Albertan*, January 24, 1964.

4 "Leadership Void," Editorial, *Calgary Herald*, January 28, 1964.

5 See "Letters to the Editor," *Calgary Herald*, January 27, 1964.

6 "Pro Con Sentiments Bared on CP Project," *Calgary Herald*, February 7, 1964.

7 Sykes Papers, Calgary Redevelopment: The City-CP Agreement, January 27, 1964. The launch of the organization was carried in the *Calgary Herald*, including a large photograph showing a smiling Carl Nickle holding a "Vote Yes" sign and surrounded by business and labour representatives and School Board trustee Wilma Hansen.

8 Jean Leslie, *Three Rivers Beckoned: Life and Times with Calgary Mayor Jack Leslie*, 192–93.

9 "CPR Referendum," *North Hill News*, February 13, 1964.

10 "New Group to Probe CPR Plan," *The Albertan*, January 31, 1964; "Pro Con Sentiments Bared on CP Project."

11 Sykes Papers, untitled map numbered and labelled with typed price-list attachment, undated.

12 "Citizens' Committee Plans to Get 'Facts' on City-CP," *Calgary Herald*, January 31, 1964; "Text of City-CPR Agreement," *The Albertan*, February 15, 1964.

13 "Committee Resists Advances of Calgarians for Progress," *The Albertan*, February 7, 1964.

14 CCA, City Clerk's fonds, box 645, file 4483, CCCD to City of Calgary, February 28, 1964.

15 Gorman had been following the debate closely and, doubtless through her good contacts, knew details of the agreement before it was published in the press in February.

16 For example, see the letters to the editor "Relocation — A 13 Point Challenge," *The Albertan*, February 4, 1964, and "How Much Will the CPR Pay in Taxes?" *The Albertan*, February 8, 1964. Both of these letters were longer than Gorman's and stressed much the same points.

17 "CP Plan Will Benefit Taxpayers," letter to the editor, *The Albertan*, January 28, 1964.

18 Sykes Papers, Sykes to Ruth Gorman, January 29, 1964.

19 City of Calgary Archives, Board of Commissioners Papers (hereafter cited as CCA, BCP), series 5, box 282, file: CPR Downtown Development Proposal, petition dated February 10, 1964; see also Peter Thurling, "CPR Plan Boils," *The Albertan*, February 11, 1964.

20 "CPR Plan Enemy Claims Consultant Has Changed Mind," *The Albertan*, February 13, 1964.

21 Sproule, the founder of J.C. Sproule and Associates, held a PhD in geology. A prominent and outspoken critic of the plan, Sproule is best remembered for his pioneering work in mapping the Arctic in advance of oil and gas exploration. For more on Sproule, see Max Foran, "Calgary, Calgarians and the Northern Movement of the Oil Frontier 1950–1970."

22 "That van Ginkel Letter," Editorial, *The Albertan*, February 15, 1964.

23 City of Calgary Archives, City Council Minutes (hereafter cited as CCA, CCM), February 17, 1964; "Consultant's Objections Technical," *The Albertan*, February 18, 1964.

24 Dimitrios Styliaras, "CPR Redevelopment Proposal: A Study."

25 CCA, BCP, series 5, box 226, file 6200.4 (file 1 of 3), DeWolfe to Steel, January 31, 1964.

26 "CPR Plans No Publicity to Sell Project-Crump," *The Albertan*, February 20, 1964.

27 "Workers Lectured on Downtown Plan," *The Albertan*, February 13, 1964.

28 These took place at a meeting at the Allied Arts Centre on February 6, at a meeting called by the South Calgary Businessmen's Association on February 10, and at the Labour Temple on February 27. See "Pro Con Sentiments Bared on CP Project," *Calgary Herald*, February 7, 1964.

29 "Aldermen Clash on CP Plan," *The Albertan*, February 11, 1964.

30 *Home Buyers' Guide* 2, no. 1 (February 1964).

31 CCA, CCM, Commissioners' Reports #28, February 12, 1964, and #29, February 18, 1964.

32 CCA, CCM, February 17, 1964; "Permanent Staff for Redevelopment — Steel," *The Albertan*, January 28, 1964.

33 CCA, CCM, February 21, 1964, Commissioners' Report #29, February 18, 1964.

34 CCA, BCP, series 5, box 226, file 6200.4 (file 1 of 3), copy of draft in DeWolfe to Steel, February 3, 1964.

35 Glenbow Archives, Calgary's Grand Story Collection, box 5, E.C. Manning to S.J. Helman, July 17, 1964.

36 CCA, BCP, series 5, box 226, file 6200.4 (file 1 of 3), text of Calgarians for Progress brief in DeWolfe to Steel, January 3, 1964.

37 "Won't Attack Plan," *The Albertan*, February 27, 1964.

38 The individual in question was Donald Fleming, the Social Credit MLA for Calgary West, who felt that several clauses in the agreement were nebulous. See "House to Eye Plan," *The Albertan*, February 19, 1964.

39 See *The Albertan* editorials "Keep It on the Rails," February 24, 1964, and "Here We Go Round ... ?," February 26, 1964.

40 CCA, BCP, series 5, box 226, file 6200.4 (file 1 of 3), notes on meeting at Municipal Affairs Building, Edmonton, on Canadian Pacific Relocation Agreement, February 26, 1964.

41 CCA, BCP, series 5, box 226, file 6200.4 (file 1 of 3), DeWolfe to Steel, February 26, 1964.

42 "A Political Kick," Editorial, *The Albertan*, March 4, 1964.

43 Leslie, *Three Rivers Beckoned*, 194.

44 "Provinces Seek CPR Land Tax," *The Albertan*, March 4, 1964; "Mr Manning's Time Fuse," Editorial, *The Albertan*, March 5, 1964. What Manning did not say was that any such challenge would probably take years and that his (and his fellow premiers') submission was but a first step.

45 CCA, BCP, series 5, box 226, file 6200.4 (file 3 of 4), City Downtown Study Agreement, "Notes Made at Public Hearing of the City of Calgary–Canadian Pacific Railway Company Track Relocation Agreement at Alberta Legislature, March 3–5, 1964" (hereafter cited as Hearing notes), 1.

46 Sykes Papers, "The City of Calgary–C.P. Railway Downtown Development Proposals: Brief Submitted by the City of Calgary to the Alberta Legislature," March 3, 1964.

47 Ibid., 33–35.

48 Ibid., 1.

49 Ibid., 44.

50 Ibid., 42.

51 Ibid., 41.

52 Ibid., 45.

53 Hearing notes, 2–9.

54 Hearing notes, 5.

55 Sykes Papers, "The City of Calgary–C.P. Railway Downtown Development Proposals: Brief Submitted by the City of Calgary to the Alberta Legislature," March 3, 1964.

56 "City's Brief Queried," *The Albertan*, March 4, 1964.

57 See Hearing notes, 10–15.

58 Questioning on March 3 lasted until 11:00 p.m. and continued the next morning following the presentation of Robert Dowling, who had to catch an early plane and was allowed to make his presentation before Sinclair took the floor.

59 Sykes Papers, "Canadian Pacific Brief Submitted to the Legislative Assembly, Province of Alberta," March 3, 1964.

60 Ibid., 8; see also "The Time Is Now — Sinclair," *The Albertan*, March 4, 1964; "CPR's Presentation Hits Home in House," *The Albertan*, March 4, 1964.

61 Hearing notes, 21.

62 Peter Thurling, "Calgary Takes Over," *The Albertan*, March 4, 1964.

63 Rod Sykes, in discussion with the author, May 26, 2011.

64 Peter Thurling, "The City's Performance," *The Albertan*, March 6, 1964.

65 "CPR's Concessions Pave Way for Plan," *The Albertan*, March 5, 1964.

66 Hearing notes, 24–25, 29–30, 33; "Dowling: Cities Just Don't Grow— They Need Tender Loving Care," *The Albertan*, March 5, 1964; "Plan Brings Tax Drop — CFP Brief," *The Albertan*, March 5, 1964.

67 The presenters were the North Calgary Businessmen's Association, Maccabees Hall, and Dale Humphrey's School of Music. See Hearing notes, 32, 34–35.

68 CCA, BCP, series 5, box 282, file: CPR Downtown Development Proposal, G.W. Kernahan, "Brief in Matters Concerning the Agreement Between the City of Calgary and the Canadian Pacific Railway," March 3, 1964; see also "Voters Fooled by CPR," *The Albertan*, March 5, 1964.

69 Hearing notes, 30–32; see also "Calgary Group Asks Commission to Study Scheme," *The Albertan*, March 5, 1964.

70 CCA, BCP, series 5, box 282, file: CPR Downtown Development Proposal, "Robert Barron to Honourable Members of the Legislative Assembly of the Province of Alberta," March 3, 1964.

71 Ibid., 1.

72 Ibid.

73 Ibid., 2.

74 Ibid., 4.

75 Ibid., 3.

76 Ibid., 7.

77 Ibid., 9.

78 "Solicitor's View Stirs Aldermen," *The Albertan*, March 7, 1964.

79 "City Official Raps Plan but Enabling Law Likely," *The Albertan*, March 6, 1964.

80 Ibid.

81 Ibid.

82 Leslie, *Three Rivers Beckoned*, 198. Leslie was quoting statements made by friends who were in attendance.

83 "Solicitor's View Stirs Aldermen"; Leslie, *Three Rivers Beckoned*, 199.

84 "MacWilliams Victim of Plot to Discredit Plan — Duncan," *The Albertan*, March 9, 1964.

85 "An Angry Council Splits over CP Issue," *The Albertan*, March 10, 1964.

86 "A Job to Be Done," Editorial, *The Albertan*, March 7, 1964. It was just a rumour, one hotly denied by the city. MacWilliams kept his job.

87 CCA, BCP, series 5, box 226, file: CPR Downtown Study — Agreement 1963 (file 3 of 4), John DeWolfe to John Steel, March 11, 1964.

88 CCA, CCM, March 30, 1964, A.C. MacWilliams, "Re: C.P.R. Development Plan," March 12, 1964, in Commissioners' Report, March 25, 1964.

89 CCA, CCM, March 30, 1964, J.P. Wilson, Secretary, Board of Commissioners, to A.C. MacWilliams, March 13, 1964, in Commissioners' Report, March 25, 1964.

90 CCA, CCM, March 30, 1964, "Re: C.P.R. Development Proposal," March 13, 1964, in Commissioners' Report, March 25, 1964.

91 Ibid.

92 Ibid.

93 Ibid.

94 See, for example, "Letter to Council Urges Three Resign," *The Albertan*, March 16, 1964.

95 "Investigate City Hall," *The Albertan*, March 7, 1964.

96 "CP Plan Unalterable, Lawyer Ruth Gorman Says," *The Albertan*, April 1, 1964.

97 See "Spur Tracks Pose a Problem," *The Albertan*, March 4, 1964.

98 "CP Plan Consultant More Enthusiastic," *Calgary Herald*, May 26, 1964.

99 "Opposition at Meeting," *Calgary Herald*, March 10, 1964.

100 "Redevelopment Plan Stirs Divergent Views at Forum," *The Albertan,* April 3, 1964.

101 "City-CPR Plan Good for Builders," *The Albertan*, March 30, 1964.

102 "Calgary CPR Project," *Alberta Homes,* March–April 1964.

103 "City Jaycees Vote Against CP Project," *The Albertan*, March 31, 1964.

104 Glenbow Archives, Calgary's Grand Story Collection, box 5, C. Baker, President, Mannix Co. Ltd., to MacEwan, April 8, 1964.

105 Letter to the editor, *North Hill News*, April 9, 1964.

106 "Voice from Arizona," letter to the editor, *North Hill News*, April 12, 1964.

107 "Enough Debate — Sykes," *The Albertan*, March 10, 1964.

108 CCA, BCP, series 5, box 226, file 6200.4, Draft Bill — Legislature.

109 CCA, City Clerk fonds, box 645, file 4436, minutes of Coordinating Committee Meeting, April 9, 1964.

110 Under the Planning Act, 10 percent was the minimum levy that could be imposed, although in actual practice, it was seen as a maximum.

111 "CP Warns Plan Dead Unless Bill Changed," *Calgary Herald*, April 8, 1964.

112 "Business Leaders Told Plan Dead," *The Albertan*, April 9, 1964.

113 "Low Hurdle," Editorial, *Calgary Herald*, April 9, 1964; "No Time to Lose," *The Albertan*, April 9, 1964.

114 "Proposal Studied by CP," *Calgary Herald*, April 11, 1964.

115 Ibid. See also CCA, CCM, April 13, 1964.

116 "Demands on CPR Cut to $360,000," *The Albertan*, April 15, 1964. The paper was assessing the 10 percent as 9 acres instead of the 11.4 figure used by the legislature. Assessment values were computed at half the estimated market value.

117 The computation should have been as follows: $33,250 times 90 plus $7,500 times 24. This gives a total assessment value of 114 acres at $3,172, 500. The recreational equivalent under discussion of 10 percent would equal $317,250. Since assessment values were half those of market values, the total amount computes to $634,500.

118 An Act Respecting the Calgary-Canadian Pacific Agreement, *Statutes of the Province of Alberta*, ch. 9, 1964.

119 "Legislature Gives CP Bill Final Approval," *Calgary Herald*, April 16, 1964.

120 Ibid.

121 CCA, BCP, series 5, box 226, file 6200.4, Crump to MacEwan, April 23, 1964.

122 CCA, CCM, April 27, 1964.

123 "CPR Plan Receives Crump's Approval," *Calgary Herald*, April 27, 1964.

124 "East End Mystery," Editorial, *The Albertan*, January 6, 1964.

125 CCA, BCP, series 5, box 229, file 6200.6, "Re: City of Calgary–C.P.R. Development Proposals, C.N.R. Land East of 6th Street East," notes of meeting between Steel, and MacMillan, January 10, 1964. *The Albertan* was certainly not as convinced as Steel. See "CNR Stand Expected," *The Albertan*, January 15, 1964.

126 CCA, BCP, series 5, box 229, file 6200.6, MacMillan to Steel, March 3, 1964.

127 CCA, BCP, series 5, box 229, file 6200.6, Steel to MacMillan, March 18, 1964.

128 CCA, BCP, series 5, box 229, file 6200.6, Macmillan to Steel, April 24, 1964.

129 One might indulge in some speculation on MacMillan's use of the word "matter" in his letter to Steel on April 24. Did it have a hidden meaning? Could he have been referring to the issue of the land sale south of 17th Avenue, still unresolved? Probably not, but it's an interesting speculation.

130 CCA, BCP, series 5, box 229, file 6200.2, R.O. Leitch, Chief Landman, to Commissioners, March 30, 1964; A.H. Nicholson, Commissioner of Public Works, to G.F. Middleton, CNR General Manager, Calgary Area, April 6, 1064.

131 See the definition of "present right-of-way" in appendix B, Agreement Between the City of Calgary and the Canadian Pacific Railway Company, Article 1.

132 CCA, BCP, series 5, box 229, file 6200.6, "City of Calgary–C.P.R. Development Proposals CP and Parkway West of 14th Street West," 2.

133 CCA, BCP, series 5, box 229, file 6200.6, "City of Calgary–C.P.R. Development Proposals CP and Parkway West of 14th Street West."

134 Ibid., 3–6.

135 "Steel Maintains CP Broke Pact," *Calgary Herald*, May 30, 1966.

136 Sykes Papers, handwritten notes, undated.

137 Ibid.

138 CCA, BCP, series 5, box 229, file 6200.6, "City of Calgary–C.P.R. Development Proposals CP and Parkway West of 14th Street West," 2.

139 CCA, BCP, series 5, box 229, file 6200.6, Steel to Sykes, March 31, 1964.

140 CCA, BCP, series 5, box 229, file 6200.6, MacEwan to Sinclair, April 21, 1964.

141 CCA, BCP, series 5, box 229, file 6200.6, Sykes to Steel, April 20, 1964.

142 Sykes Papers, Crump to MacEwan, April 27, 1964.

143 CCA, CCM, April 29, 1964, Report of Special Coordinating Committee, April 28, 1964. The later plebiscite date of May 27 had been necessitated by the delay in securing CPR approval.

144 CCA, CCM, April 29, 1964, Commissioners' Report, April 28, 1964.

145 "CP Says City Stuck with $250000 Bill," *Calgary Herald*, April 29, 1964.

146 CCA, CCM, April 29, 1964.

147 Leslie, *Three Rivers Beckoned*, 203–4.

148 Lynne Cove, "3 Aldermen Given CP Land Problem," *Calgary Herald*, April 29, 1964.

149 "What a Mess!" *Calgary Herald*, April 30, 1964.

150 "Wisdom and Foolishness," Editorial, *The Albertan*, May 1, 1964.

151 "City Outplayed in Poker Game for CP Plan," *The Albertan*, May 14, 1964.

152 "Russell Forced to Leave Job," *Calgary Herald*, May 19, 1964. Interestingly, Russell was philosophical about his dismissal, noting that, for the most part, he had been given a lot of freedom. He was also not overly surprised, since his outspoken behaviour had already been noted by his employers.

153 "The Russell Affair," *The Albertan*, May 22, 1964.

154 "Russell Forced to Leave Job."

155 Quoted in Leslie, *Three Rivers Beckoned*, 213.

156 David Russell, personal communication, September 4, 2009.

157 "Starr Wants Province to Study Russell Case," *The Albertan*, May 26, 1964.

158 CCA, CCM, May 29, 1964, W.T. Paterson, Secretary, Calgary Labour Council, to H. Sales, City Clerk, May 29, 1964.

159 CCA, CCM, May 29, 1964, Ruth Gorman to Members of City Council, May 28, 1964.

160 "The Russell Affair," *The Albertan*, May 22, 1964.

161 See CCA, BCP, series 5, box 226, file 6200.4. The breakdown was as follows: land acquisition, $4.4 million; bridges and bridge extensions and approaches, $1.5 million; interchanges, $1.3 million; parkway, $1.6 million. It was also noted that the existing debenture debt was $92 million, none of which was in arrears.

162 "City CN Meeting Slated Soon," *The Albertan*, May 14, 1964.

163 "City Handling of CP Plan Rapped," *Calgary Herald*, June 2, 1964.

164 CCA, CCM, May 29, 1964.

165 Ibid.

166 "City CPR Plan Alive City Asks Delay," *The Albertan*, May 30, 1964.

167 "Opportunity," Editorial, *Calgary Herald*, May 30, 1964.

168 "CN Won't Negotiate," *The Albertan*, May 30, 1964.

169 CCA, CCM, June 8, 1964, G.R. Graham, CNR Vice-President, to G. MacEwan, June 5, 1964.

170 CCA, BCP, series 5, box 229, file 6200.6, R.O. Leitch, Chief Landman, to J. Steel, June 8, 1964.

171 CCA, CCM, June 8, 1964.

172 Ballard and Deyell are both quoted in Lynn Cove, "Cost of CP Project Hiked by $5m," *Calgary Herald*, June 9, 1964.

173 Grant MacEwan, diary entry, June 8, 1964.

174 CCA, CCM, June 8, 1964.

175 CCA, City Clerk fonds, box 641, file 4399, MacEwan to Crump, June 12, 1964.

176 CCA, CCM, June 22, 1964, R. Gorman to City Council, June 17, 1964.

177 "City Morality Probe Asked," *Calgary Herald*, June 11, 1964.

178 CCA, CCM, June 22, 1964, R. Gorman to City Council, June 17, 1964.

179 "Herald Severely Censured," *Calgary Herald*, June 11, 1964; "A Complaint," Editorial, *The Albertan*, June 12, 1964.

180 "Challenge to Calgary," Editorial, *The Albertan*, June 17, 1964.

181 See CCA, CCM, June 22, 1964, delegation report to City Council, June 20, 1964.

182 Ibid.

183 CCA, City Clerk fonds, box 641, file 4399, N.J. MacMillan to G. MacEwan, June 18, 1964.

184 CCA, City Clerk fonds, box 641, file 4399, Crump to MacEwan, June 18, 1964.

185 CCA, CCM, June 22, 1964, delegation report to City Council, June 20, 1964.

186 Sykes Papers, "Notes on Special Meeting of City Council on the City-CP Redevelopment Scheme Held at City Hall at 10:00 a.m. on June 22, 1964." Sykes obviously secured a copy of these proceedings, which contain handwritten marginal comments and a handwritten note: "To be retyped single spaced and carefully set up." The writer, probably a city official, is unknown. The handwriting does not belong to Sykes.

187 CCA, CCM, June 22, 1964.

188 "City Fumbles Ball, Claims Nickle," *Calgary Herald*, June 22, 1964.

189 "Plan Opponents Cheer Scrapping," *Calgary Herald*, June 22, 1964.

190 Grant MacEwan, diary entry, June 22, 1964.

191 CCA, CCM, July 3, 1964, N.R. Crump to Mayor and City Council, June 26, 1964.

192 "Death Blow," Editorial, *Calgary Herald*, June 23, 1964.

193 "Derailment," Editorial, *The Albertan*, June 23, 1964.

194 "As the People See It," *The Albertan*, June 23, 1964.

195 "Council Kills City CP Plan," *South Side Mirror,* June 25, 1964.

196 "$40m Plan Along the Bow Bared," *Calgary Herald,* July 2, 1964; "Place d'Eau Claire," *The Albertan,* July 2, 1964.

197 Glenbow Archives, Calgary Grand Story Collection, box 5, W.G. Morrow to Robert Barron, July 2, 1964.

198 Glenbow Archives, Calgary Grand Story Collection, box 5, Barron to Morrow, July 9, 1964.

199 "Mayor Strikes Back at Council's Critics," *Calgary Herald,* October 10, 1964.

200 Grant MacEwan, diary entry, November 13, 1964.

201 Grant MacEwan, diary entry, January 6, 1965.

202 "Civic Official Raps Plan but Enabling Law Likely," *The Albertan,* March 6, 1964.

203 See Statutes of Alberta, 1951, c. 9, "An Act Respecting Cities," s. 67, Duties of the Chief Solicitor.

204 The Commissioners' Office wanted the Stampede to expand into the deteriorating suburb of Victoria Park to the north. When this happened, it created another major controversy that, in its social implications, rivalled that of the project under discussion. See Max Foran, "Coalitions and Demolitions: The Destruction of Calgary's East Victoria Park, 1960–1998."

Conclusion

1 David Cruise and Alison Griffiths, *Lords of the Line: The Men Who Built the CPR,* 423.

2 Ibid., 420–21.

3 Sykes Papers, handwritten draft of letter to CPR vice-president Fred Stone, undated [ca. early 1964]. In this letter, Sykes describes the depth of his frustration over the CPR's unwillingness to provide the support he felt was necessary to sell the project to the city.

4 Glenbow Archives, Calgary Grand Story Collection, box 5, E. Manning to E. Helmer, July 17, 1964.

5 Other examples include the decision in January 1964, when, following the seeming defeat of the agreement, a few aldermen reconvened an adjourned meeting in order to secure it. In March 1964, City Council asked the city's chief solicitor to evaluate both the agreement and the project and then chose to shelve his powerful negative arguments on both counts.

6 There was a strong parallel to the Calgary experience in Winnipeg in the 1970s involving redevelopment in the downtown core by the major property developer Trizec Corporation. In his excellent account of the issue, University of Manitoba professor David Walker, in discussing compliant civic administration and supportive outside consultants, noted: "City politicians were not in

the same league as the corporations with which they were bargaining. They were poor negotiators on point after point at a high cost to the tax payer." David C. Walker, *The Great Winnipeg Dream: The Redevelopment of Portage and Main*, ix.

7 Quoted in Ruth Gorman, *Behind the Man: John Laurie, Ruth Gorman and the Indian Vote in Canada*, 110. In his introduction, Frits Pannekoek, the editor of this volume, refers to "her single-handed successful opposition to the relocation of the CPR rail track in Calgary" (xiii).

8 "Council Kills CP Project: Cost Found Too High," *Calgary Herald*, June 22, 1964.

Epilogue

1 "Bow Village Project Flops," *The Albertan*, April 3, 1968; "'Village' Property Price $1.3 Million," *Calgary Herald*, April 3, 1968.

2 "Canadian Pacific Railway Corridor Plan (Background Information)," City of Calgary, Land Use Planning and Policy, November 2010, 1.

BIBLIOGRAPHY

Atkinson, Wallace. "Urban Transportation Problems — Solutions." In *Canada: An Urban Agenda,* edited by H. Peter Oberlander, 199–224. Ottawa: Community Planning Press, 1976.

Baine, Richard Paul. *Calgary: An Urban Study.* Toronto: Clark Irwin, 1973.

Barr, Brenton M., ed. *Calgary: Metropolitan Structure and Influence.* Western Geographical Series, vol. 11. Victoria: Western Geographical Press, Department of Geography, University of Victoria, 1975.

Bunting, Trudi E., and Pierre Filion. *The Changing Canadian Inner City.* Waterloo: University of Waterloo, Department of Geography, 1988.

Chodos, Robert. *The CPR: A Century of Corporate Welfare.* Toronto: James Lorimer, 1973.

Clark, Joseph S., Jr., and Dennis J. Clark. "Rally and Relapse, 1946–1968." In *Philadelphia: A 300-Year History,* edited by Russell F. Weigley. New York: W.W. Norton, 1982.

Cruise, David, and Alison Griffiths. *Lords of the Line: The Men Who Built the CPR.* Markham, ON: Penguin Books, 1988.

Evenden, L.J., and G.E. Walker. "From Periphery to Centre: The Changing Geography of the Suburbs." In *The Changing Social Geography of Canadian Cities,* edited by Larry S. Bourne and David F. Ley, 234–51. Montreal and Kingston: McGill-Queen's University Press, 1993.

Foran, Max. "Calgary, Calgarians and the Northern Movement of the Oil Frontier, 1950–1970." In *The Making of the Modern West,* edited by A.W. Rasporich, 115–32. Calgary: University of Calgary Press, 1984.

———. "Coalitions and Demolitions: The Destruction of Calgary's East Victoria Park, 1960–1998." *Prairie Forum* 30 (May 2005): 17–45.

———. *Expansive Discourses: Urban Sprawl in Calgary, 1945–1978.* Edmonton: Athabasca University Press, 2009.

———. "The CPR and the Urban West, 1881–1930." In *The CPR West: The Iron Road and the Making of a Nation,* edited by Hugh A. Dempsey, 89–106. Vancouver: Douglas and McIntyre, 1984.

Goliger, Gabrielle. "The Changing Canadian Suburb." *Habitat* 26, no. 2 (1983): 20–23.

Gorman, Ruth. *Behind the Man: John Laurie, Ruth Gorman and the Indian Vote in Canada*. Edited by Frits Pannekoek. Calgary: University of Calgary Press, 2007.

Grant, Jill. "Shaped by Planning: The Canadian City Through Time." In *Canadian Cities in Transition: Local Through Global Perspectives,* 3rd ed., edited by Trudi Bunting and Pierre Filion, 320–37. Don Mills, ON: Oxford University Press, 2006.

Gutfreund, Owen D. *Twentieth-Century Sprawl: Highways and the Reshaping of the American Landscape*. New York: Oxford University Press, 2004.

Hallendy, Norman. *Housing a Nation: Forty Years of Achievement*. Ottawa: Canada Mortgage and Housing Corporation, 1986.

Harasym, D.G. "The Planning of New Residential Areas in Calgary, 1944–73." Master's thesis, University of Alberta, 1975.

Harasym, D.G., and P.J. Smith. "Planning for Retail Services in New Residential Areas Since 1944." In Barr, *Calgary: Metropolitan Structure and Influence,* 157–91.

Harris, Richard. *Creeping Conformity: How Canada Became Suburban, 1900–1960*. Toronto: University of Toronto Press, 2004.

Hodge, Gerald, and David Gordon. *Planning Canadian Communities: An Introduction to the Principles, Practices and Participants*. 5th ed. Toronto: Nelson, 2008.

Leslie, Jean. *Three Rivers Beckoned: Life and Times with Calgary Mayor Jack Leslie*. Bragg Creek, AB: Far-Ma-K, 2004.

Lucy, William H., and David L. Phillips. *Confronting Suburban Decline: Strategic Planning for Metropolitan Renewal*. Washington, DC: Island Press, 2000.

Magnusson, Warren, and Andrew Sancton, eds. *City Politics in Canada*. Toronto: University of Toronto Press, 1983.

Masson, Jack K. *Alberta's Local Governments and Their Politics*. Edmonton: Pica Pica Press, 1985.

Mawson, Thomas H. *City of Calgary, Past, Present, and Future: A Preliminary Scheme for Controlling the Economic Growth of the City*. London: T.H. Mawson City Planning Experts, 1914.

McKee, Guian. "Blue Sky Boys, Professional Citizens and Knights-in-Shining-Money: Philadelphia's Penn Center Project and the Constraints of Private Development." *Journal of Planning History* 6, no. 1 (February 2007): 48–80.

Miron, John R. *Housing in Postwar Canada: Demographic Change, Household Formation, and Housing Demand*. Montreal and Kingston: McGill-Queen's University Press, 1988.

Muller, Edward K., and Joel A. Tarr. "The Interaction of Natural and Built Environments in the Pittsburgh Landscape." In *Devastation and Renewal: An Environmental History of Pittsburgh and Its Region,* edited by Joel A. Tarr, 11–40. Pittsburgh: University of Pittsburgh Press, 2003.

Nader, George A. *Profiles of Fifteen Metropolitan Centres*. Vol. 2 of *Cities of Canada*. Toronto: Macmillan, 1976.

———. *Theoretical, Historical and Planning Perspectives*. Vol 1. of *Cities of Canada*. Toronto: Macmillan, 1975.

Nelles, H.V. "How Did Calgary Get Its River Parks?" *Urban History Review/Revue d'histoire urbaine* 34, no. 1 (2005): 28–45.

Norris, Marjorie. *A Leaven of Ladies: The History of the Calgary Local Council of Women*. Calgary: Detselig Enterprises, 1995.

Peach, Jack. *The First Fifty Years: A Chronicle of Half a Century in the Life of the Calgary Real Estate Board, 1943–1993*. Calgary: Calgary Real Estate Board Co-operative, 1993.

Peacock, Don. *Barefoot on the Hill: The Life of Harry Hays*. Toronto: Douglas and McIntyre, 1986.

Pickett, Stanley H. "An Appraisal of the Urban Renewal Programme in Canada." *University of Toronto Law Journal* 18, no. 3 (1968): 233–47.

Rogers, Ian MacFee. *The Law of Canadian Municipal Corporations*. 2nd ed. Toronto: Carswell, 1971.

Roweis, Shoukry T., and Allen J. Scott. "The Urban Land Question." *Urbanization and Urban Planning in Capitalist Society,* edited by Michael Dear and Allen J. Scott, 123–58 London: Metheun, 1983.

Sandalack, Beverly A., and Andrei Nicolai. *The Calgary Project: Urban Form/Urban Life*. Calgary: University of Calgary Press, 2006.

Sewell, John. *The Shape of the Suburbs: Understanding Toronto's Sprawl*. Toronto: University of Toronto Press, 2009.

Simmons, James W., and Robert Simmons. *Urban Canada*. Toronto: Copp Clark, 1969.

Spurr, Peter. *Land and Urban Development: A Preliminary Study*. Toronto: James Lorimer, 1976.

Stamp, Robert M. *Suburban Modern: Postwar Dreams in Calgary*. Calgary: Touch-Wood Editions, 2004.

Stanback, Thomas M., Jr. *The New Suburbanization: The Challenge to the Central City*. Boulder, CO: Westview Press, 1991.

Styliaras, Dimitrios. "CPR Redevelopment Proposal: A Study." *Royal Architectural Institute of Canada Journal* 41, no. 3 (1964): 53–56.

Walker, David C. *The Great Winnipeg Dream: The Redevelopment of Portage and Main*. Oakville, ON: Mosaic Press, 1979.

Wiesman, Brahm. "A New Agenda for Cities." In *Canada: An Urban Agenda,* edited by H. Peter Oberlander. Ottawa: Community Planning Press, 1976.

Wolforth, John R., and Roger Leigh. *Urban Prospects*. Toronto: McClelland and Stewart, 1971.